**Lesley Abdela** is a well-known jou~~~~~~~~~~~~~~ ~ho has worked as a parliamentary researcher in both the ~~~~e of Commons and the House of Lords. She stood for Parliament herself in the 1979 election. In 1980 she founded the all-party 300 Group which campaigns for greater representation for women in politics and public life.

3 50

# WOMEN WITH X APPEAL

## WOMEN POLITICIANS IN BRITAIN TODAY

LESLEY ABDELA

An OPTIMA book

© Lesley Abdela, 1989

First published in 1989 by
Macdonald Optima, a division of
Macdonald & Co. (Publishers) Ltd

A member of Maxwell Pergamon Publishing Corporation plc

British Library Cataloguing in Publication Data

Abdela, Lesley
    Women with x appeal : women in British politics
    today.
    1. Great Britain politics. Role of women
    I. Title
    323.3′4′0941

    ISBN 0-356-17184-1

Macdonald & Co. (Publishers) Ltd
66-73 Shoe Lane
London EC4P 4AB

Typeset in Century Schoolbook by
Leaper & Gard Ltd, Bristol

Printed and bound in Great Britain by
The Guernsey Press Co. Ltd., Guernsey, Channel Islands.

# CONTENTS

For all the women candidates who've ever stood for election, to local councils, Westminster, and the European Parliament — for those who were elected, and those who weren't.

# ACKNOWLEDGEMENTS

This is my first book. I have always said I was a doer not a book-writer so I owe very special thanks to the good-humoured support team who kept me going and nursed me through an experience I found far tougher than pregnancy.

A definite thank you to all the women I interviewed for the book, for giving me so much time and taking such care in helping me to get things right. Grateful thanks also to John Weller of Dunham Consultants in nearby Devizes who taught me how to 'fly' a word-processor; to management consultant Sue Morse; to Sharon and Bob Lomas of R and S Consultancy Services in Bratton, Wiltshire, who transcribed a quarter of a million words from over thirty interview tapes and handled the hi-tech back-up disc business which provided such comfort in case I lost all the copy on my machines; and particularly to fellow journalist Ann Hills who enabled me to interview so many women at the House of Commons by letting me stay at her London home.

And thanks to my patient editor, Harriet Griffey at Macdonald Optima, for being so continually encouraging and positive. As weeks beyond the deadline passed, it must have been nerve-wracking. I shan't forget Harriet's exasperation: 'Lesley, I hope you aren't *one of those authors* who won't let go of the typescript!?' Thank you David Beamish at the Public Information Office at the House of Lords for all the calm assistance over many months, checking facts, and to Avis Furness at the European Parliament for checking the appropriate chapters.

To my teenage son Nicholas, what can I say but thank you for spending your pre-GCSE Easter school holidays encouraging your mother with a diet of hibiscus teas and chocolate biscuits. And thank you Tim for advice, encouragement, organising, editing and generally keeping me going.

# PREFACE

Many of the frank insights in this book show what life is like for any politician, female or male. More than that, they describe the many extras women in a political fast-lane still have to cope with. It is written directly from the point of view of women in, or trying to get into, the House of Commons and the European Parliament, and the town halls around the country.

Before writing this book, I often listened to women politicians telling groups of women about their lives in politics, what it had been like once they stuck their heads above the proverbial parapet. It struck me as a great pity that the public didn't see their more human side too. I have known a number of these women for many years and watched their progress or otherwise up the political ladder. They talk of the good and the bad and the highs and the lows, the funny moments and the sad moments and their hopes for the future, the support, or lack of it, they receive from family, friends and political party. This book reveals keenly held political ideals, beliefs that range right across the political spectrum. What brought them into politics? What are their backgrounds, their ambitions, weaknesses and their strengths? What is it like living in the public eye, and what *extra* angles are there as a woman no-one ever seems to mention?

The aim of the book is to present snapshots of what it's really like to be active in a political party, a town hall, the House of Commons and The Lords, and in the European Parliament in Brussels.

Edwina Currie reveals how she and her family coped with Christmas just days after she was forced to resign as Junior Minister. Lynda Chalker talks about the threat she has lived with for years as a Government Minister and, on the lighter side, about the Iranian Minister who could not touch her body. There are some truly shocking revelations about the behaviour in the House of Commons of what I have called 'Yahoos'. Clare Short, Jo Richardson and others describe the gross behaviour of male chauvinists in the House of Commons.

Shirley Williams talks about Crosby and Cabinet. Teresa Gorman and Doreen Miller speak bluntly about Conservative selection committees. Polly Toynbee describes the blood on the floor as she and Roy Jenkins battled over the entrails of the Alliance. Recollections are vivid. Rosie Barnes describes the dual role of moving within minutes from heated discussions with Liberals, to Lego and lesson books with children at home. Angela Rumbold describes what it's like to fight a by-election when you have never been the centre of national media attention before, and recalls the constituency chairman who told her she was the wrong age *and* sex to be their parliamentary candidate. Joyce Quin gives the low-down on surface-swimming demersal fish in Brussels. Joan Ruddock and Ann Clwyd reveal how they were persecuted by the press (and in Joan Ruddock's case, probably MI5) and how they dealt with it. Zerbanoo Gifford reveals racism in Harrow. Ray Michie and Carole Tongue expose the loneliness of these long distance political runners. Maggie Ewing gives a poignant description of what it was like to lose her seat in Scotland. Betty Boothroyd describes what it's like to sit in 'Madam' Speaker's Chair.

The title *Women with X Appeal* is a tongue-in-cheek swipe at the way some sectors of the press still perceive women politicians. It comes from a headline in the *Daily Mail* in the early-morning edition on Election day in 1979, above a centre-spread feature about six women candidates (including yours truly, standing as Parliamentary candidate in East Herts).

Although this book is primarily written for women interested in the lives of other women, I hope men will read the book too, especially male politicians and the gentlemen of the press. It may give them a much greater understanding of their female colleagues and the people they write about. Ideally, I would like this book to be given to every paid-up member of a political party who may one day have the opportunity to be present at the selection of a woman candidate.

Lesley Abdela, Potterne, Wiltshire, 1989

# 1.
# PUBLIC EYE —
# *PRIVATE EYE*

EDWINA CURRIE

'I'm not a woman, I'm a Conservative.'

'It's always said in Parliament, the three ocupational hazards for a politician are arrogance, alcoholism and adultery. I think I'll admit to the first.' (BBC Radio 4)

'Good Christian people who wouldn't dream of misbehaving will not catch AIDS.'

'The strongest piece of advice I could give to any young woman is: don't screw around and don't smoke.' (Talking about cervical cancer, March 1988)

Edwina Currie is without doubt the best-known woman Member of Parliament in the country after the Prime Minister. She is also the first women politician in this country to fully understand and *act* on the weakness of the age we live in — the Media Age with its restless search for 'sound bites', the 'headline-speak' system successful politicians develop to get more than their quota of press and media coverage. Her skill raised hackles and dangerous jealousies. She says: 'For a politician, the media is a weapon. It's part of the way of life.'

Edwina Currie was born Edwina Cohen to a Jewish family in Liverpool on 13 October 1946. She grew up in Toxteth, winning a scholarship to the grammar school. She blossomed into the most controversial and media-mentioned woman politician of the late eighties. For a while her newsworthiness was to eclipse even the Prime Minister's.

She met her husband, Raymond, at Arthur Anderson, an international accountancy firm where she worked as a student trainee, and married him in 1972. They have two daughters, Debbie and Susan.

In 1975 she was elected a Birmingham City Councillor, and became Chairman of Bromsgrove's Housing Committee.

After her election as the Member of Parliament for South Derbyshire in 1983, her rise in the Conservative Party was meteoric. She became Parliamentary Private Under Secretary to Sir Keith Joseph at the Department of Education. In 1986 she was appointed Parliamentary Under Secretary at the Department of Health. Her resignation in late 1988 was brought about specifically by the furore she caused among egg producers and egg eaters, especially the elderly, with her statement that most egg production in Britain is contaminated with salmonella, but she had long since begun to unleash primal forces among important and not always friendly segments of Party, press and populace.

The high profile didn't arrive by accident. She set about it professionally and worked hard for it. 'An ego certainly,' wrote the perceptive journalist Edward Pearce in the *Sunday Telegraph*, 'but a buzzing worker, a good technician.' Or as *Elle* put it, comparing her to two other formidable media people: 'Take two parts of Joan Collins and three of Mrs T and you have Edwina Currie.'

Behind her, she left a trail of people who admired her or loathed her. Alan Cochrane in the *Mail On Sunday* stated: 'Keen swimmer, jogger, rifle-shooter, "Vindaloo", tactless, tireless and, as her friends admit, tiresome.'

However, BBC journalist Polly Toynbee, herself a recent parliamentary candidate, says: 'I think she's clever, funny and good. A lot of the abuse she gets is because she's a woman. I don't see why she should be abused in that kind of way. A lot of the things she says are very straightforward, just good sense, said in rather a right-wingish way. It doesn't seem to me she often says anything that is seriously wrong. It's something to do with the way she says it and who she is that gets up people's noses. She does it partly because she has a genuine lack of pomposity and therefore is willing to make a bit of a fool of herself. Once you get that reputation, then any stray remark you make — and you don't know which one — might suddenly splash across the tabloids. If you suddenly picked on even somebody ultra low-key, like Geoffrey Howe, if he became a monumental figure of fun, an extraordinary, bizarre character and people began door-stepping him and following him back and splashing what he said across headlines, he too could be made to appear a total idiot, a buffoon, or anything else. I think she's been hard done by.'

Although in-house power struggles and character assassinations are rife in political life, they are at least relatively private. This isn't true when an MP loses their seat or a Minister has to resign in the glorious glare of the TV lights. It is a mortifying blow. It brings a deep sense of personal failure, loneliness and bereavement, compounded by public humiliation. Unlike the company executive who can slink quietly away, politicians have to cope with these cataclysmic events in front of family and colleagues and readers of newspapers, listeners to radio, and vast TV audiences. Few misfortunes happen to politicians in private. Personal misery is broadcast in the sort of blaze of publicity that in other circumstances politicians would pursue and welcome. Politics is a very ungrateful business.

Edwina Currie's swift passage through the revolving doors of ministerial office was of Profumo Affair magnitude, made slightly risible through the humble breakfast egg being the *cause célèbre*, not sex. Over Christmas and New Year 1988 at parties and dinner tables up and down the land, Edwina Currie and salmonella roared past house prices and AIDS to become top of the pops in the conversation ratings chart, and was a major story in both the national quality and tabloid press. Not a bus-stop chat could go by without the topic coming up. Meanwhile egg farmers went out of business and legal writs fluttered into Edwina Currie's postbag. It overshadowed completely the 'Look After Your Heart' and drugs programmes she had worked on with considerable success.

Conservative colleague Lynda Chalker observes: 'I much regret Edwina's gone. I do actually think it was partly the campaign certain male-dominated groups ran against her. It was partly that, and it was partly jealousy. I know she was totally sincere in what she was saying.'

Throughout the storm Edwina Currie kept her fighting spirit in public. 'If the end result of all I've done as a Health Minister is better health — and we won't know for five or ten years — I would like to be able to put my finger on it and say I had a little bit to do with that, I'm pleased I did that.'

Unsurprisingly, she was shaken and chastened by what by all accounts was a relentless Force 12 battering by colleagues,

Opposition, egg lobby, press and media. She resigned as a Minister just before Christmas 1988. Hoist with her own extraordinary publicity petard, Edwina Currie's descent from public office was a public schuss down the mountain in the full glare of television cameras and popping camera bulbs.

In 1986, as though by the stroke of a wand — a call from Number Ten — she had risen to a position of real power and privilege as a Minister. She had had a large staff, two secretaries, a salary increase from an MP's £24,107 a year to £36,367, plus a ministerial car with chauffeur. On 16 December 1988 almost all of it disappeared. The Minister's salary went; the chauffeur went, the ministerial car turned into a pumpkin, the civil service flunkeys vanished.

Throughout the whole Salmonella Affair a very shaken Edwina Currie kept up a tough persona in public. She quipped, 'One of the advantages of not being a Minister any more is that I've swapped the ministerial Montego for the family Jaguar. It's a darn sight more comfortable!'

However, all was not lost. A stream of book offers, with interesting price tags poured in; 'The most bizarre offer was for my life story for the *News of the World*,' she said.

Four weeks after her post-salmonella resignation, she told me, 'There is only one thing I have ever said in my life I regret.' And added, 'The past few weeks were an interesting experience I would not wish to repeat.'

I asked her what she would do with her energies now. She replied, 'First, recover them. Then I'm going to write myself a little note and stick it on the back of the kitchen cupboard. It will say "It's very nice *not* to have ambition."'

Enlarging on the kitchen cupboard note, she says: 'It's not until things come to a dead halt you realise how much you were driven by ambition before. You begin to understand what other people wrote about you. What they had the luxury of mocking, however, is if you're going to get into parliament, whoever you are — male or female — there is only one way to do it and that is to be totally single minded. *Everything* you do has to be directed towards that end.'

She was interested in politics for as long as she can remember. 'I suspect now, looking at my younger daughter, I had always been interested in politics because she's been fascinated by the whole business since she could toddle. I have two daughters; the other isn't interested at all. She is 14 and she's likely to be found sticking pictures of Marilyn Monroe in a scrap-book, but the little one is 11 and she is likely to say, "I'm not going to bed yet, I'm going to watch the news first." She has to be dragged away kicking and screaming from discussions about Chernobyl and so on. She wanted to know all about it, and who Arthur Scargill was, and all the rest of it when she was 7. If we'd let her, she would have taken part in the 1983 and the 1987 General Elections. I suspect I was like that because I can remember Suez, I can remember the Korean War, I can remember the air-lift. I can't have been more than a small child and those things stuck in my head. I can remember the Coronation very clearly indeed and I can remember sticking lots of scraps in a scrap-book. The Coronation was a tremendous PR campaign.'

Edwina Currie's determination is by any standards truly formidable. She freely admits that, from the age of 19 onwards, every move she made was designed to advance her one goal of getting into the House of Commons.

'Before I became an MP what I did quite consciously was write my CV. If something came up which was interesting and worthwhile I would say yes to it, and then I would drop whatever I'd been doing for two or three years if it wasn't achieving very much or I wasn't learning any more. Gradually the portfolio of things I was doing, or had done, got more and more solid and more and more interesting to the point of writing a CV for a selection committee so it really did look as if I'd achieved something.'

After years of such slog, the respite on resigning her ministerial post and slipping away to the back-benches seemed almost welcome. 'One of the nice things about this little bit of my life is that for the first time ever (though I suspect it won't be for very long) the shackles are off. I am completely a free agent. I'm a Member of Parliament, but I'm not fighting an election for a couple of years, so I'm all right as far as that's concerned. I'm not under pressure to resign from my constituency, in fact they're very supportive, so I'm all right as far as that's concerned. I'm not short of money because I have my parliamentary salary, so I'm all right as far as that's concerned, and I can do whatever I like.'

In 1983 she had hurtled through the narrow St Stephen's entrance into the House of Commons Calamity Jane-style, in a flurry of publicity, posing for press photographers, guns poised in the Commons' shooting gallery. Male Tory MPs were unprepared for what hit them. It must have been like the words of the song 'when an irresistible force meets an immovable object'. Her style unnerved many of them.

Edwina Currie lacks the inhibitions that make many other women keep their heads down and 'behave well'. This absence of inhibition is a double-edged sword. The traditional upbringing for girls, where they are praised for good behaviour more than for achievement, has led women to assertiveness classes in droves as they aim to lose those inhibitions and gain the very courage required to stick heads above the parapet of twentieth-century life. Once they do pop their heads up over the trenches, it can shock and unnerve and destabilise other people's personalities.

Even as a school-girl Edwina knew she wanted to get up and out of Liverpool. 'When I was at school doing O Levels and A Levels, I knew I was going to leave home — apart from anything else because Liverpool was going downhill fast. In fact there were a whole batch of us in the sixth form at that sort of time who knew if we were going to make anything of our lives in the way we wanted to we were going to have to leave Liverpool.'

It was a headmistress and the Liverpool Institute for Girls that switched her life on to the upwards and onwards path. 'When I was 11 I won a scholarship to what was a slightly unusual grammar school. It had been one of the first proper schools in Liverpool long before the Education Act of 1870, and drew a lot of pupils from aspiring lower middle-class families all over the city. Nobody ever said, "What are you going to do?" as they do now. They said, "Which college are you going to?" Or "You're going to a college, aren't you — which one?" '

Her best subjects were maths and sciences. 'I thought I'd do chemistry at university. It wouldn't be too difficult for a Northern grammar school girl scientist to get into university, and it wasn't.'

At a careers advice session with the headmistress, she remembers saying, ' "My parents would like me to go to Liverpool or Manchester — Liverpool because I can stay at home, Manchester because we've got close family there I could stay with." She said, "Have you thought of going to Oxford or Cambridge?" I said, "Well, I'm not sure my parents would let me." She said, "Well, would they stop you from trying?" '

Her parents were not strict in their religious observance, but uneasy at the idea of their daughter leaving a community atmosphere for the non-Jewish culture of Oxford or Cambridge. They were afflicted with the fears shared with many other Jewish families in post-Hitler Europe. 'In their eyes, it wasn't *kosher* down there at Oxford. My parents had this bizarre cultural mix of keeping Jewish rules but not believing in them. People were feeling terribly insecure still — it wasn't that long after the war, nor was it that long after the foundation of the state of Israel. I was 10 years old at the time of Suez, when Israel had been bombed. Jewish people did feel very insecure and I understood that when I was at university.'

When she married a non-Jew and converted to Christianity, her father never spoke to her again. He died four years after her marriage.

Before the war, her father, like most Jewish people of that period, was a socialist, but he had changed his views by the time she was born, after he had become an employer himself in a tailoring business. 'He was disabled, so he hadn't had to fight during the war. He'd worked in a factory. The moment the war was over he and a couple of friends came out of the factory and set up in business. He was then in a position of being an employer with staff, having to try to deal with wage councils and trade unions and the environmental health officer and all the rest of it. He became very hostile to all kinds of authority and bureaucrats and became, I suspect, a classic small businessman.'

She remembers animated discussions with her father. 'He was a very argumentative character and I didn't entirely share all his views. Like most teenagers, I was much more idealistic than that. But I could see the point he was making about how the trades unions were ruining the docks and ruining Liverpool and all the rest of it and enterprise was being stifled.'

At school most of her fellow pupils were Labour. Former Labour leader of Liverpool Council, Derek Hatton, was a contemporary of hers at school though she doesn't remember meeting him. In school debates she was invited to put the opposing arguments. 'They'd ask me if I wanted to do the other side. I read it up and I got very convinced. By the time I got to university I knew where I stood.'

Before going up to Oxford, she worked in Distillers' biochemicals factory to save enough money for a seven-month trip to the East Coast of the United States. Like other women MPs —

Marjorie Mowlam, Teresa Gorman, Betty Boothroyd — the prolonged visit across the Atlantic had long-lasting effects. 'Being in America was very influential. I was at a key age, 18 years old. I saw this tremendously successful society which was nevertheless struggling to cope with social change, struggling and openly discussing and arguing how they were going to integrate people. I've always thought you should treat people as individuals, which is why racialism doesn't fit, it's why feminism doesn't fit, which is why patriotism is a difficult concept.' Edwina Currie viewed some of the 'women's lib' stands in the 1960s with grave suspicion: 'In the sixties and seventies, with Germaine Greer and Betty Friedan, women's issues were being raised in a way I disagreed with very strongly. They seemed to say "Men are the Establishment and we're anti-Establishment and we're therefore anti-men and while we're at it we don't approve of marriage." I thought "Blow this. This is not for me, I don't fancy this at all! There was no way I was going to have children unless I was married, and God willing, if I was going to be married I wanted to have children. I'm very glad I've got two daughters. There was no way I was going to be anti-male. I like men and always have done, and back in those days I think I probably found the company, the working environment of men, as councillors or often as colleagues in the university, more stimulating. I can still be the only woman around a table of men and taking part in the discussion. I enjoy it.'

Edwina Currie felt the United States outshone the Britain she had grown up in. 'It was a much more confident economy and society than ours. Ours was struggling — it was all about Britain's economic decline and we hadn't the foggiest idea how to sort out the long-term problems. Back here, there was nothing but all this short-term stuff about pay and prices control.'

New York was definitely Edwina Currie's kind of town: 'I loved New York and still do — to be in charge of a great city like that, I thought *that* would be tremendous.' American electioneering razzmatazz impressed her too. 'The New York Mayoral candidate had a band and a bandwagon, we'd never seen anything like that in this country. We do it all the time now but then it was very fresh.'

However she was not blind to the conflicts in the American Dream. 'On TV I saw the Watts riots in Los Angeles. When they set fire to the town area, I thought to myself that that could never happen in England!' The Vietnam War was intensifying.

'I listened to President Johnson talking about Vietnam. When he doubled the draft, all my friends got call-up papers and went out and got drunk. I said to them, "You're going to get killed, this is no game out there — do you know what you are going for?" They said, "Don't know, don't care, pass the bottle." '

Edwina was appalled. 'They had no idea what it was about and fifty odd thousand of them went off and got killed. I thought that, if we got involved in something like that in England, at least people would talk about it. These guys never talked about it, they hadn't the faintest idea where Vietnam was, they didn't know what the issues were, they didn't know whether they agreed or disagreed. All they knew was they were being sent. I realised then that one of the key things about a successful democracy is that people must be interested and talk about politics, even if the only time they do it is on a Saturday night in the pub.'

She admired the way Americans she met didn't depend on the State. 'I asked friends and relatives out there how they coped without a National Health Service. My aunt said people didn't depend on the government in that sort of way. You saved in order to pay for things like operations or eventualities and you took full insurance, that's how it was done in America. They were English and had gone across to America after the war. My aunt said that in England if somebody had got a problem they said, "Gee I've got a problem, the government's got to do something about it." In America they said: "Gee I've got a problem, maybe other people have got the same problem. Maybe I can do something about it and make a bit of money about it." And they did and they'd see a gap in the market and they'd say, "Wow, this is terrific!" '

After the excitement and glitz of New York, she sailed back across the Atlantic. Gloom settled in on her as the ship reached Merseyside. 'The boat docked in Liverpool and I walked out at six o'clock in the morning. I looked at Liverpool and straightaway I thought that there had got to be something better than this.'

Edwina had won an open scholarship to St Anne's College. A couple of weeks later she left Liverpool for good, first stop Oxford University.

'I came back from America thinking there were aspects of a democracy that had to be preserved and encouraged — that meant people should talk about politics, people should stand for election. If the good guys don't stand for election, then the bad guys will. Societies are kept free and uncorrupt in all sorts of ways, but one of them is because good people are willing to give up their lives in order to stand as representatives. You care about your own people and the people who are elected to look after you. In my view the welfare of the Party and the welfare of the country are the same thing.'

She joined all the political party clubs at Oxford, including Labour. 'The political clubs had closed meetings for members only. If you wanted to hear a Cabinet minister, you had to be a member of the Labour group. We were all members, it was hilarious because we were only members out of convenience. I remember getting into a Labour Party meeting, as a card carrying member, and heckling Dennis Healey. He got very indignant about it. I can't remember if they threw me out or not. I think I got a bit cowed and shot out after a bit.'

By Christmas 1965 she had mapped a path in her mind. She knew she wanted to become a Member of Parliament. 'I would have been 19 then. I'd come back from America. I switched from reading science to politics, philosophy and economics. At my very first chemistry lecture, I listened to a wonderful man called Sir Lawrence Bragg who, when he was young, had been an assistant to his father. The two Braggs had discovered the crystalline structure of metals. He was wonderful. I knew I would never make a contribution to science like that. I didn't want to spend my time in a laboratory.'

She worked hard on her new subjects. 'I'd never even heard of Gladstone. When I had to do an essay on Gladstone I had to go and read *everything*. I also had a struggle for the first year because the tutor I was allocated to was a lady called Jennifer Heart who was a Marxist — and here was I, a Tory!'

Edwina combined political theory with practical pavement politics by joining the local Conservative Association. 'I went to a Conservative fayre in Oxford Town Hall where I was accosted by a young councillor called Michael Pinto Duschinsky who asked me to come and have tea. Michael, it turned out, was a Junior Research Fellow at Merton and tea in his rooms was really quite something. I'd never seen such a beautiful place as Merton.'

Tea led to a dinner invitation. 'I asked: "What do I wear?" He said, "You can wear anything. Except jeans is not a great idea, this is one of the slightly better dinners." I was a Scholar and one of the things I had long discovered was that if you wore your

Scholar's gown, doors opened.'

She wore her Scholar's gown to the dinner. 'It was a guest dinner and he met me at the gate and took me in through a door into a room full of old gentlemen wearing gowns. They were all chatting terribly nicely. Then a gong went and a door opened and we were on high table. I said to Michael, "Who are you?" He said, "I teach here." '

The Scholar seized the chance. 'I asked, "Could you teach me?" "Of course," he said. And he did. He introduced me to Robert Blake and to good sound, solid teachers. Bob Skidelski taught me for a while. Bob is not Tory, but he's a sound teacher — if you wanted to do a certain topic he would do it thoroughly.' She had become part of the Oxbridge 'old boy network'.

'In '83, there were 17 of us who came into parliament at that General Election who had known each other at Oxford. I'm the first woman who was active in the Oxford Union to become a Member of Parliament. William Waldegrave was President of the Union the year I was Treasurer. Douglas Hogg had been President before him; Douglas is very underrated, he's very good indeed. Tim Smith (Member for Beaconsfield), Chris Murphy (Member for Welwyn and Hatfield) and Steve Norris (Member for Oxford East) came in too. Steve Norris and I were also at school together. He was Head Boy and I was a Deputy Head Girl. The Cambridge Union was more successful at producing women. People like Ann Mallalieu, and Helene Hayman who became an MP too.'

It took Edwina Currie twelve years from first being elected as a Birmingham City Councillor to her appointment as Junior Minister for Health. When the Prime Minister has a reshuffle to bring in new Ministers (and to let serving Ministers go), she informs the in-coming (and out-going) Ministers herself.

'I could see the gentlemen of the press and television hanging about outside my home. They all knew because No. 10 had told them. *They* said the telephone call was coming. The phone went. It was Nigel Wicks who was then the Prime Minister's Private Secretary. He said, "The Prime Minister would like to know if you can spare her some time today or tomorrow?"

'I said, "What did you have in mind?" and he said, "Could you come down?" I said, "Yes, when?" He said, "It's all right, there's no hurry, but if you could come down reasonably soon she'd like to have a word with you." I said, "Do you mean this evening?" and he said, "Yes, that'll be fine, we'll see you at about 7 p.m. then."'

The exchange baffled Edwina. Had it been *a* call but not *the* call? 'I put the phone down and thought how odd it was. I thought what you got was "Hello, this is Margaret here." The TV people came to the door and said, "You've had your phone call?" I said, "No, I don't think I have to be honest." So they played around taking pictures of me and I said "Look, if there's no announcement, will you promise me you'll not publish them?"'

Edwina telephoned a friend. 'I said I'd just had a phone call from Nigel Wicks who works at No. 10 and he had asked me to come down to London. My friend went, "Eek!" I asked what that meant. He said, "It means you get in the car and you drive and drive and get down there!"'

She got in her car and ran straight into a traffic jam. 'I turned on the car radio. It was about 5.30. At 5.00 they'd started saying, "We're expecting the announcement of the ministerial reshuffle at 5.30 this evening and we'll bring it to you when we've got it." And here was I stuck in a great fat traffic jam. 5.30 comes and goes. At 5.50 I'm *still* stuck in this traffic jam and they come on the radio again and announce, "We were expecting a ministerial reshuffle, but we gather the Prime Minister hasn't been able to contact everybody." By then, I thought I did not have a ministerial job. Maybe she wanted me to do something like recruit more women MPs or doing something in Conservative Central Office. I thought she'd actually done the reshuffle. At 6.50 I was in Swiss Cottage. I thought, "This is great, I've been stuck in a traffic jam the whole way." I parked the car at Swiss Cottage, phoned Downing Street and said I was sorry and they said, "Don't worry, take your time." I said, "I'm coming down on the tube," and they said, "Just take your time." There was no point in taking a taxi because this road was solid.

'I bunged the car in a car park, got on the tube, came out at Parliament Square, told myself I was *not* running down Whitehall, strolled down Whitehall, smiled at everybody, walked in and she was standing in the doorway saying, "Come in, my dear, come in, you're the last one. I want you to be Minister at the Department of Health, is that all right?" She repeated it because I must have looked absolutely stunned. What she'd done was spend the morning seeing off the old ones — she'd had them all in round the back room to have a drink and a talk. That must be an awful thing. From five o'clock onwards she'd had all the new ones in. The Prime Minister opened the door and there were all my pals standing there, grinning from ear to ear and asking what I had got. It was hysterically funny. Then she rang up and said, "Come on, Dennis, they're all here now." I said to the others, "As far as I'm concerned you can stay put, but I've got work to do" — and ran.'

In an interview with Anthony Clare on BBC Radio 4 when she was Junior Minister of Health, Edwina Currie said: 'The reason I do this crazy job, and I work 100 hours a week, and put up with the pressure — pressure is not quite the same as criticism because pressure can come when things are going well and you are under pressure to do even more of it — the reason I put up with the pressure is I believe in what we're doing. I'm quite sure, with a degree of certainty that perhaps I try and communicate in the way I do things, that most of what we're doing is not only right, but it's going to be very effective. Maybe this is part of a style of a government of our particular colour at the moment. It leads me therefore to have a kind of protective coating. You don't stand up and say rude things about people's eating habits in Newcastle and expect them all to jump up and down and say great we agree with you — you do it because it's necessary and you do it in the hope and the prayer you're actually going to *convince* people. While all the flak's going on you stick to that, you cling to it and you cling to it as a person. There isn't a separation between me as a person and my job. I am that same person. If you're asking, does one never get hurt the answer is, of course I get hurt. Yes, *of course*, one gets hurt.'

## CLARE SHORT

'Clare Short is actually a very attractive personality. She is the sultry Anna Magnani of the backbenches; earthy, gutsy and a very good contributor to debates.'

*Teresa Gorman*

When Clare Short launched her Page Three campaign against pornography, she unleased a nuclear salvo of sexist ridicule against her from the chauvinists in the House of Commons, and the tabloid press, who cruelly dubbed her 'Crazy Clare'. At the same time she became a heroine for millions of women across the country. 'I was a woman and wanted to stand on women's issues but I wasn't as conscious of it as a firm part of what I bring with me as I am now. I now feel enlarged by it and it affects all my politics. I'm interested in many issues that go beyond what people would call classical women's issues, but the perspective that comes with it affects the whole of politics. This might sound romantic. But it's about a more caring politics and a more democratic politics, looking for a style of politics and of organising society that is less egotistical and hierarchical, and more open and inclusive of people. I suspect, but don't know, that the Tory women are less close to this burgeoning new outlook amongst women. It isn't there as a supportive mechanism for them so strongly and clearly as it is for women on the Left, because that's broadly where the women's movement puts itself. You get little flashes of it across the floor but not strongly.'

Clare Short scores very high marks with women, both inside and outside the House of Commons, and especially those in the centre or left of politics. She has championed causes of fairness and justice for women and ethnic minorities. 'You realise you're feeling differently than most of them in here, most of the men MPs. You bring your womanness with you. If you didn't have it there all in a package before, you find it once you get in here. You're responding in a different way and you have a different understanding.'

Her Catholic father came from a village just north of the border in Northern Ireland. 'He was angry about partition.' Clare Short recalls: 'I remember Suez. I was 10 then and I knew they were entitled to have their canal. All the kids would say rude things about Nasser and I had to put them right. As a kid I delivered leaflets and things and I joined the Labour Party formally in 1970.' Her own uncompromising support for the reunification of Ireland makes some people uneasy. Clare is a battler against injustice and her Irish republican background informs her sympathy with human rights struggles of peoples all around the world — whether Palestinian, Turk, Chilean, Nicaraguan.

She still seems surprised to find herself a Member of Parliament. Like many women she always thought of MPs as a special breed. 'I come from a tight, confident, strong sort of family, but people like us aren't MPs. We do all sorts of other good things in life, but we're not those kind of people. There was plenty of discussion at home about national and international affairs, but nobody had stood for public office.

'I remember when I went to grammar school, I was looking for those teachers who appear in books, the ones you get really close to and really admire. Although I liked quite a lot of them, I didn't find one. I thought that when I went to university I'd find these heroic, intellectual figures. I didn't really. I got on and respected some of the people who taught me, but not on that heroic level. I had this sense of a search for heroes which was constantly disappointed. I'm at the end of that journey now. I understand that there aren't any heroes. We've all got feet of clay, we've all got good and bad qualities.'

The university grant system meant Clare and her older sister were the first generation in the family to go to university. 'Like my Dad, who was a natural intellectual, we used to talk with great awe about university people and then you found you could be one — it was mind-blowing. It was the sixties when you didn't worry about jobs, so because of my natural interest I did a degree in politics.'

After a year at Keele University, she transferred to Leeds and then did research for a couple of years. 'Then I thought I'd better get into the real world. I thought I would go and look at the British Establishment. I didn't have the commitment to be a life civil servant, but I took the exams and went to work in the Home Office. It was extremely interesting.'

Although a staunch Labour supporter, she found no difficulty in maintaining the neutrality demanded of a professional civil servant. 'If you're a political person and you do understand your politics, you understand neutrality much more thoroughly than people who think they're not political.'

She was one of the privileged graduate entry, entering as an Assistant Principal. 'You get moved to four different jobs and you get into a Ministerial private office and you're going to be promoted. All but me were male or Oxbridge. I *saw* the Establishment. I ran a couple of Ministers' private offices.' Clare stayed on through to the election in 1974 with Conservative Minister, Mark Carlisle. When the Labour government came in, she began to work for Alex Lyon, minister at the Home Office. (In a true-life *Yes, Minister* script, she later married him.) 'I was there for five years, including the three-day week in 1974. We were sitting there while the country ground to a halt.'

During the three-day week, she began to think about standing for Parliament. 'We had time to sit around and discuss the situation. I felt the strain of the pseudo-neutrality of the Civil Service. I'm more of a person of strong views, who wants to do things and make things better. I was very interested in policy and changing things. I had this secret thought in my mind: "I'll pack this in and perhaps come back honestly and do the job from the other side of the fence."'

Civil Service Private Secretaries have a special observers' box reserved for them in the House of Commons Chamber, immediately on the right as you enter the Chamber, at the opposite end to the Speaker. She frequently went and sat there to watch the debates. 'I realised I could do the job better — that's the crunch thing that happened to me. I thought that these people weren't particularly impressive. I knew now I really did fancy being an MP, and because I had seen the feet of clay, I knew I was competent to do it. I marched out of the Civil Service over a difference about inner-city deprivation. Those were the days of full employment and I got another job within months.'

The five years in the Civil Service had been good training for parliament. 'All these people are aspiring to be Junior Ministers, but I actually know all about it. That sounds a bit arrogant, but I do know how it works. I was lucky in a number of ways. I knew what the job of an MP was like, I knew it wasn't scary, and Alex firmly encouraged me. The hardest thing of all for women is to come out and confess or say I actually *might* be able to do this. That's quite unlike most men.'

At her first attempt at selection for a Parliamentary seat, she lost out to Peter Tatchell for the Bermondsey by-election.

'People say women have to fight lots of hopeless seats and struggle and fight for it. I didn't. It just came right. A safe seat just came up, and it was in the place I grew up. My folks lived there. Luck, or the gods, were just on my side. Sheila Wright, the MP for the seat, had been unwell and had bad things happen to her family and she stood down.'

Due to boundary changes in 1983, a frantic 'musical chairs' game of seat switching was taking place ahead of an anticipated general election. Seat disruption caused by boundary changes throws a number of senior MPs and Ministers on to the Parliamentary job-search market, looking for another safe seat to occupy. This stacks the odds very high against the selection of a novice candidate for a good seat. A winnable seat coming on the market will attract up to 300 candidates. This time luck was on Clare Short's side. 'Some of the big tanks didn't come for Ladywood because they thought the constituency might disappear completely in the boundary changes. I put myself forward.'

Clare Short soon found herself the parliamentary candidate,

but she was not home and dry yet. Another hurdle arose. In the musical chairs of the boundary changes, two constituencies were merged into one. It left Albert Bore, a sitting candidate, and Clare Short, a parliamentary candidate, competing for the one constituency. 'It became a run-off between us. We had all the meetings and I came out on top. I had already started working with Sheila Wright, doing the advice bureaux with her.'

Within days the election was called, and Clare Short became Labour MP for the multi-ethnic inner city constituency of Birmingham, Ladywood, with a majority of over 9000. Husband and wife had hoped to work together in the House of Commons but in a left-hand-of-God swipe, Alex Lyon lost his seat at York after seventeen years as an MP.

Soon after, Clare started to take up the women's angle for which she is now widely admired and respected. There had been five girls and two boys in her family. 'When the women's movement was growing and women were belonging to women's groups, I was quite sympathetic to it all, but never actively belonged to a women's group. I was always proud of being a woman, but it hadn't ever been one of my sort of top issues. My brothers grew up with us, sharing the washing up and making the beds, and then they left home. When all these women started to say stop oppressing us, my brothers said, what a swizzle, we've had big sisters pushing *us* around all our lives.

'Then after I was elected, I can remember saying something about low pay and I got this letter from a woman saying, "Thank you so much for being there." She said, "Low pay is women's fate in employment — it's been mine, and I'm now thinking of my daughter and the future." I was very moved by that letter. Increasingly I had a very enlarging, lovely sense of being there for all those women who weren't in the Commons, because that agenda needs addressing and isn't being addressed. That's the thing you find. On some issues that you care about, you get the odd male goodie on the other side. You just get this sense you can trust someone, pop into another issue — and you can't, they've let you down. Robert Adley is quite good on South Africa, for example, but he was the MP who spoke against my Page Three Bill. At the end of his speech against it, Robert Adley said, "And this Bill gets the booby prize". That kind of double innuendo. You could hear the sniggering. Mention *anything* to do with breasts and they all double up!

'On the occasion of the Page Three Bill the Labour MPs were

being fine and supportive. Some of that was the nature of the Commons. You broadly have a sense of loyalty to your side — and also I think that because the women's section in the Labour Party is strengthening, the Labour men are becoming educated and know they have to be a bit careful and respect the women or they might get into trouble when they get home. That process is working very well in the proper democratic way. They come up to you and say they're thinking of doing something and ask if you think it's all right — just checking out — which is rather sweet in a way. It doesn't mean they're perfect but they're trying because they have to.'

On Thursday afternoons and Friday mornings, Intercity trains abound with MPs returning for the weekend to their constituencies. Clare Short is usually one of them. But one Friday, instead of boarding the British Rail Intercity to Birmingham, she stayed on in the House of Commons to fight a battle on behalf of her sex and finished up on the front pages for fighting a totally different one, after a spontaneous outburst against Page Three of the *Sun*. She had originally stayed in the House on the Friday morning because Enoch Powell had introduced a Private Member's Bill on embryos. 'They called it stopping embryo research, but what it meant was an end to help for women or couples with infertility problems. Those sorts of things come up and you just feel passionately about them.'

After Enoch Powell's bill, Winston Churchill was bringing in a bill under the Private Member's procedure to reform the Obscene Publications Act. 'It was the famous "laundry list bill", a nonsense bill, that would have outlawed most sex education material, most medical text-books, and even war reporting because it included extreme violence.' Opposition Parties saw Winston Churchill's bill as a certain danger to real freedom.

'I stayed because we had to prevent it going through and that meant, in all the weird procedures of this place, we had to keep the discussion going. I was sitting there and all these MPs were getting up saying that women throughout the country feared sexual attacks and that people who didn't pass this bill had to be in favour of sex attacks. It started to make me really angry. So I just got up and made this speech about how it was a nonsensical and dangerous bill. It was true women certainly do fear sexual attacks, but if MPs really cared and wanted to do something about it why then didn't we start with something practical we could get rid of, which wouldn't endanger any liberty or freedom, like carving the Page Three thing out of the press! There are dozens of copies of every type of newspaper lying around the various rooms of the House of Commons for Members to read, and since I'd come in here I'd tended to flip through a lot of newspapers. It hits you and hurts you when you go through them and all those images pour out of the newspapers. And as I spoke against the Churchill Bill I found myself saying: "Indeed, I think I'll introduce my own 10-minute-rule bill on this."' When women heard about the debate, Clare Short was inundated with letters of support. Shortly afterwards she introduced her Bill.

'Following that I got *hundreds* of letters and cards from women saying, "I was just doing the ironing and I had to stop and I'm quivering with anger and are you OK and don't worry, we care about you." Not just trying to say we agree, but also this enormous sense of worry and concern for me, to look after me, which ♦was just lovely. The Page Three argument enlarged women's sense of confidence, finding we all felt the same thing. That was a liberation in itself — to protest and push it back. There's heavy porn on the top shelf at every single little newsagent in Britain. You just look up and look away and feel offended.'

Clare Short happily wears short skirts which a High Court judge might well describe as 'provocative' rather than 'fragrant'. 'I think where we are on women's clothes is brilliant now because we can wear anything. We can wear short skirts, long skirts, trousers or get dressed up. Women are entitled to feel good and be beautiful or be scruffy, whatever they're feeling like doing. I do think in that we're freer than men. They have to wear suits. I'm so glad I'm not a man, having to put that uniform on every day. We do things with our clothes that say things about our mood. The suggestion that if women dress in an attractive way they're making themselves vulnerable to sexual attack or even advances is intolerable. You've got to shift public perceptions of what's acceptable.

'You need a whole series of steps, it seems to me, using public opinion and women's perception to take us forward. Maybe in time we could say you can only have heavy porn sold in licensed shops, and, just a minute, we'll have a look at the Advertising Standards regulations. But because we're turning over something so deep, we've got to go a step at a time, using law, using public opinion, using women's buying power, using our power to protest. But it's hard to measure what you're doing if you stand up and speak for something. Over time public opinion switches. You can never measure what any one of us did towards it. Sometimes you feel despondent. This is a bad era for anyone broadly on the Left who considers themselves a Radical.

'Once my father died (and I think this is a common experience when one of your parents dies), I really felt that sense of mortality. When you're young, you feel as though you're going to live for ever. I'm 43, I know I'm pretty fit and healthy and vigorous and I think I've got twenty good strong years left. I'm not going to disappear after that, but presumably I'll slow down a bit. I think I have ability and caring — I'd just like to be able to pour it into some creative space so that something better can happen, rather than protest against badness.

'I could give you a list of things I hope for in my lifetime. I think it's possible we'll see peace in Ireland. I hope there'll be a Palestinian State and a transformation of the situation in the Middle East. I hope there'll be a transformation in Europe, East–West relations move towards an end to the Cold War, cuts in arms spending and then much less poverty in the world. Now the issues most important to me are: women, unemployment, low pay, equal opportunities, training and the whole package which could make this a much more open society for everyone, but especially the disadvantaged.

'Everything interests me. In terms of my constituency, housing is very serious, poverty is very serious, I care about disarmament and I care about South Africa. I haven't really done anything apart from being supportive about Chile and Nicaragua and Central America, but I feel for them. But it's a real problem if you're that kind of person. You have to rein yourself in or you're going to splatter yourself everywhere and be ineffective.

'I love the constituency work. Times are hard in Ladywood and lots of people come to see me. In a surprisingly large number of cases, you can get what they want sorted out because they're entitled to it, but the system's malfunctioning so badly that alone they can't get what they're entitled to. Just that sort of affection and the sense of little victories keeps you going. I like that.

'Sometimes I think I've only got one life, I've got this vigour and my brain. Maybe I could have done more or had more impact or more satisfaction by working in another job. I do think that sometimes. I feel at the moment a lot of my ability is not fully used as creatively as it could be used — that's one of the things about this job. If we're going to be in Opposition for a long time that harps back to that thing about maybe I could be doing more good somewhere else.

'I'd like to be a senior figure in a Labour government that dispersed power throughout Britain, that started a kind of transformation. It's not just bringing in a better benefit for those poor people down there. It's dispersal of power, engaging the people more. Sixth-formers are very perceptive. When you go and give a talk they ask if you are going to be the leader of the party. My emotion about that is that I'd rather not be the leader. I'd rather be a centrally powerful figure. That might have something to do with the woman ducking out thing. Some of it is just not liking all the flummery that goes with it.'

# 2.
# THE YAHOOS — A WOMAN IN A MAN'S PRESERVE

Attitudes towards women inside political parties are without a doubt improving. But on an individual basis, in constituencies and in the House of Commons itself, there are still handfuls of 'Yahoos' around. Some are pale imitations of Rik Mayall's slimy character Alan B'stard in the TV series *New Statesman*. Others never forgot schoolboy ritual or behave to primitive tribal rules. But Yahoos give women politicians an exceedingly unpleasant time. The word Yahoo is defined in Colling English dictionary as a 'crude, brutish or obscenely coarse person' and comes from the name of a race of brutish creatures resembling men in Jonathan Swift's *Gulliver's Travels*.

The Yahoo manages to get away with his behaviour in the House of Commons partly because his remarks and jibes at women and women Members of Parliament do not get into the Hansard reports and are not picked up clearly by the broadcasting microphones. Few of the Yahoos' voters know about their shocking, offensive behaviour. This irritating and destructive handful of male MPs gets away with behaviour in Parliament that is despised in the lager lout.

The Yahoo is known to hurl snide comments and insults like 'slag' at women MPs across the Chamber. He demands 'Tell us your age, love!' This nasty and intimidating school-boy behaviour of a handful of male MPs can make life a misery for too many women MPs on both sides of the House. Usually the Yahoos make downright offensive personal attacks on a woman's physical appearance.

The majority of the worst offenders sit on the Tory benches but there is Yahoo behaviour from the Opposition too. A Tory woman was aghast — and badly hurt — when a Labour back-

bencher called across the Chamber to her, 'You're all plastic.
You're kept together with hormone implants. Which part of you
is real and which is plastic?' When Labour MP Joan Ruddock
was protesting about police strip-searching women at Greenham
Common, other women MPs were shaken to hear Tory men
MPs opposite make remarks like 'Cor we'd like to strip-search
you too!'

Teresa Gorman, Conservative MP for Billericay, is not a wilt-
ing daisy. But even she is shaken by the sheer crudity and
cruelty of some of the men in the House of Commons. 'Shortly
after I got in to the House of Commons, Dennis Skinner would
shout across the Chamber to me, "Tell us your age! Where's
your birth certificate? Here she comes, Harvey Proctor in drag!"
It was all quite intimidating. But of course the majority of men in
the House behave impeccably and treat women as equal
colleagues.

'At first the Chamber of the House is a cockpit designed for men
to attack each other with words. That is why the two sides are
seated face to face. The whole structure of competitive debate is
alien to a woman's nature. When they are given the verbal equivalent of a punch on the nose, their instinct is to retreat, shocked by
the aggressiveness of the unsolicited attack.'

Mitcham and Morden MP Angela Rumbold was perfectly
accustomed to working with male colleagues in business and
town halls, before she entered Parliament with a stunning by-
election win in 1982. But nothing had prepared her for her first
encounters with the male tribal territory of Westminster. 'Parliament — now there's a culture shock! You get in and there are
all these people who look at you and think "Oh God, a *woman*
who's won a by-election, a woman who's been feted, a woman
who's going to come and disrupt our lives — we've already got
enough of them (they'd only got about 20 women MPs when I
entered the House in 1982) and she's going to bounce all over
us." It took me a week to realise I mustn't bounce, I must sink
into the woodwork. The whole atmosphere was one of slight
condescension. We must be nice to you — but please do go away.'

Clare Short agrees with Angela Rumbold. 'Just the style of
the House of Commons makes you very aware you're a woman,
actually acting in it rather than observing it from outside. It's all
these hundreds and hundreds of men — more than 600 of them
— in grey suits with blue or red ties. We stand out because there
are so few of us women MPs, and we wear different clothes.

Even the rituals reinforce it. For example, if you make a point of order while a division is on, you have to sit down and put a top hat on. One night I put on the top hat to make a point of order and the male Members went wild! It was obviously something to do with top hats and cabaret — the Folies Bergère. It made them have those kind of associations! It seems a lot connected to certain articles of clothing — certain things trigger some sense of woman as different.'

In his biography of Margaret Thatcher, *One of Us*, Hugo Young writes: 'This exceedingly male establishment took time for a woman even so forensically skilled as Margaret Thatcher to master.' One of Margaret Thatcher's colleagues observed: 'She is often formidable, but only in the afternoon. At night the Commons becomes a much more masculine place, and she fades.'

Though they shy away from stating it publically, women MPs privately admit the very close association between an excess of alcohol in the blood and the loutish behaviour. There is general agreement that Yahoos are at their worst whenever there is a debate on issues of particular concern to millions of women around the country, but Yahoo-ism rises to a crescendo in the long after-dinner debates. Labour MP Maria Fyfe said, 'I notice if a woman is speaking at the despatch box late at night they talk loudly and misbehave. Men get this too, of course, but there's that extra edge of hostility in remarks to women and they do it more often to the women.'

Shouts and screams directed at other male MPs do not seem to concentrate on the man's physical appearance or deformity — a large nose of a bald head, for example. But when directed at a woman MP it goes straight to her looks or femininity. Teresa Gorman recalls the occasion when a women MP on the Opposition benches was on her feet speaking in the Chamber. 'She's tall with short, cropped hair. Men on my side were saying, "Do you think she's a woman or a man? Don't you think she looks more like a man than a woman?" That kind of talk. And I turned round and said "Well, some of you are no picture post-cards." I mean, there are plenty of fairies here who would pass for a woman in a skirt.' Teresa Gorman does not like the treatment meted out to Labour women by a handful of loutish MPs on her own side. 'When a woman on the other side gets on her feet to say something, there's always a group of men sitting near you who will comment loudly. For example, when a Labour woman

MP was talking on the Abortion Bill they would say, "I wonder how many times she's been through the back-streets!" I found this particularly offensive and I've always been slightly ashamed for not reporting it to the Speaker.'

Debates on issues of importance to women like Abortion, Parental Leave, Equal Pay or Pornography bring out the Yahoos in force. Labour front-bench Spokesperson on Women Jo Richardson readily picks out some of the men who have given her a tough time: 'Male MPs like Tony Marlow, Nicholas Soames, Eric Forth. When we've had a special debate with a real perspective to it and I'm answering from the front bench, or Ann Clwyd, my deputy, is doing so, they'll come in to take the mickey. It's horrible. It just makes me so angry and it is so puerile and juvenile. They came into a serious debate on parental leave last year. The speeches from our side were very serious, from both men and women. But there was this gang on the other side who came in to the Chamber to have a bit of fun: "What's all this about parental leave? We don't want men to be at home!"'

'Teresa Gorman has found this difficult too, I understand, because she is not into rubbishing women or issues of concern to women. Indeed, though her political views on the market and on hanging, for example, are diametrically opposed to mine, she was part of our team on the Alton Abortion Bill Committee, and she was brilliant, and a real "sister".'

Getting away with Yahoo-ism in the clubby secrecy of the benches will continue unless disapproval of colleagues becomes widespread, or direct sanctions are levied by Party whips. But being exposed to voter disapproval is the ultimate pressure on any MP. I was in the House of Commons when Jo Richardson introduced her Sex Equality Bill. The Yahoos went straight into their mocking and jeering act. But the instant she read out a letter of support for the Bill from the huge National Federation of Women's Institutes you could have heard a pin drop in the Chamber — it suddenly dawned that over 300,000 constituency stalwarts were taking the Sex Equality Bill very seriously indeed. If such behaviour towards women MPs — and women's interests — was more widely publicised outside the House of Commons, it could lead to immediate voter-rejection at the next election.

Journalist Lesley White in a feature in *Elle* asked MP Marjorie Mowlam what effect she thought it would have when

TV cameras invaded that sanctuary of prep school protocol. 'Good thing,' Mo Mowlam replied. 'It might quell the worst excesses of male carry-on. You know, all the put-down shouts of "Sit down, what do you know?" when I'm speaking on steel or shipbuilding.'

Such feelings are perhaps encapsulated by John Carlisle, Conservative MP for Luton North. The *Evening Standard* of 2 February 1987 quoted him as saying: 'Women are natural bitches. They mistrust other women and have a general sense of insecurity about their representing their interests. The day's work here at the House of Commons is more naturally tackled by a man. Once you start giving women special privileges and pushing them forward — and it's the same with ethnic minorities — you give them a false sense that they are equal to the task.'

The behaviour of Eric Forth, Conservative Member for Mid-Worcestershire and now a Junior Minister, is notable. His misogynist behaviour at the time of Clare Short's motion on pornography was so outrageous that political columnist Edward Pearce wrote in *DX* magazine: 'The awful Eric Forth, representing designer bad taste, responded to Clare Short's motion with an offensive display of changing-room humour.'

Clare Short still remembers how unpleasant it was. 'When I did my Page Three Porn Bill I thought I was just making a little protest but it all escalated. I got these juvenile, hysterical, bawdy, leering remarks about me. Tory MP Peter Bruinvels was the centre, but there was a clump of Tory MPs. The House of Commons is a cruel place if you lose your way. If you get upset and distressed by it they go on, but if you can go through it then you can shut them up.' Observers in the Press Gallery say that one Conservative Member was so proud of his performance during the Page Three debate that he has been known to wear a gold chain with a gold model of a topless woman as a battle trophy.

Clare Short feels male MPs reflect a lot of what goes on in the country at large. 'You do get some rough behaviour but I think most women get it in their life anyway, and you have to deal with it. Soon after I arrived at the Commons I became perceived as a strong feminist, probably before I used that same label about myself. It was both their reaction to me, and other women's reaction to me, that strengthened the very joyous sense in me of being a woman, of being different, of being there connected with lots of other women who aren't in, and who ought to be here, in the Commons. For me that was a very lovely experience.'

Silvia Rodgers in the book *Women and Space: Ground Rules and Social Maps* compares the male tribal territorial possessiveness of the House of Commons to male cults in other societies, specifically to the ones considered to be the most primitive. 'The men of New Guinea and of lowland Latin America protect the boundaries of their men's houses by the deterrence of violence. The Members of the House of Westminster cope with the intrusion of women by more subtle strategies. Common practices include attempts to throw doubts on a woman's femininity, to question her legitimacy in the House, to place her on a different plane of reality. Even today, women in the House are seen as alien, as children, or as unreal. None of these categories has the legitimate right to be in the House.'

Teresa Gorman echoes this idea. 'It really upsets me, but I think it's part of the nastiness of male coteries. There's a very powerful sense of male coterie in the Commons. That's why I think I quite like the Labour women. You get a feeling and you can talk a different type of talk. In the debate which Edwina did on women's health, we had practically all women speakers. The whole debate had an entirely different tenor. There was a different feeling of camaraderie among us women.'

Maggie Ewing was away from the House of Commons for eight years. She's noticed a genuine improvement since her re-entry. 'I don't think there's as much sexism in the House now as there was in the seventies — I don't find the comments and the conversations anything like as sexist as they were. Male MPs would pat you on your head, they'd pat you on your bottom. In the seventies I was conscious of the general attitude of "You're young, you're female, you're attractive" and you did have to fight to be taken seriously. I think they've got more used to women MPs. There are more of us around. We're part of the scene, we're not unusual anymore. There are a lot of young men here and I imagine many of their wives are working wives, that helps. But maybe I'm just older and I don't get the same remarks! Dawn Primarolo very much has that problem because she's a very young attractive-looking woman and there's just this assumption women don't know and don't understand the issues, and it really is infuriating.'

Edwina Currie is more entertained by the spectacle. 'You get someone like Dawn Primarolo who's a very, very attractive girl sitting right at the top of the back-benches with a short-skirt, crossing her legs. Every time she crosses and uncrosses her legs all these lads on our side go "mmoooorre"! It's really very funny! She probably isn't quite conscious of what's happening when the back-row opposite sways. One day one of my colleagues sitting next to me was murmuring gently, "Oh don't do that, don't do that!" and I said, "What's the matter?" and he said "Dawn's crossing her legs again." Dawn Primarolo has problems because she's young and attractive and very bright. But don't overlook the fact that being a woman here has its benefits, because you are noticed very quickly, and you're more likely to be called if you want to speak. If you want to make the most of opportunities like that then you probably have more opportunities than an exactly equivalent man in the same constituency in the same Party would have. You're certainly much more interesting to the media and for a politician the media is a *weapon*, it's part of the way of life.'

Speaker Bernard Weatherill says he has never received any complaints from women MPs. 'I feel quite sure no one would hesitate to raise it as a point of order,' he states. He admits he only hears what comes through the two microphones on the Speaker's Chair. 'On the whole I only hear the Member who is speaking on their feet and not the extraneous comments. I would take it up at once if anything like that came to my attention.'

But several targets of the Yahoos say they feel too intimidated by the male public school atmosphere to raise the issue. As a woman MP remarked, to bring a complaint — either as a point of order, or by informing the Party whips — could bring about the type of unpleasant face to face confrontation no woman particularly wants. Nor do women MPs want the charge 'She can't take it' levied at her, despite the fact women MPs have universally had to show terrific guts and stamina to get into the House of Commons in the first place.

There seem to be fewer complaints about sexist Yahoo behaviour on Labour's benches, almost certainly because of the born-again reforms on equality within the Labour Parliamentary Party over the past couple of years. Thirteen women now sit on the Labour front-bench, and one of the whips, Llin Golding, is a woman. I have heard no complaints of sexist behaviour at Westminster about Nationalist, Irish, SDP or Liberal Democrat MPs.

One certain way to improve behaviour on the Tory side would be to promote more Tory women MPs to senior positions starting with that all-male bastion, the Tory Whips' Office. Yahoos understand nothing better than schoolboy lines of authority. We all know the House of Commons has an outdated male oriented air. We seem to take it for granted that as a matter of tradition the Palace of Westminster has been dominated by men. It positively bristles with barber shop, shooting gallery, and wafts of after-shave. Reforms are desperately needed to make it a more human place to work.

Change does certainly seem to be in the air. On Radio Humberside recently, the Conservative MP for Beverley, James Cran — certainly not a Yahoo himself — said, 'I want my daughter to be an MP when she grows up, but I wouldn't want her to be exposed to the sort of behaviour we occasionally see in the House.'

# 3.
# CLASS OF '87

There has been a marked change in climate in the late eighties. The all-male ozone layer that hung over the parties has developed a hole that is rapidly opening wider. Practically every week, in every political party, people are saying, both at internal meetings and in public, they hope far more women will stand for elected office and especially for Parliament.

The motivation? It is right and fair and proper to have an equal balance of women and men working together to shape society. There is a large pool of female talent as yet untapped. Parties are embarrassed at their small number of women MPs. And practical as ever, they are also just waking up to the importance of wooing the female vote.

This is not to say there aren't some serious obstacles remaining. These obstacles are partly a consequence of attitude and partly a consequence of structure. Only a handful of winnable seats come vacant at each election — there is no retirement age for Members of Parliament and despite all their moaning and groaning about the hard work and the long hours. MPs really do seem to die with their boots on — and it is usually boots, not high-heeled shoes. This means there is hardly a vacuum into which large numbers of women can move.

Attitude is the other serious block. There is a need for sufficient numbers of women to realise they can stand for Parliament. At the same time there are still far too many party members on selection committees and at selection meetings who need to update their attitudes. At candidate selection the underlying image of a Member of Parliament in too many people's minds still seems to be that minority human being, the white male in his middle-thirties with a wife (i.e. two for the price of one in the constituency) and two children. A family dog is an extra plus for pulling in the animal lovers' votes.

The different party cultures have responded in different ways. Labour constituencies must have at least one woman on their short-list of candidates for selection. At the last election some Labour constituencies had all-women short-lists. Out of 633 candidates Labour fielded 92 women in 1987. The Liberal Democrats must look for two women and two men on their short-lists. The Conservatives have so far shunned equalising action and point to their high-flyers' conferences for recruiting more women candidates.

Seventeen Conservative women were elected to Parliament in 1987, 21 Labour women, and Ray Michie from the Liberals, Rosie Barnes from the SDP, and Margaret Ewing from the Scottish Nationalists. The interesting difference between Conservative and Labour is that nine of the Labour women were total newcomers to the House compared to just four of the Tory women. The main reason for this difference is the Labour Party made a conscious choice to select women for a number of their winnable and Labour-held seats. The nine new Labour women MPs were Mildred Gordon (Bow & Poplar), Dawn Primarolo (Bristol South), Hilary Armstrong (Durham NW), Joyce Quin (Gateshead East), Maria Fyfe (Glasgow Maryhill), Diane Abbott (Hackney North & Stoke Newington), Alice Mahon (Halifax), Joan Ruddock (Lewisham Deptford) and Marjorie Mowlam (Redcar). The Conservative Party, with the greatest number of winnable seats to offer at the 1987 Election, fielded half the number of Labour's women candidates — 46 out of 632 candidates. And just four new women were chosen for seats already held by the Conservatives: Emma Nicholson in Devon West, Teresa Gorman in Billericay, Ann Widdicombe in Maidstone, and Gillian Shephard in Norfolk South West. Maureen Hicks won the Conversative marginal seat in Wolverhampton, previously held by the retiring Labour MP Renee Short.

## TERESA GORMAN

'An irreverent individualist on the libertarian Right of the Party,' is how Beatrix Campbell described Teresa Gorman in her book *Iron Ladies*.

Teresa Gorman's story is as unlikely and astonishing as the story of Cinderella. She went from playing on the rubbish tips of Essex as a child to driving past them as Member of Parliament for Billericay, one of the safest Conservative seats in the country. 'Saturday mornings we all climbed on the lorry and off we went to the sites to pay the workmen and that was our Saturdays. If we were really lucky we climbed on the back of one of the lorries on its way to one of the gravel tips in Essex, where we tipped the rubbish — that was our version of the huntin' shootin' fishin' brigade — rubbish tips in Essex. It was wonderful, I can smell 'em now!' Rubbish tipping is one of the major industries in her constituency.

Instead of a glass coach to transport her to the House of Commons, Teresa Gorman was swept in by the sex-scandal which toppled MP Harvey Proctor just before the 1987 General Election. She went from being a candidate sitting at home believing she had no hope of getting chosen to stand for election to a fully-fledged Member of the House of Commons in two-and-a-half weeks flat. Teresa Gorman is perhaps one of the most interesting of the new intake of women MPs: she is a convinced right-wing libertarian on the one hand and a staunch feminist pro-abortionist campaigner on the other, as well as being one of the few Conservative women who is proud to boast of 'drinking cups of coffee happily' with her Labour counterparts in the House. When I talked to Labour women and men, they all expressed an admiration for this gutsy right-winger. The story of how she got into the House of Commons reads like an Arthur Rank movie script.

Until very recently the Conservative Party was not inclined to allow people over 40 years of age on to the approved candidates list. Over and over again women over 50 with oodles of experience and ideas to contribute were complaining that they were being told by Party officers that they were too old to be considered as potential MPs. Apparently constituencies wanted young men who would stay MPs for thirty years, whereas many women, especially if they were working and bringing up children, found it was only practical to consider standing for Parliament once their families had grown up and they had a bit more money and time.

Ageism is rife in politics as elsewhere but, unlike racism and sexism it is never discussed. The hidden age barrier militates against many women who would make excellent MPs. Full of experience, with a great deal to contribute, these older women are brushed aside by the stampeding male young Turks in the parties.

At selection meetings party members have in their minds a clear imprint of what a candidate must look like — a Kinnock/Ashdown/ Owen/Dan Quayle animal — although the electorate clearly does not hold to this image. How do women fit into the picture?

I once heard Baroness Gardner complaining about the difficulties faced by women candidates over 50 in the Conservative Party, the disgraceful way in which they are rarely even invited to be interviewed for a seat despite all their experience. Her advice to Tory women on that occasion was to leave their ages off the application form completely (in the United States, it is illegal to ask for an age on a job application) or actually to lie about their date of birth.

Teresa Gorman seems to have overcome this problem. Elected in her fifties with two careers — in teaching and business — behind her, she has plenty of time, she says, to make it to the top in politics. 'Churchill was in his seventies when he first became Prime Minister' she says, and she intends to use her political opportunities to promote the image of older women as interesting and highly effective communicators.

On Guy Fawkes Day, 1985, Teresa Gorman had a suitably explosive feature in the *Daily Mail* under the headline 'Why the Tories are *really* failing women'. In the article she attacked sexist attitudes to selecting candidates in the Conservative Party. She recounted some of her own experiences, and those of fellow Conservatives, including how the chairman of a selection committee had been staring at her during the interview: 'He finally put the question that made me realise I would not be chosen to fight an election for the Conservatives in his town. "We liked your speech," he said. "But tell me, why did you wear high heels?" For a moment I was speechless. I'd expected him to ask my views on the economy, Northern Ireland, the police. "I mean to say," he went on, "you couldn't go canvassing around the streets in those, could you?" Another Conservative woman candidate was told: "We didn't like your hairstyle." "Aren't you too *small* to be an MP?" a five-foot-tall woman candidate was asked. She has now risen to a very senior position at the BBC. "We thought you were jolly but a bit fat," one experienced GLC Councillor was told. Another woman candidate was even informed that "the Committee thought you were a bit too glamorous to go around the factories." One exasperated woman candidate was asked at the end of her interview whether she was on the Left or Right of the Party. To which she replied through gritted teeth, 'If only you'd asked me some political questions, you would have found out."'

Ironically, six months before the 1987 General Election,

Teresa Gorman had given up applying to fight a seat. Instead she had re-directed her energies into raising money for the Amarant Trust, a charity she set up to support work on Hormone Replacement Therapy and particularly the work at King's College Hospital in London. Her interest in hormones was to become an election issue.

'The *Daily Mail* suggested that Mrs Thatcher might be getting her energy from HRT and then linked this to me as Chairman of the Amarant Trust. The *Independent* weighed in with speculation about my age and whether I was held together with hormones. I soon learned that once you put your head above the parapet in politics some elements of the media will treat it as a coconut shie and try to knock you off your pedestal. But the *Daily Mail* came to the rescue. I did an article for them in which I admitted to being over 50 but feeling 20 due to HRT. The *Mail* got over 10,000 letters from women who were desperate to relieve their own middle-age problems. I had found my first, populist political cause.'

Luck plays an important part in everyone's political career, but especially in Teresa Gorman's. In an astonishing quirk of fate, on the Saturday in late May, just 19 days before election day, Harvey Proctor, the MP for the Essex Constituency of Billericay, resigned after press reports of involvement with rent boys. It left one of the safest Conservative seats in the country looking for a candidate in a hurry. In the aftermath of the Proctor scandal, they could be especially predisposed to a woman candidate. She had already been in the final selection for the two adjacent seats of Thurrock and Chelmsford.

'On the day Harvey Proctor resigned I was telephoned by local people and invited to put in my CV. Three days later I was adopted as the candidate. Friends had been on the telephone all day saying, "Have you heard? Harvey Proctor's resigning — are you going to put in for the seat?" I kept saying no, Conservative Central Office will have somebody ready for that — it'll all be stitched up. But the Tories in Essex are very independent-minded and they anticipated Central Office wouldn't send them anybody they actually wanted. My intuition is I'd have been very surprised if my name was one of the ones Smith Square [Conservative Party Headquarters] sent to Billericay.'

She didn't think she would stand a chance. 'I said to Jim, (her husband) "Oh I can't be bothered, I can't be bothered."'

She went to bed, but woke up in the early hours and changed her mind. Shortly after dawn on that late May Sunday morning, a lone figure sped out of London towards Essex. Teresa Gorman remembers that morning vividly: 'At five in the morning I got up and went to my office and duplicated my CV. Then I got in my little motorcar and tootled down the A12.

'I arrived ever so early in the constituency and at eight in the morning delivered the copies. They were laid around the table so in addition to what Central Office were putting around the table, my CV was seen by the Selection Committee too.'

Teresa drove home to wait. 'My husband spent the afternoon trying to calm me down. When I'm nervous, I shriek a lot! I kept jabbering on about it, saying I wonder whether they will or whether they won't choose me.' Thirteen hours after she had delivered the copies of her CV, Teresa Gorman got a telephone call to say she was the only woman on the short-list of 12. 'At that stage, I knew I'd got a pretty good chance.'

Conservative candidates from all over the country had rushed to apply for the plum seat. 'Do you know, there were people literally coming to that meeting clamouring to have their CVs considered? It was incredible, it was like the opening day of the sales. They were having to hold people out of the hall.

'In the semi-finals in the morning, there were 12 of us. Out of that they chose three, including me, to go on to the final selection a day or two later.' Teresa knew arriving without her husband at that all-important jump-off would certainly not be seen as a plus mark, but Jim was stuck on Jury duty. 'In the Conservative Party, your spouse is supposed to come with you, so they can have a look. The other two naturally brought their very nice wives with them, looking impeccable.'

Each short-listed candidate in turn delivers a speech and answers questions from the audience. Questions put to Teresa Gorman were par for the course for the constituency — 'The usual, you know, where do you stand on capital punishment? Where do you stand on immigration? Are you a supporter of Mrs Thatcher? What do you know about Essex?'

She did know something about Essex. 'My husband's family were living in Chelmsford. We used to take them out for a ride on Sunday afternoons around Essex so I knew all the little villages and names and if you can say the name of somebody's village in the audience, you've got that vote! Another friend of mine had worked as a plastic surgeon for three or four years in the burns unit of St Andrew's Hospital at Billericay and we had spent a couple of Christmases with them. So I was talking all about the burns unit in Billericay and how wonderful it was — lots of local colour — I think I just talked their kind of language.

'I gave my little spiel at the selection, along with the other two. A lot of people who go to these interviews are very hoity-toity and talk frightfully grandiose politics, but most people in a selection meeting don't really want to hear that. Whenever I went for interviews for a seat, I never talked politics, I always tried to entertain people a bit and to put across the kind of person I am, because I think that's actually what they are buying.

'They had only phoned me up on the Sunday. On Wednesday evening, three days later, I was adopted.'

So nineteen days from polling day Teresa Gorman found herself chosen to stand in one of the safest Conservative seats in Britain.

The strong influence in Teresa Gorman's life has been her mother. 'My mother wasn't happily married. What I took in with my mother's milk, was the message I must be independent. She used to say to me, "Don't you ever depend on anyone else, certainly not a man." She had been trapped into marriage very early and had spent all her young years raising three kids.'

Teresa Gorman and her husband decided not to have children. 'It didn't seem to me any great treat to be saddled with a load of small children of my own. My husband is the eldest of eight in a Catholic family and he maintains he's already raised half a dozen — the little ones as they came through, because it was the older ones who looked after them. I have never had children so I've always done what I want to do. Women's ability now to control their family sizes, and not being tied up so much domestically with cooking and doing all the chores, means they can come home, have dinner with the family and then have time to go off and be on the council or whatever. The two great leaps forward for women in this century have been contraception and the legalisation of abortion; the ability to regulate the size of the family which you're prepared to devote *your* life to rearing is absolutely essential.'

Her mother is still alive. 'She is only 17 years older than me. Funnily enough, she isn't all that thrilled at me being an MP, she just thinks I'm very wilful. The other thing she was always saying to me was, "You'll come a cropper, my girl!" because I was always taking chances, I imagine.'

Her parents weren't interested in higher education. 'My mother thought it turned you into an old maid and my father's idea of progress was to open your own shop or be somebody's secretary, so I battled to go to even the grammar school. I've always worked myself up by my bootstraps.'

It was natural for her to think of being in business — 'That's my whole family background. Every Friday evening we cleared the table after we had our high tea — we didn't use to have dinner in working-class households — then we did the wages for the men. We all sat round with my Pa and counted up and made up the pay packets.'

She had a grammar school education in Fulham — 'more in spite of my parents than because of them. Then I did teacher training because I thought that would be a secure kind of job. I taught secondary modern and comprehensive off and on for the best part of ten years. I decided while I was teaching I wouldn't get very far without a degree so I went and did a university degree part-time.' She got a first class honours degree in zoology and botany.

'My life is made up of what I would call serendipity — the unexpected juxtaposition of circumstances. I don't think I've ever really planned to do something, like going into politics. Going to the States, I think that was the beginning of it all.' She and her husband taught in the United States in the mid-sixties on an exchange programme. 'I wanted the experience really of going to America — the great dreamland. I hadn't been before and we were there nearly two years, it was wonderful, I adored it. I'd love to be an American if I weren't British. If we could have stayed, we would have stayed, but we had two-year visas.

'We encountered a completely different attitude in America. I learned for the first time that making profit and being successful was actually a good thing, whereas in this country it was considered to be reprehensible. If you were doing well in this country and working hard, which my husband and I had always done, people would say "Oh, it's all right for you, *you're* doing all right" — that horrible attitude that you've got to disguise your success, you couldn't share it with people in this country. But in America, everybody was delighted.'

While she was in the United States she came into contact with 'the free market movement'. 'People kept telling me that I'd been reading Ayn Rand. Ayn Rand is an American woman novelist who shot to fame in the United States around the 1960s with her free market philosophy. She was actually raised in Russia and escaped and settled in America. She wrote classic books, such as *The Virtue of Selfishness*, and *Atlas Shrugged*, in which she postulates that all the businessmen run off to a mountain top and leave the rest of us to stew in our own juice, to demonstrate the importance of the free enterprise system in support of society. I thought this was terrific stuff, it really turned me on.'

When Teresa came back to London in the late sixties, she couldn't face the prospect of going back into school — teaching. 'I knew I wasn't going to get promoted because I was 30-ish — still of child-bearing age — and in those days they used to ask you, "Mrs Gorman, if we give you this job, can you guarantee you won't go away and have a baby?" so I thought I wasn't going to hang around for the next twenty or thirty years to get promoted.

'If feminism means being on the side of your own sex and wanting to see them get a fair crack of the whip, then I'm a feminist. I'm not a feminist in the left-wing sense of demanding special privileges for women, I don't agree with legislating. My feminism is entirely consistent with my Conservative politics. The Industrial Revolution and the free market have done more to emancipate women than a hundred years of feminist cant. Capitalism has provided the machines which have emancipated us from the drudgery of domesticity. The hoover, washing machine and now the microwave oven have completely changed a woman's domestic role. *I* didn't just say that, Simon de Beauvoir said capitalism has done more to emancipate women. Microwave, birth control and abortion — regulating families and not having to spend all your time over a hot stove. I emphatically reject government support for crèches, equal pay legislation etc. I believe this to be counter-productive and anti-feminist. Instead we should press for equal tax treatment for women so that the support skills they require in the form of home help or help with children can be paid for out of income before tax just as a man pays for his secretary or driver. I've always battled through and I've come up against prejudice. When I was a school-teacher they wouldn't promote me because

I was a woman. When a door closes like that — firmly — I don't hang around banging on the door and demanding to be let in, I go off at a tangent and achieve something another way. Going into free enterprise and into business on my own was one way of dealing with the frustration of being within a corporate structure where women were discriminated against.'

She had started a Master's degree in History and Philosophy of Science at University College, London. 'At the same time I'd got ideas for low-cost, simple teaching materials for biology and nursing courses that I had developed when I was teaching in London, so I decided to try and use these in a commercial way.'

She and her husband mortgaged their home to raise the money. 'Eventually we got the business off the ground. I can't say I actually starved in a garret, but on the other hand I gave up my wonderful teaching salary and the security and the pension. I was about 32 or 33. We built things by elbow grease, we've never had any family money either of us.'

The introduction of VAT was the beginning of her move into politics. 'VAT came in, which didn't please me because there was a lot of paper work involved. I hated that — in those days I was still doing all my own books. Then under the Labour government, Barbara Castle introduced this so called eight per cent levy. All of us self-employed people had to pay eight per cent on our net income as an extra contribution to the DHSS, but we didn't get half the benefits. We couldn't register for unemployment pay and lots of other things and there was a great upsurge of protest about this in the country. It wasn't just me, there were thousands of self-employed people protesting.'

She read an article in the *Daily Mail* and wrote off to join the National Association of Self-Employed. 'From that I started to go to meetings of the Adam Smith Club over at the Institute for Economic Affairs. They used to have speakers from America like Milton Friedman. Some of the stuff was really terrific, telling us how the state was the ultimate parasite and how we could run things much better ourselves. It was very inspirational and I still find it so. I still find it a turn-on to be with a crowd of people who think like that. I always ask myself, "Will this mean less government intervention?" '

Suzie Mackenzie wrote in the *Independent* magazine: 'In Mrs Gorman's version of the perfect state, nothing would be provided beyond the most basic public services.'

Teresa retorts: 'The poor are doing badly because the system is bad and that's how I view the Welfare State. I think the Conservative Party is coming round to that, but it's a difficult position to articulate publicly, so the senior level of the Party feel they must tread very carefully. I wouldn't. I'd say we believe this is wrong, we believe this is the way to do it, so let's chuck out all that middle-man garbage and get down to the nitty gritty. I would give the money direct to the schools and make them all self-funding, I'd cut out all this nonsense of the local education authorities. Or I'd find a way of getting it into the pockets of the people so they could purchase. The same with health care, because the middle layers are basically a barrier between the people and what they are actually paying for through their taxes — supporting this huge parasitic layer of administrators. I call them poverty pimps.

'When this eight per cent tax levy came in, then I came out with my free enterprise ideas because otherwise I could see this new self-employed movement developing into yet another pressure lobby for more government intervention which I knew to be quite wrong.'

She was running the Alliance of Small Firms and Self-Employed People, one of the pressure lobbies representing small businesses that grew out of the protest movement of the mid-1970s. 'That was my first move into active politics. We used to take up cases for people against the bureaucracy when people were being dunned by the Customs and Excise. Speaking on platforms didn't frighten me at all. I'd been speaking in class-rooms for a long time.'

She hadn't yet joined a political party. 'At that stage I despised all the political parties. We thought Heath was going to usher in the new free-enterprise system and then when he got in, he did his little U-turn and spoiled it all.'

When Edward Heath called a second General Election in 1974, 'some of us were so brassed off with the whole political structure, we decided we'd put up our own candidate. We drew straws and I got the short straw so that's serendipity at work. We stood for Parliament on a Free Enterprise platform. I actually used my maiden name, Teresa Moore, because I didn't want the neighbours to know what I was up to. I thought it was a kind of embarrassment. I was kind of shy about it.'

William Shelton, the Conservative candidate in her constituency, was indignant. 'He said to me, "Why are you doing this?" Pompous little creature that I was, I raised my nose in the air and said, "Because *you* are not doing it in the Tory Party!"'

She polled only 350 votes, 'but we had a great time. The Institute of Economic Affairs thought it was a great jape. They kept sending me telegrams from the Reform Club [associated with Left of Centre and Liberal politics] urging me on, and I didn't even understand the significance of the Reform Club, but I thought it was very flattering! They invited me up to a lunch at the Institute of Economic Affairs which is a sort of free market (though not *very* free market) think-tank where I met all sorts of journalists. I was terrified, but I knew I was moving in high circles. In those days Thatcher and Keith Joseph and Nigel Lawson and Geoffrey Howe and Alan Walters all used to go to the Institute of Economic Affairs.'

After that General Election Teresa Gorman received an unexpected invitation. 'Shelton masterminded Thatcher's campaign for the leadership. He invited me up to the House of Commons in a nice friendly type of gesture. Jim and I went up there, we thought it was a great treat. I think it was my first visit to the House. We had tea in the Pugin Room as I now realise it to be, but it might have been Buckingham Palace for the impact it had on me. Shelton asked me why I didn't join the Party under the new leadership. Soon after that Thatcher made a speech in which she used the very slogan we'd made up for our campaign: "We need less government, less taxes and more choice." I thought that was an omen.'

While on Westminster City Council she was an advocate of privatization. 'I think I'm a person in politics for a principle rather than for a political package of deals. What attracts me to the Conservative Party is clearly that they are the Party moving towards the free market solution to everything, which is what attracts me to politics. I've long thought that Mrs Thatcher won't retire for some time. But if something awful happened and she went under a bus then her immediate successor would probably be someone fairly bland, or the new PM will come out of the generation around and about mine.'

Will Teresa ever get to the top of Conservative Party politics one day? 'If Mrs Thatcher is looking for a Green Queen I'd be the perfect choice, but I don't think she knows who I am! There are lots of areas where I think I could usefully bring her solutions to problems, but I think that Whitehall and the Whips' Office are likely to take a different view. Political preferment is for conformists and that I am not. But I still think that I can contribute to the sum total of human happiness by exposing the humbug and the authoritarianism which is ripe on the front benches.'

In two short years at Westminster Teresa Gorman has already put herself on the political map as someone prepared to engage in controversial causes. 'Any old backbencher will make a speech in support of three legged dogs or one-parent families, but it takes more imagination to stick up for the rights of people to trade tickets on the pavements at Wimbledon, or to face the displeasure of Central Office by championing the right of Conservatives in Northern Ireland to vote for Conservative candidates. I'm known in the local press as Controversial Teresa Gorman but politics is all about controversy so I regard it as a compliment. Backbenchers are there to keep an eye on the executive and criticise whenever it tries to clutter up our lives with more unnecessary regulations. That, and preventing the professions and other trade unions from dictating to the rest of us, is the essence of Mrs Thatcher's brand of Conservatism. I want to help it along.'


## JOAN RUDDOCK

There is one area of south London where you can drive continuously through constituencies represented by women MPs. Solicitor Harriet Harman was the first of the current clutch of South London MPs to get elected, in a by-election in 1982 made famous because she was expecting her first child. In Greenwich, Rosie Barnes is the SDP MP and alongside them is Lewisham–Deptford, represented by Joan Ruddock. Kate Hoey represents Vauxhall. A short drive across the Thames brings you into the East London constituency of Bow and Poplar, represented by Mildred Gordon.

People become Members of Parliament by a variety of routes. Some, like Janet Fookes, Teresa Gorman and Edwina Currie, serve on local councils first. Others, like Harriet Harman of the National Council of Civil Liberties, come from a background of campaigning pressure groups. Joan Ruddock, too, was first known nationally as chair of the Campaign for Nuclear Disarmament.

Well before Joan Ruddock became famous through CND at the time of Greenham Common, she was a Labour Party parliamentary candidate. 'It wasn't as though I saw the light on the road to Damascus or I fell to my knees at Greenham Common and worshipped the ground and said, "This is it!"' she says. 'No, I first got into defence through pure academic interest — what will parliamentary candidate Joan Ruddock say when she's asked a question on defence in the next General Election? I was already in my thirties and I'd been selected to stand for Labour at Newbury for the 1979 General Election. But I knew nothing about defence. At the Party conference I went to a fringe meeting that was organised by CND to try and get myself better informed about it. I was amazed to find that CND made a lot of sense. I thought these were the only people who have got something coherent to say about defence, so I then became a member, not out of absolute conviction but simply because I wanted to get information. I approached the whole thing very much intellectually.

'Amazingly, the first question I was asked by the first person who came up to me on the first day I went out to canvas and present myself to the electorate was: 'What's your policy on the Falkland Islands?'' He was a man who had relatives in the Falkland Islands and objected to having to fly to Argentina to get to the Falklands. I was able to answer the question, but I don't think there could have been many candidates in Britain in 1979 who had a clue where the Falklands were, but even I could not have predicted the significance of the Falkland Islands to the future of British politics.'

Joan Ruddock values highly the skills and knowledge she learned on the pressure group circuit. 'Working for Shelter, the campaign for the homeless, in my early twenties set the pattern for the rest of my life. It was the first campaigning pressure group to use new techniques. By the time I was 25, I was head of a department. I had 25 staff, four offices and a fleet of cars. Clearly I was going to sink or swim. Fortunately I succeeded and I learned a lot about campaigning.'

When I met her, the quietly spoken, determined, slightly shy air was not what I'd expected from someone who has addressed open air audiences of 200,000 in Hyde Park, has been hounded by the secret service, and threatened with sex scandals by the tabloid press.

Her father and mother were active Conservatives. 'My parents collected membership subs and things like that. My father was quite strongly political and was always giving me Sunday afternoon lectures about Reds under the beds.'

When Joan decided to stand for Parliament she received an unenthusiastic response from her father. 'My father's view was that this was a silly thing to do because Labour is a dreadful party. He took a rather patronising attitude — "She'll get more sense and she'll actually learn what's what and then she'll become a Tory." I think he felt that for a woman politics was probably a bad business anyway.'

She remembers being politically aware by the time she was 11. 'One of the very first issues which affected me was race relations, which is really strange as I lived in an almost wholly white population. In the late 1950s I went to see a film called *She Passed For White* with my parents. There was a romance between a woman who looked white, but had black ancestry, and a white man. It was an American sob story really — the marriage became impossible and broke up because of her terrible fear she would have a black baby. It had an amazing effect on me. At the end of it, the only question in my mind was *why* couldn't the love story continue? My parents simply said well it wasn't possible, as black and white people just couldn't live together because society wouldn't accept it. I remember being profoundly affected by that and thinking it just didn't make sense.'

When she was 16 she heard Shirley Williams speak at a sixth-form conference on race relations. It inspired her to join the Labour Party. 'The things she said, which were essentially about values, were the things I knew I believed in but had never had a convenient framework in which to present them. I'd never heard a live politician address a conference, certainly never a woman, certainly no-one who called herself a Socialist, which she did in those days. I was just bowled over. Shirley talked about equality — not discriminating between people — and about recognising human value and worth in people regardless of their colour.'

From an all-girls grammar school in Wales, Joan entered the male atmosphere of a science faculty at London University. 'I read Science at Imperial College. There were 160 women and 3,000 men. Coming from an all-girls school, this period was clearly an influence on my life — having to make it as a woman in that environment.'

At Imperial College, she became politically active, joining the Labour Club and becoming president of the International Relations Club. 'It was a club which focused on foreign affairs because, as a science, technology and mining college, Imperial had a huge proportion of overseas students. I was constantly meeting people who were coming to Britain as young Socialists from Third World states. It was an extremely formative part of my life.'

Within the year she married her childhood sweetheart, Keith. 'We met when I was at school and he was at university. It was regarded somewhat as a cradle snatch by some of his relatives. Indeed my choice of Imperial College over some of the other colleges, like Oxford where I might have got a place, was very much because he was at Imperial and I was already quite sure I wanted to spend the rest of my life with him.' They have been married for 25 years. He is now a Professor of Biophysics at Imperial College.

'I began to travel during that period as well because Keith is very, very keen on travel. We spent our summer vacations travelling, with a hundred pounds in our pockets to survive. We went to Western Europe, Eastern Europe and to the United States. We went twice to the Middle East, three times to Turkey and then in subsequent years we have been almost everywhere including Central and South America. The Middle East interested me mainly then.'

Joan Ruddock planned to become a teacher when she graduated from Imperial College in 1965, but her plans didn't materialise. The Inner London Education Authority was the only authority in Britain which wouldn't accept graduate science teachers without an extra teacher training course. 'We couldn't afford the money for me to study another year — that hitch determined the course of my life.'

Instead of a quiet career as a teacher, she was propelled into the world of pressure group campaigning which ultimately led her to become Chair of the Campaign for Nuclear Disarmament and one of the best-known women campaigners of the 1980s. At first she had taken a junior job at Imperial College doing practical teaching for a couple of years and then started doing research full-time. 'I hated it. I decided to quit science altogether and work for a United Nations agency. It was the spring of 1968, the twentieth anniversary of the Declaration of Human Rights. I organised a big exhibition at Imperial about human rights violations around the world. I suddenly thought the important thing concerning human rights violations in Britain was homelessness. Keith and I got all the material from Shelter, which was a newly emerging campaign at that time, and I ended up working for Shelter instead of working in a UN agency. Shelter was an organisation which offered their young staff enormous responsibility.'

From Shelter she moved to become the Director of the Oxford Housing Aid Centre. 'One of the things Shelter pioneered and of which I am eternally proud, was the whole housing aid advice movement. I was responsible for setting up one of the first Housing Aid centres, the one in Oxford, right from the drawing board. It was a very important time for me. I loved the job and I thought it was a wonderful project. I learned an enormous amount about people and legislation and the whole housing field and it has proved very useful politically.

'At that time, I had absolutely no interest in CND. All my interest was in foreign affairs, and strangely enough, CND was more like a domestic issue in those days. The Vietnam War was essential to my politics at that time. When we heard Wilson support the Vietnam War, and Callaghan's attitude on immigration policy, frankly I decided the Labour Party wasn't for me. I left, but I didn't join any other party. After Labour's 1970 defeat, like many others of my generation I began to feel the Labour Party needed to be *changed*, not left at the side-lines. It was important to go back into the Party and to try to begin the process of democratising the Party and broadening its horizons. I decided to rejoin. It was then I went out to live in Burghfield. Keith and I became extremely active, we started a local Labour branch, built up the membership, I stood for council elections. No chance there of getting elected, of course.'

When Celia Fletcher, a trade union activist who had stood for Parliament for Labour in Newbury in both elections of 1974, decided she didn't want to stand for the 1979 Election, members of the local party suggested Joan Ruddock should stand for Parliament, which she did, coming third and failing to get enough votes to avoid losing her deposit. 'It was a vicious campaign. The Liberals fought a very, very bitter campaign for second place. I was impersonated — some unknown people said Joan Ruddock wants all Labour voters to vote Liberal. They organised a telephone trick. Nothing was done officially by the Liberal Party, but it clearly was done by a group of activists. The worst thing was just before the election they actually printed a leaflet saying Joan Ruddock is calling on all her Labour supporters to vote for Tony Richards who is a fine man. I had to take it to the Director of Public Prosecutions, and it became a court case which I won.'

After the 1979 General Election she moved to become manager of the Citizens Advice Bureau in Reading. Within months, the unknown, quietly spoken woman at the CAB metamorphosed into the centre of attention of not just Tory MP Michael Heseltine — then Secretary of State for Defence — but the press and media, the Pentagon and M15.

It all started one day when she came out of a meeting and glanced at a local newspaper. The headline stated: 'Cruise Missiles for Greenham'. Her house at Burghfield Common was close to Greenham Common. 'I thought no, I am not going to get involved, I'm just not going to. I'd fought the election and worked hard. I wanted a holiday that summer, a proper holiday.'

By the time she got home, the telephone was ringing. 'It was the secretary of the local Labour Party asking what action we should take about the Cruise missiles coming to Greenham Common.' Her first reaction was to say, 'We aren't going to do anything.' She saw her dream of a summer holiday fade away. She actually said, 'Give me a couple of hours. I'll just have supper, then I'll write a press release.' That night she and a colleague issued a press release which said: '*We have set up a campaign of opposition to Cruise missiles at Greenham Common or anywhere else in the UK.*'

The Newbury campaign took off, followed by a campaign right across Berkshire. 'I became the focus of CND nationally because I was the one person who could do the sort of job they needed PR-wise who was on the spot.' She was invited to stand for the National Council of CND and got elected. 'Within a year they asked if I would stand for the Chair and I did, having no expectation of winning whatsoever.' She was elected Chair of CND.

'It changed my life. CND took over my life totally. And it put tremendous pressure on me as a human being. We were the support group for the women's march from Wales which became the "Greenham Common Women" — and history.'

Burghfield Common, the village where she lived, is sited conveniently from CND's point of view between Newbury and Reading and Joan's non-working hours were completely taken over with Greenham. She would get a call from CND Head-quarters saying, 'We've got an Australian film crew arriving who want to be taken to Greenham, when can you see them?' I would have to say things like, "Well, they'll have to be here at 7.30 am because I have to go to work." I would get up, drive through the mists out to Greenham — that was very good for photography, all misty and evil-looking, just what the Australian TV crew would want! There I would stand in front of the TV camera pronouncing upon the fact there was this base in this isolated spot.'

In 1980, long before she became a Member of Parliament, Joan Ruddock was asked to speak in front of 80,000 people at a CND rally in Trafalgar Square. 'It was the first major rally CND had held for about ten years. We had no idea what was going to happen. Although I had spoken at meetings in both university and election campaigns, I don't suppose I had ever spoken to more than about 100 to 200 people. I had to get on in front of this rostrum at Trafalgar Square, on the plinth and face 80,000 people. Just a sea of faces. I felt so physically sick. As I stepped forward this huge wave of nausea came over me and I thought I was going to fall right off the end of the plinth, I thought I was just going to faint. I don't know how I began speaking because I have always been nervous. I was terrified. My whole body was shaking from head to foot. At that stage there wasn't any way of overcoming that, it was so extreme and there was no comfort to be gained anywhere. It was just such an incredibly terrifying thing to do and as soon as I had started speaking, there were hecklers there as well, right down at the front.'

This was Joan Ruddock's most 'unforgettable' occasion. The other memorable time she recalls was at Greenham: the first of the non-violent direct actions, when the women sat down in front of the gates of the vast missile base. 'I was there all night. We had no idea whether everyone would be arrested immediately or what. It must have been March '82. It was dark and the women just moved forward and sat in the television arc lights, absolutely silent. The suspense and the sheer emotion . . .'

It was good television, too, in 1982 when winter drew in and the nights grew cold. 'The Greenham women were now certain they were going to stay. I remember getting their first portacabin. They'd been living in tents. I had to negotiate with this portacabin owner, trying to make an arrangement whereby it wouldn't be a problem to have his portacabin sitting on the nicely cut front-lawn of RAF Greenham Common which had become a focus for national media attention.'

The emancipation of women as individuals and politically was as strongly interwoven into the Greenham tapestry as their passionate feelings against nuclear weapons. 'That was very much part of the British peace movement. For any major political movement that was extraordinary. At first I was in two minds about a women-only peace camp, but the women used to say in political activities women never have a space. We're always expected to compete. I identified very strongly with that. Later, when I saw how it developed and how women did develop and increase and the campaign took on a particular ethos, I became quite certain I'd made the right decision in giving my support, as CND chair, to a women's only camp.'

Becoming a frontrunner in a campaign which touches such raw nerves as defence inevitably brought problems. 'Yes, I've had hate mail, death threats, everything, yes, of course.' Not only death threats. For a long time Joan Ruddock and other members of CND suspected their telephones were being tapped. 'We knew a lot of things were going on. We had a real sense of being constantly monitored — phones and our mail interfered with.'

One day she got a phone call from a TV producer at 20/20 Vision. 'A woman I didn't know said would I have a meeting because she had something she wanted to discuss with me. I was invited to go to her house.' At the meeting the producer told Joan Ruddock they had an affidavit from Cathy Massiter, an MI5 employee, who had decided to spill the beans. 'The affidavit said MI5 had opened a file on me, and that phone calls were being intercepted. I felt a sense of tremendous horror and chill go through me.'

Although Joan Ruddock had suspected for some time that CND was being monitored, she hadn't wanted to think it was possible. 'You don't want to believe that in Britain, people in the highest positions of responsibility actually decide that individuals like me, who have never done a criminal act in their lives and who have engaged openly in legitimate political activities, can be targeted by the security apparatus and someone could tell me that my movements were monitored, that people recorded where I went, and that I was being followed. Just the horror of her saying the file had grown and grown. The absolute horror of feeling that your life was totally invaded. It was quite shocking.'

She felt saddened at the intrusion too. 'There were things that had happened in my life which were to do specifically with family crises, in particular, my sister being very seriously ill. If I felt at all bitter it was the thought that people could so invade my life that in moments of extreme personal hurt and misery there could be a third party there.'

After four years as Chair of CND she was ready to ease out of the leadership. 'I'd been in the Chair of CND from '81 through to '85. When I first took it up, I thought three years was enough and I was then persuaded to do an extra year. I began to feel it wasn't good for CND to be totally identified with Bruce Kent and myself.'

She was aware that once she was no longer Chair of CND, she would be free for party politics again, but was uncertain whether she would be acceptable as a candidate because she had withdrawn from Labour Party politics over the past few years. But she need not have worried. When Leo Abse announced he was retiring as MP for Pontypool, the town where she had grown up, Joan Ruddock was invited to apply for the seat.

She narrowly missed winning the nomination after a gruelling four months' selection process during which she commuted to South Wales and back to her job in Reading. 'It cost me a huge amount of money and an enormous amount of time and energy, and in the end it cost me a lot emotionally. I came out of that feeling I had really done my best and given everything but this time, when I didn't quite get it, I felt rejected. I knew it wasn't logical because the local CLP Secretary was a man and had always been better placed. I suspect men feel rejection as much as women, although they probably don't admit it in the same way. The other thing it meant to me was my final break with Wales.'

She then tried for a London seat. 'I have to say if anyone is responsible for my being the MP for Lewisham Deptford, it's Harriet Harman, the MP for Peckham. It is the neighbouring seat to hers. She wanted more women in London.' Joan Ruddock got two letters from Harriet Harman, urging her to apply for the next door seat of Lewisham Deptford. 'The first letter said, "Go for Deptford, it's wide open!" Then I got another letter from Harriet saying, "Joan — GO FOR IT!" underlined about twenty times.'

This time, Joan Ruddock found herself commuting for nine months from her home and work in Berkshire, 45 miles to Central London and then to South London. She was a lone figure, late at night, waiting around on draughty South London railway stations or sitting half-asleep on the bleak train journeys home.

'Some of the time I thought I was completely mad. How could I have taken this on? I used to go to meetings at night and I would take really late trains on the South London lines where people were raped and mugged and I would be the only *person* — not just the only woman but the only person — sitting on the station waiting for one of those late-night empty trains.'

## MAGGIE EWING

Scottish Nationalist MP Maggie Ewing returned to Westminster in 1987 after an absence of eight years. She has experienced the poker game of politics in full, from extreme emotional highs when her name was read out by the Returning Officer as 'the new Member of Parliament for Dunbarton East', to that most devastating blow for any MP, losing the seat. 'When your name is read out as the newly elected Member, that's always great,' she recalls. 'But I've had everything. Winning, losing, losing my deposit, and winning again — in that order.'

She was 29 in 1974 when, as Maggie Bain, she was first elected to the House of Commons as Member for Dunbarton East. 'It was a handicap coming into politics as young as I was, because people think you don't have any life experience.' In an interview in the *Glasgow Herald* she commented: 'It certainly is the only profession you enter without training. Suddenly you're confronted with a postbag of 200 letters a week, endless committee meetings, constituency meetings and surgeries, plus attending debates in the House of Commons and learning your way through a maze of parliamentary tactics.' With a touch of irony, she recalls her first encounter with the barracking in the Chamber of the House of Commons. 'It was over Scotland's North Sea oil. The whole House broke into uproar. I just stood there and said nothing: that's the way as a teacher I used to quieten down noisy classes. It works in the House of Commons too!'

She first came in contact with politics at Glasgow University where she was reading English Literature and History. 'Scottish universities have a tendency of being very political. Glasgow University in particular has been a breeding ground for a vast number of Scottish politicians. Because I enjoyed debating at school, I wanted to debate at university and ended up joining the Scottish National Association at Glasgow. Then it snowballed — it was the mid-60s, and the SNP came racing to the front in 1967 when Winnie Ewing won the by-election in Hamilton.' (She would later marry Winnie Ewing's son, Fergus.)

She readily acknowledges her debt to the women who would become her mother-in-law a decade later. 'It was Winnie who persuaded me to stand for Parliament, after she won the by-election to Westminster and became Chair of the SNP selection committee. She went around to everyone she thought had any ability in the Party and seized on them. She was particularly determined she would have a lot of women. She's a persistent woman. Of course I did the usual shrinking violet bit and said, "Who, *me*? Don't be ridiculous, I couldn't do that." I had never thought of myself as one of the standard-bearers, I was more a worker behind the scenes. Winnie just kept on and on at me. I was going to all these party meetings and speaking — usually about education — I was gaining confidence and becoming a public speaker and handling questions and so on. It all came together around 1972 or 1973 so I went onto the candidate's list.'

'At first I think my parents found it quite difficult to cope with the fact they had someone who was so involved in politics. My father was a farmworker and my mum was a housewife. Like a lot of Scottish working-class rural people they voted Conservative because the Labour Party was seen to be only interested in the cities. They just accepted I had always had a very independent mind and there was nothing they would say which would ever stop me from going into politics. I remember my mother saying, "But you are not likely to win, are you?" I think she just thought I was just going to have fun and enjoy myself, and that it wouldn't uproot me at all. They had mixed feelings of fear and pride — they were frightened what it might do to me, and at the same time they were very proud that "their wee girl" had done so well. And I just gave them back the old Scottish phrase they had drummed into me: "If you want something doing well, do it yourself".'

After teacher training, her involvement with the SNP escalated when she married the Party Research Officer, Donald Bain. 'Part of the reason I automatically became more involved in the SNP was that Donald had to go to all these meetings as he was involved in committee work.' For the next six years Maggie Bain divided her time between secondary school teaching, the

Scots Nats, and studying part-time for a further degree in Economic History at Strathclyde University, where she specialised in ship-building industry on the Clyde.

In 1974, still in her 20s, she stood for the Scottish Nationalist Party in Dunbarton East in a cliff-hanging election and after three nerve-wrenching recounts, won her first seat. After the first count she was 11 votes behind the Conservative. 'Because the margin was so incredibly tiny we immediately asked for a complete recount. It was in the recount they found 33 votes which belonged to me in the wrong box, so that gave me the majority — by 22 votes.'

Maggie has never been anything but SNP. 'I suppose that's partly because of when I joined and what was happening to the Party at that stage. Lots of politicians in other parties who were in the Scottish Nationalist movement at university went off and joined the Labour Party or the Conservative Party. I didn't think about going into any other party. I think Scotland should have its own Parliament. Like every other European country we should be allowed to rule our own affairs — it seems to me a perfectly logical argument. I suppose if there hadn't been an SNP I might have been a Liberal because I'm very similar to some of the people in the Liberal Party in Scotland, but the SNP seemed to me to be the one that put the priority on establishing a Parliament.

'There must definitely be economic powers for a Scottish Parliament. I don't want just a talking shop. We've got to really achieve social and economic change for the community, and the opportunity for Scotland to be out in the international community. I do think we have very different viewpoints on a lot of issues in the international context, particularly under the Thatcher government. We are almost at total extremes: a Scottish Parliament would by now have economic sanctions against South Africa, and we would not have supported the Falklands mission.'

Five years after her astonishing victory, in one of those lurches of fate so typical of political life, on May 4 1979 the bottom fell out of the Scottish Nationalist vote and out of Maggie Bain's life. At general elections voters can and do shift away, on a national basis. Support for a political party first melts, then drops like a stone. Members of Parliament can see it happenings. If they won their seat with a slim majority there's nothing they can do but watch the seat slipping away like quicksand.

Maggie has never forgotten the experience of becoming the ex-MP for Dunbarton East. 'It was clear the national trend was moving away from the Scottish Nationalists from around about 1977 onwards. I knew during the campaign that there was just no way I could hold my seat. I don't even think it would have made any difference if I'd stayed at home and not done any campaigning at all, because we lost nine seats in that election. I felt really dreadful on election night. All the TV cameras were there. They were transmitting live because the Scots Nats were in the news and the media knew I had this tiny majority and I might lose. And I did.

'I had to make a brave speech as the losing candidate. I kept wondering how the electorate could *do* this to me. For five years I'd been slogging my *guts* out for them as their MP. But they did. And we all packed up and went back to my Agent's house and drank a considerable amount.' As she was later to be quoted in The Glasgow Herald, 'There is nothing more ex than an ex-MP.'

Overnight she went from being the Member of Parliament for Dunbarton East, to being a very lonely figure. She couldn't share the loss with her husband. He had left her a short time before, though she states her marriage didn't disintegrate because of political pressures — 'that would have happened anyway.'

She had no job, no income, no home and no immediate prospects. 'I really had no income at all. Worse, to my horror I discovered that when I started work in the 1960s I had opted to pay the Married Women's Insurance Stamp which meant I wasn't entitled to proper unemployment benefit. I had about £1500 severance pay after five years in the House. It was nothing, especially as I was paying a mortgage. I just didn't know what to do with myself. It's appalling — you think you are so organised and confident and that you'll know how to handle it, but you're not really any different from anybody else.'

Terribly hurt by what she saw as voter disloyalty, she was determined to return to Parliament. 'I gave my all to them,' she repeated. 'I spent my life worrying about their worries, charging up and down on the midnight trains to London and back, eating reheated food from Chinese take-aways when all the grocery shops had shut. I slogged my guts out, but in 1979 they simply voted for someone else. In a feature entitled 'Much More Than Just A Pretty Face', *Glasgow Herald* journalist Ann Shaw

looked back on that time: 'The media predictably had less interest in her now. More hurtful though has been the way people
avoided meeting her because they were embarrassed. They
would dive into shops rather than pass her on the streets.
Employers were suspicious about offering work to an ex-MP.'

As Maggie Bain struggled to earn a living and pick up the
pieces of her life, politics was forced to the back-burner. Courage
and determination came to the front. 'I really drifted around for
a while. I knew girls in London and asked if I could share their
flat. I kept on my mortgage on my flat at home in Scotland, and
I did a lot of freelance journalism, working nightshift subbing for
BBC Radio News, and doing articles for the *Observer*. I did find
it hard and it wasn't a good living and it wasn't an easy living. I
had to work the most outrageous hours at the BBC — sometimes getting up at 3.00 in the morning to go and do shifts.'

In the 1983 General Election she gallantly stood in her old
seat again. 'It was very depressing. The Party was going through
a low time, and this time — far from winning — I lost my
deposit. But I stood because I have a commitment to what I
want to see achieved in Scotland.'

Then life brightened up. 'As my personal life started to stabilise again, so too my political life started to stabilise. I'd known
Winnie Ewing's son, Fergus, for years, but we met up again at a
wedding of Nationalist friends. Winnie was thrilled. Fergus and
I got married in 1983, shortly after that disastrous election.'
Maggie Ewing took a complete year out from politics. 'We
bought this grand old house which needed a terrific amount
done to it and it just seemed very sensible to have that time. I
must admit I suffered from withdrawal symptoms. The temp-
tation when invitations came in to go to such and such a thing!
But I'd made a decision to take a year without anything at all.
My father died shortly after I got married too, so I had a lot of
personal commitment looking after my mum and so on. There
were lots of things I needed that year for.'

When the year was up she was persuaded to go back into
active politics and stand for a senior position in the Scottish
Nationalists. 'I became Deputy Leader of the Party, and then
the Moray constituency said they would like me to be their
candidate. I accepted. Moray has always been an area where the
SNP's been strong. We have a very strong base built there. Even
when votes were crumbling elsewhere in Scotland, there was
always a very solid base, and I like the people there.

'We found it hard at that time. We were living 200 miles away. It cost a lot of money to travel that amount every weekend and nurse the constituency. The Party gave me petrol money but that doesn't come anywhere near meeting expenses, though second time round, like marriage, you certainly know all the problems and the drawbacks and the difficulties to overcome!'

Her second husband is a perfect political match. He is possibly the first man to be both son and husband of women Members of Parliament. Margaret Ewing appreciates the advantages of a man equipped by background and temperament to be the husband of a woman MP. 'Because Fergus comes from a background with his mum always being in political life and having been away so much when he was young, he's not in the tradition of expecting everything to be in a great routine. It's not just that he came from a background where he was used to his mother being in politics, he just sees it as natural that he should share the housework with me. If I'm cooking and there's ironing to be done, he'll just go and do the ironing. He just sees that as part of life, he doesn't have any macho problems about that at all.'

By 1987 the standing of the Scottish Nationalists in the polls had risen dramatically. By now a seasoned trouper, Maggie Ewing stood for the Party in Moray — and won. When she arrived back at the Commons there was some confusion as to whom she was. 'Because of my new surname, people thought my mother-in-law, had come back. They were all a bit confused, even the Speaker called me Margaret Bain! But it was nice because so many people from all parties genuinely welcomed me back.'

Margaret Ewing has a dynamic-duo political partnership with her mother-in-law who is now a Euro-MP. The two women share the expenses of a house in Lossiemouth. 'It really is a working base for us, because my constituency actually comes within Winnie's Highlands and Islands Euro-seat. Winnie and I are there quite a lot at weekends working.'

Now she has fought her way back to the House of Commons, is she pleased that she did it? 'There are times when the paperwork piles up and the phone never stops ringing and I'm working Saturdays and Sundays — I think, O God, what am I doing this for! But I must really want to do it. I do enjoy aspects of it. It is a hassle and it's a tough life, not easy. It's even difficult to point to particular achievements. I get great satisfaction from things. I've had a major campaign on maternity facilities in my constituency, and we've actually forced the Scottish Office into doing an independent study to investigate the situation. *That* was a great achievement, because originally it just looked as if the Health Board was going to close our units and we weren't going to get anything else.

'I don't know that you end up picking up issues because you are a woman. I think you probably identify more with some issues — like arguing for better screening facilities for cervical cancer and breast cancer and so on, because you have a natural identity with them. I wouldn't describe myself as an out-and-out feminist although as I get older I sometimes feel more of a feminist than I was when I was younger.

'Apart from a Scottish Parliament, I've always been interested in education, and I've always been interested in social work. The new European dimension is becoming more and more exciting. If Scotland were independent from England, I'd like to get into a Commission post, in Brussels. Something like that. Being a roving Commissioner for Scotland would be *super*.'

# 4.
# TALES OF THE UNEXPECTED — BY-ELECTIONS

By-elections are the spice of politics and can cause sea changes. They often take place when and where you — or party leaders — least expect them. What's more, by-elections, particularly in the 1980s, have been central to the now-rapid advance of women in politics.

'Where there's death, there's hope.' A process begins even when an MP falls seriously ill. The political cycle mimics nature's cycle — a great tree in the forest falls and a set of seedlings springs up in the space. An MP who dies during a parliament's life, as happened at Greenwich, provides a God-sent chance for a new political star, like Rosie Barnes, to rise. Winning at a by-election, with its huge press and media coverage, campaigning with Party stars deferentially at your side, means instant national recognition.

For candidates and constituency parties by-elections are far more exciting than General Elections. At weekends hundreds, sometimes thousands, of party workers stream in from across the country to help. All the big-time pundits from the major newspapers and television stations and press agencies check into local hotels to begin their watch, like hunters in the reeds at dawn, themselves not averse to being recognised by the person in the street. This press army is viewed with contradictory emotion by candidate and party worker. Do they bite? Are they open to stroking?

Usually the campaign gets into top gear once polling day has been announced. By the strategic tenth day before the election, all the gloves come off in a crescendo of local opinion polls, quotes, misquotes, daily press conferences, accusations, counter-accusations, poster wars, temper tantrums among the campaign teams, and, in filthy British weather, yet more soggy leaflet delivering in the rain, followed by the relaxed and enjoyable cameraderie of late night Chinese and Indian take-aways. The gentlefolk of the press and media start to look even more self-important, as though they bear great secrets. Over cracked mugs of foul tasting instant coffee, seasoned by-election campaigners relive old battles fought shoulder to shoulder over the years: 'Were you at Fulham? Berwick? Hillhead? Vauxhall? Remember that dog-ridden council estate up at Knowsley . . . ?' For the smaller parties, by-elections are the only chance their candidates have to fight a properly financed campaign with a full complement of helpers.

Politics under Margaret Thatcher is passing through a tense and polarised time. Because the stakes are high, a by-election campaign is a no-holds barred affair, fuelled by the much higher national media and press coverage given even to previously unknown candidates. All sides ritually complain about the other side's 'dirty tactics'. Occasionally over-zealous party activists can go well past acceptable behaviour. Harriet Harman rightly complained bitterly at Liberals who knocked on doors during her Peckham by-election telling voters they oughtn't to vote for a pregnant woman. Liberal women as well as Labour women were very angry at that particular tactic.

Unfortunately, if the American experience is much to go by, such knocking copy can be unpleasantly effective in a short, sharp campaign, though not in Harriet Harman's case. For a long time after the last war, it suited an anti-woman element (and not just male misogynists either) to put about the effective and damaging charge 'Voters won't vote for a woman.' Sometimes it became even neater: famed political lecturer Dr Elizabeth Vallance discovered, 'Farmers' wives won't vote for a woman'! Crucially and historically, a group of women of many political parties disproved the myth once and for all: Harriet Harman (Lab.), Virginia Bottomley (Con.), Llin Golding (Lab.), Angela Rumbold (Con.), Shirley Williams (SDP), Elizabeth Shields (Lib.), Rosie Barnes (SDP) and Kate Hoey (Lab.) were the by-election victors of the 1980s who did it.

## ANGELA RUMBOLD

In the curious twists of fate which shape political destinies, Angela Rumbold might never have got into Parliament if the

Gang of Four, plus the Polly Toynbees, Rosie Barnes, and Celia Goodharts, and 60,000 others, hadn't launched the SDP.

Angela Rumbold is a founder member of NAUTCH, the campaign for parents to be allowed to stay with their children in hospital. She was co-founder of 'Women and Families for Nuclear Defence'. She is on the right of the Conservative Party on most of the touchstone issues, including bringing back the death penalty. Her first experience of elected politics was in 1974 when she won a seat on Kingston Borough Council. She became Chairman of the Council of Local Education Authorities for 1979-80.

From Kingston-upon-Thames, Angela Rumbold decided to apply to be the candidate for the by-election caused when Labour MP Bruce Douglas-Mann, in nearby Mitcham and Morden, felt he should put his decision for the voters' endorsement in May 1982 after moving to the SDP.

'The first round of the selection came at a ghastly time for me, as we were having a big dinner party. I had Janet Young, who was then Minister of State for Education, and her husband, and other people coming to dinner. I was into cooking that Saturday morning, I wasn't into being interviewed.' En route to the interview, Angela drove through some council estates, gloomily thinking: 'This place will never go Conservative.' Arriving at the Conservative Club in Mitcham and Morden, she was shown to the bar along with two other contenders for the seat.

Parliamentary candidates come to recognise the peculiar smell of stale ale and stale cigarettes which inextricably attaches itself to the candidate selection process. There is always a dreary bar where you have to sit and wait your turn, making awkward conversation in an embarrassed and nervous voice with rivals for a seat which may one day lead you through the needle-thin portals of St Stephen's Gate and up the stony steps to the lobbies and the debating chamber of the House of Commons. As Angela came into such a gloomy atmosphere, she noticed two photographs above her, one of the Queen when she was about 23, and one of Margaret Thatcher when she was Leader of the Party in 1976. There was also a notice in large letters saying, 'LADIES SHOULD NOT COME TO THE BAR UNLESS AC-COMPANIED BY A MAN'.

There were about 15 people on the selection committee and 30 approved candidates had been short-listed from about 150 applicants. Eventually Angela Rumbold's turn came. 'I wanted to get back to the cooking, so I socked it to them. I was really rather right-wing and truculent and I complained about the notice above the bar: "Fancy asking a woman to come and be interviewed and then confront her with that!" They all laughed. They thought it was quite funny!'

The Chairman of the Association had been an undertaker. 'And he really was a lugubrious man. He said to me, "We've got this by-election, Mrs Rumbold, and we've had some very unfortunate experiences with Conservative Central Office with by-elections. Candidates have not been suitable and the media have found them out." Then he said, "Two questions: have you any experience of the media and have you any skeletons in your cupboard?" Well, I'd had a lot of experience with the media. As Chairman of the Local Education Authorities, I'd actually appeared on programmes like Robin Day's *Question Time* and I'd done quite a lot of television so I wasn't worried about that, but the skeletons in the cupboard really floored me! I didn't know what he meant. I said I don't think so, I'm boring, I've only been married to the same man for heaven knows how long, I've had a very boring middle-class upbringing, I have three boring middle-class children, it's all very dreary. It seemed to satisfy them and then they asked about capital punishment. They were hangers and floggers. I was able to go for that. I'm keen on deterrence. They were very keen on law and order. They still are.'

The interviewers asked how she managed her domestic situation. Her youngest son was 14. 'They wanted to know what would happen. I said I had coped with that in the past and I wouldn't be here if I hadn't considered it. I didn't resent being asked; I thought it was a perfectly legitimate question because they needed to know. Women on the committee particularly wanted to know. By that time I had a "treasure", beloved Nora, who is still with me and runs my home. I found out afterwards some of my answers at that interview had been very good from the women's point of view, they were very convinced. And one of the things they had liked was my rather truculent attitude to the fact that women weren't allowed to go to the bar. They felt there were all sorts of prejudices about age and being a woman.'

The next thing that happened that day was about 4.30 pm, when the Chairman rang up. 'He said, "We took a vote and you came top, so can you come next Thursday?" During the evening I remember raising this with Janet Young and saying, "Of course, it won't happen because they'll find someone else suitable and I'd like to start a business," Janet Young said "You're just about to start a parliamentary career." To which I replied, "You're daft, it'll never happen."'

On the Thursday, Angela Rumbold went along with her husband, John. 'He wasn't invited to say anything, they just had him sitting there and we went through the same ritual, the same questions again, and at the end of that they had to take a vote on the final candidates to come up for the final selection which was going to be the following Thursday, so it was quite important.'

She went home and sat around and nothing happened. 'When you're me and you are naturally pessimistic you say, "Oh well, they've chosen somebody else and nothing is going to happen."' Nevertheless, she didn't sleep much that night. 'I worried. I wanted to know desperately badly what had happened.' Still nothing happened the following morning. 'Then at midday the ex-undertaker with the lugubrious voice rang up again. "Mrs Rumbold?" he said. "Yes," she replied nervously. The voice continued, "I've got some very bad news." Angela replied, "Don't worry, it's all right. I'm quite prepared. You've obviously found the two other applicants you want. I'll try somewhere else."'

'"No, No!" he shouted. "It's not that at all. We wanted one of each, a man and a woman. And we really didn't want your age at all. But we've ended up with two women and you're one of them. Please will you come next Thursday?"'

'I thought, what a funny way to invite you.'

The next session was in front of 22 people. 'By that time, I actually wanted it. I prepared for the final interview, I practised and practised my speech. I thought, now this time (a) you mustn't have notes and (b) you must really come over well as a friendly, warm person. John said, "Don't get bogged down, don't try and tackle too many subjects, do a fairly general political speech and just stick with the things you know really well. You know local government, you know the social services side and go for law and order 'cos they'll love it. And be loyal to the government." So I did all those things and I didn't have any notes and that impressed the audience. We were kept in the kitchen of this rundown and horrible hall while the other candidate did her thing and then we both ended up in the kitchen drinking filthy coffee waiting whilst they stuck their hands up to vote. Then somebody came in and asked me to come back, which meant I'd won and she'd lost.

'The constituency agent instructed me "You'd better get back into the body of the hall and press the flesh, dear." So I did, that was it.'

The by-election hadn't yet been called. She faced a dilemma, 'the do I stand for the local authority again, or do I pack it in and just wait for the by-election to come? You have to make up your mind a month before. I didn't want to lose a power base so I stood again for Kingston as a local councillor. I've never been so frightened.' She realised it would undermine her credibility badly as a parliamentary by-election candidate if she lost her local council seat. 'I just had no confidence, again this awful lack of confidence. I don't know why, but those '82 elections were awful. I just thought the Social Democrats were much stronger than they actually were. I thought they were going to win and the build up was tremendous and I remember going to the count that night and shaking — literally *shaking* — with fear that I'd lost my local council seat, because by that time I knew we were definitely going to fight a by-election a month later.

'Geoffrey Seeton stood behind me and said, "You're joking, you've won two to one, just look," He took me round the count and showed me the little piles of votes. "When you see the figures like this," he said, "this means you've won!"

'When I saw what had happened in Merton where we had won a significant number of seats, I realised for the very first time I could make it into Parliament in this crazy by-election!'

One week later the Mitcham and Morden by-election campaign began. 'I thought, I'm not going to allow *anybody* to get between me and being elected. All these men in dark suits who looked like more undertakers who came down to organise me and said, "We are going to put your press conferences on at five past ten," and I said, "No, no, I want it at 9 o'clock." I wanted to set the agenda each day. "Oh we can't do that!" they said. "We've organised it with the Labour Party." I said, "You make it at 9 o'clock or I won't do them." They said, "We've never had a candidate say that to us before." I said, "Well, you've just met one!" They said, "Why?" and I said, "It's *my* by-election and I want to win it."'

They changed her press officer and brought down a very experienced press officer from Manchester to advise her on what topics to take. 'We talked about it the evening before, from about 9.30 onwards. We looked at the news and we would say, what's going to be in the newspapers?'

The next morning the team would meet early. 'I would cook breakfast at half-past seven at the constituency offices. It was the only way to get them to meet early.' No-one thought of offering to cook the breakfast. 'I got them to do the shopping and I took my own home-made marmalade.'

The team went through the newspapers at the breakfast meetings to pick the topics for the day's press release. 'The weather was beautiful. It was a lovely early summer, so I was able to put on nice, easy simple shirts and skirts.'

Press conferences at by-elections can be very hairy, the press versus the hapless candidate. It may be the first time a candidate has had to face such a nerve-wracking situation filled with pit- (or prat-) falls. One awful blunder and your entrails are plastered all over TV and newspapers, to lurk in the nation's archives, on film or in print for any 'Political (or Comedy) History of the Twentieth Century'. They are probably the most testing situation a candidate can undergo — a pitting of wits and questioning to rival the Jesuits in the Spanish Inquisition. I watched an excellent by-election candidate, Rosie Cooper at Knowsley North, totally flummoxed when asked by a male journalist if she could tell him how many miles a Cruise missile can fly.

'I did find the press tricky. They were trying to trip me, but it was interesting how press interest grew. Journalists started coming down to do single face-to-face interviews. And although they were trying to trip me they were actually, I think, a little engaged. I would joke with them and call them "the bloodhounds" and they liked it and I wasn't nervous about it at all. I actually enjoyed the press, I always have enjoyed the press, I like the press and I have no problems with the media at all.'

Angela Rumbold won by 4,274 votes. It was the first by-election gain by a party actually in government in over twenty-two years.

Her rise since winning has been rapid, possibly because she was an experienced woman already in her fifties. Nicholas Ridley soon offered her a role as his Parliamentary Private Secretary — good training ground for a future Minister. Seven years after winning her by-election she became Minister of State for Education. The future? 'I've always wanted to go into the Treasury. Chancellor of the Exchequer? I don't think that will happen in my lifetime, but I'd very much like to see something of the Treasury.'

## ROSIE BARNES

When Rosie Barnes was first selected to stand as the SDP parliamentary candidate for Greenwich in November 1986 ready for the General Election in 1987, there was no hint of a by-election. She stepped in as candidate when SDP candidate, Tim Ford, who had come third in the 1983 General Election, stepped out of what he saw as a 'no-hope' seat. Rosie Barnes was under no illusions about her chances of winning Greenwich for the SDP at a General Election. Guy Barnet was the well-respected, well-entrenched Labour Member of Parliament. She thought she had been chosen to fight a seat which would take at least two elections to win. It would fit in well with her children growing up. She was still very much a political novice with a year or two's experience on education policy committees in the SDP and very, very little public speaking experience.

'I hadn't spoken up very much. When we had my candidate adoption meeting late in 1986 it snowed heavily, so not many people came. I spoke to a virtually empty room about how proud I was and how I was going to do A, B and C.'

Three months later Rosie Barnes was the centre of press and media attention right across Britain. She was intriguing packed meetings of Greenwich voters and winning the admiration of even hard-bitten political pundits like Hugo Young of the *Guardian.* He described her as 'a classless strong-minded, political ingenue of no fixed political allegiance who has discovered in the politics of the SDP a way of life that turned out to suit her temperament perfectly'.

A former market researcher, Rosie Barnes was already a mother in her thirties with two children before she joined any political party. She recalls, 'The by-election campaign was to be the most exhausting two months of my life. I had less sleep in that two months than I've ever had before or since.' It was in December 1986 that Guy Barnet, Labour MP for Greenwich for 15 years, died suddenly of a heart attack. His death caused the by-election that rocketed Rosie Barnes, 'political ingenue', into the House of Commons and on to the front pages of the British press.

'Christmas Eve was in full swing. The children were at home and excited. Joseph must have been about 20 months — it was his first Christmas tree — the ham was in the oven and the mince pies were cooking. I'd forgotten something I thought I might need over Christmas, so I nipped down to the chemist's.'

By the time she returned home, she noticed a complete change of atmosphere. 'The music was off and everybody was quiet and our two mothers, who were staying with us for Christmas, were sitting on the stairs with glasses of sherry. They're not the sort of mothers who would normally sit on the stairs and I looked at them with their glasses of sherry and thought, I know, there's been a death in the family.'

Her husband Graham broke the news. '"I think you'd better sit down, too, Rosie. I've just heard on the news that Guy Barnet's died, which means there's going to be a by-election." Talk about being dumbfounded. It was Christmas Eve. There was nobody at the SDP Headquarters at Cowley Street or in the House of Commons for me to contact. Everybody had gone. I didn't know what to do. I wondered if I was going to be in a by-election or if they would choose somebody more experienced?'

Soon the press started to phone her. 'The *Sunday Times* rang straight after Christmas to ask if they could come and do a photograph of me and the children in a relaxed holiday setting.' But she still didn't know if she was to be the candidate. She rang her political mentor, John Cartwright, the SDP MP in next door Woolwich, to ask his advice. 'When he told me to go ahead with The *Sunday Times* picture, I realised I was going to be the candidate. The *Sunday Times* headline read: "Greenwich SDP Hopeful". It had me in a track suit with two of the children and the dog. All very exciting.'

In a by-election the parties' national campaign teams flock into a constituency and seize control of campaign and candidate. But, like Angela Rumbold, Rosie Barnes was determined to be in charge of her own campaign. 'I was a more assertive candidate than they'd had in the past. If you're female and you smile a lot and you've got curly hair, people think you're light-weight and you're a push-over. If you're tough, it takes them totally by surprise, they're not expecting it.'

She laid down ground rules. 'Not one piece of literature was to go out that door without my having read and approved it. The candidate in Fulham had found himself on a platform defending things on leaflets that had gone out without him seeing them.'

The worst night of the campaign came with less than two weeks to polling day. 'We had to make the breakthrough into second place in the straw polls. We just *had* to get ahead of the Tories, to be the main challenger to the Labour Party and get voter momentum going.'

The following day was the crucial Vincent Hanna all-party, all-candidate television debate, recognised as a true make-or-break occasion. Rosie Barnes was well aware that by-election candidates had been crushed on such occasions. 'I was extremely nervous, so we had a mock debate where Roger Liddle, who stood as candidate in Fulham, pretended to be my Labour opponent, front-runner Deirdre Wood. We had an audience and we did the whole thing. I didn't think I did very well and *everybody* was coming at me with briefings — you *must* know this and you *must* know that — and I was trying to retain it all, but I couldn't. I was exhausted and in the end I thought I had to go to bed and sleep. About 12.30 Graham woke me up and said, "I thought you'd like to know that someone's just phoned, there's a new poll coming out tomorrow. The Labour Party is still in the 50s, and the Tories are still 27 and we're only at 25 per cent." We were still running third and it was going to be disastrous. I couldn't get back to sleep again then, after all the turmoil of this news.'

How did she cope with the Party's pre-press conference briefings? 'I used to turn up with my tape recorder and record things. I began to find my way around the people of the SDP. There was the policy secretary, Wendy Buckley, and she was excellent but I couldn't actually understand her very well. She spoke at slightly above where I was in political terms. She had an assistant called Andrew Cooper who was very calm and very relaxed and I understood every word he said. When some issue suddenly blew up, he had the gift of giving me three sentences which would carry me through. So I commandeered Andrew Cooper and he stuck with me through the whole by-election.'

Rosie Barnes calls herself a pavement politician. 'I get my political theory on the doorstep. I'm a grass-roots politician. There has been a lot of debate about the Charter for Human Rights recently, but in a way that kind of politics doesn't interest me at all. What really concerns me is the damp on the housing estates, the ill-fitting window, the bad housing.'

She prepared hard for what she was going to say at the Vincent Hanna BBC TV debate. 'Despite my fears, I did comparatively well. Deirdre Wood did rather badly. She blew it on the issue of lesbians adopting babies. There was a question about whether lesbians should be allowed to adopt children or not. I said my view was no, apart from exceptional circumstances where maybe a woman who was a lesbian and a child's aunt and already had a very good relationship with it. Just to take a child to a couple who were lesbians, who didn't have any connections with that particular child, as a social experiment without knowing quite what effects it was going to have, would be unfair to a child who had been unfortunate enough to need adopting.'

Her memory of polling day itself is one of extreme and utter exhaustion. 'The day I won the by-election was very exciting, but was I exhausted! Although I looked elated on all the pictures, I've got one or two which show what I really felt like. I was shattered! I only went to bed for about an hour before I had to drag myself out to be chirpy and elated on TV AM. I took off my make-up and my clothes and lay in bed for about an hour. Then I got up, had a shower, washed my hair and put all my make-up and clothes back on again and went off to the TV studio.

'Although I'd won, I didn't actually feel I'd won. I thought I'd got it temporarily and had to hang on to it. I knew I was going to fight a General Election very soon and I knew lots of people in small parties win at by-elections and then lose in the General Election. It was a peculiar anti-climax. I had a huge support system up to the day of the election and then the by-election team disappeared. It just went away.'

Rosie Barnes's worst experience came in the autumn of 1987 at Portsmouth when she stood up to speak at her Party Conference during the agonies of self-destruction of the SDP. She was hissed by party members who just months before had been fêting the 'Winged Victory of Greenwich'. It shook her badly. 'I was hissed before I said anything. It was just a few months after I'd won a by-election and a General Election at great personal cost. I thought: "What am I doing? Who ARE these people?"'

Like other public figures, Rosie Barnes has developed her own tricks to help her when things hurt. 'I've coped by sometimes being slightly detached and seeing it as a performance going on on the stage and I'm somewhere else watching.' She found it extremely painful. 'I didn't want to be in the firing line. It was the letters from people telling me how dreadful I was. It went on for quite a while, we still get the odd one. My secretary, Vanessa, is very good — if I get a sort of little wodge of hate mail about anything, I suddenly find it's at least three weeks old and she decided I wasn't feeling robust on the day it came. I'm probably tougher than she thinks. But I do get wounded.'

# 5.
# DYNASTY — THE POLITICAL HERITAGE

Although British politics has no Kennedy clan, there are some almost dynastic political families in the UK, where the succeeding generation is heavily influenced towards politics by being brought up in a political ambience from the moment of birth. The Churchill family very nearly qualifies. The Oppenheim family has made a start with Sally and her son Phillip. Baroness Summerskill and daughter, Shirley, were Members of Parliament. Daughters do well — selection committees and political parties often plump for dynasty over gender. Emma Nicholson, Shirley Williams, Virginia Bottomley and Ray Michie are all women whose family background shaped their future politics.

## EMMA NICHOLSON

Conservative Member of Parliament for Torridge & West Devon since 1987, Emma Nicholson was 'to the manner born'. Political blood courses through her body. She waxes lyrical about the House of Commons: 'Being in the House has fulfilled what I hoped and more — the depth, the richness, the intricacy of the work, the extraordinary satisfaction of getting something right, which will improve people's lives in some way or another. Life in the House is fascinating, absolutely fascinating. It is also very hard work — you need the stamina of an ox. Health is one of the great difficulties. Members of Parliament do tend to die young. There's a medical study being carried out on the new Members, a survey which they're going to carry on for some years because they're concerned about early deaths amongst parliamentarians.

'Lots of my family have been in politics — my father was a Member of Parliament from about ten years before I was born and he eventually retired in 1966 — a grandfather, three of my great-grandfathers, two of my uncles, about half a dozen of my closest cousins, myself, my brother-in-law. Three or four cousins are in the Commons, and several in the Lords. The family's been in politics on both sides, Mother's and Father's sides. My mother's side goes back in politics to the eleventh or twelfth century.

'I was brought into politics in the first place because when I was a small child I saw my father effecting change for the better for his constituents through the parliamentary process. There was always room in the car for a companion. He always wanted a daughter to come with him. Later I was the first woman in my family to be actively involved in politics and my mother didn't like it at all. She saw it as an activity that was too ego-centred. She was a very unselfish woman and she did an enormous amount of work for handicapped people and children. She was Deputy Chair nationally of Dr Barnado's. She poured herself into that, the sacrificing side of life.

'By the time I was born my father's constituency was Farnham in Surrey, but before that he was Member of Parliament for Morpeth and Northumberland. I remember seeing real poverty with elderly people, post-war poverty. I remember seeing homes with very badly handicapped, grotesquely deformed children and adults and I remember saying to myself, never forget how lucky you are, your job is to try and give as many people as you can the luck that has come your way. I can't recall a moment when I didn't feel like that. It was certainly not inevitable I became a Conservative. My father stopped politics when I was 21. I then looked very closely indeed for a long period into the other parties. One of my great-grandfathers was a Liberal Member of Parliament. He crossed the floor of the House to join the other two Conservatives in 1871. So we had quite a strong Liberal tradition, but what I would call pre-1900 Liberalism and perhaps I'm really a Conservative because I believe many of those stands now form the bedrock of modern Conservatism. Freedom of the individual. I think that's my beginning and ending. I suppose I was always part of the Conservative Party, but I backed off when I was 21 and I remember saying to myself very consciously, now my father's retired I must step back and see what I really believe. I mustn't just follow the family line because they all happen to be Conservatives. I had listened to all my relations make speeches throughout my childhood and adult life. I've knocked on more doors than I can count and begged everybody to vote for my relations, mainly my father, and now I've got to think for myself. And so I suppose I started collecting knowledge and information. I didn't sever my links with the Conservative Party, but I built up a lot of knowledge and understanding, I saw things from other people's points of view, other politicians' points of view. Again I had a head start because I knew so many of the Opposition politicians here.

'I left school when I was 16 and went to the Royal Academy of Music. I left the Royal Academy with my qualifications when I was 21 and went straight into computer software with ICL. It was clear I wasn't going to fulfil my ambition of filling the Albert Hall playing my piano and I think the sensible thing, when you realise that, is to turn in another direction. I didn't give up music. I love it, it's my life-line but I'm not a professional musician, I haven't got that great art.

'What made me decide to speed up my route to parliament was having a Marxist couple to dinner. I had learned that politics is a practical matter and not just a philosophical matter. That's why I could never join the Labour Party. I could never be a Socialist, because although some of the aspirations could not be higher, could not be more knowledgeable — the brotherhood of the system of men and women, for example — what it leads to is the centralisation of domination which militates against the individual. For all its faults, conservatism underneath is a practical philosphy for the ordinary person and it only fails when it gets away from that grass root.

'I invited this couple and three or four other friends, and I thought it would make an interesting and constructive evening. The husband was rock solid Communist, possibly even a Marxist Communist, not that I use labels in any denigratory way in that sense, but he had been taught to see things very much from the then closed Russian viewpoint. He'd done a lot of work in and out of Moscow. It was really his hatred that shook me, the way in which he wanted to destroy so much in the United Kingdom. I've no respect of institutions per se, but it was his total destructiveness. It's interesting he hasn't managed to get into parliament, although he tried very hard. I remember I'd spent my small salary on the dinner. I was not at all a well-off person and you know how tough it is to get flats if you're a girl and how high the rents are and how women, certainly then, weren't paid the same as men. I remember I was so proud of the fact that I'd managed to find avocados, very expensive, very rare — and how rude he was about them! He didn't know how to eat an avocado, he was the son of a miner. Had he got to use a knife and fork? What was this disgusting luxury food he'd had put in front of him? It was horrid — he was positively fuelled by hatred. I was so appalled at their hatred and distortion of reality. It was listening to him which made me reach for the telephone at 9.00 the following morning to call Conservative Central Office and ask if I could go round and have an interview and be considered as a candidate. I asked to speak to the Vice Chairman of the candidates, the first person to contact if you want to be considered by the Conservative Party as a candidate.'

It took about a year to go through the mechanics. 'The forms were clearly slanted at men, asking for your wife's maiden name, but that didn't floor me because I'd been working in a man's world in computers, in business and industry, travelling all around. It didn't worry me.'

She was placed on the approved list in about 1975. 'I knew what I wanted to do was to fight a hopeless seat for experience — that's a first step on the ladder. So I ticked every single box and, to my horror, I was called for interview by 25 different seats in roughly the same fortnight and I had to take 10 days' paid leave to cover the interviews.

'I went to everything. That's the secret, to do everything. Don't miss a trick, don't drop a chance, try everything. It was great fun and I ended up being offered two seats at once. One in the North and one in the Midlands. I took Blythe in the North East because my father had been Member of Parliament for Morpeth and the current Blythe seat contains half the old Morpeth seat, so I had a reason to be there. In politics that's vital for your own self-respect and understanding as well as the point of the constituency linking in with you.

'I had a very happy three-and-a-half years in Blythe. I spent every weekend and all my holidays bankrupting myself getting on the train ninth class. I dread to think what it cost me — I didn't add it up. I stayed in a £3 a night bed and breakfast and my landlady and her husband were strong Conservatives. They looked after me very well and I still keep contact with them. I built up a mass of friends in Blythe and got about 12,500 votes, the highest Conservative vote they'd ever had. I doubled the previous Conservative vote. It was tremendous fun and a great experience.

'I missed the 1983 General Election in terms of getting a safe seat or getting any seat. By then I was one of the directors of the Save the Children Fund and I was responsible for raising many, many millions of pounds a year — £30-£40 million a year by the time I left. And I was responsible for raising at least £25 million of that rather more than a full-time job — plus I had a mass of international involvements.

'After the General Election I put my name down for Willie Whitelaw's seat when he moved to the Lords. I came second there. Directly after that Cecil Parkinson, the Party Chairman, sent for me and said the Prime Minister had asked him to invite me to be a Party Vice-chairman with special responsibility for women, to bring more women into politics, and specifically into the Conservative Party.

'I replied: "I'm a director of fund-raising for the Save the Children Fund, which is a full-time job. You have many Members of Parliament's wives who could do this job for you. They have time, they're not working. I don't." He said "Well, the Prime Minister has asked me to say she wants a working woman because women now work, because women have changed, and she wants a younger working woman." And Cecil Parkinson said I was the only one who fitted. I asked if I could think about it and he said yes — until tomorrow morning. This was about 6.00 in the evening. I take my work, whatever I'm doing, with total seriousness — I never got married until I was 45 because of that — I had always taken my work as my priority. So I went home and rang up my brother-in-law, Richard Luce, who's an Arts Minister now, and said. "Richard, I've been asked to become a Party Vice-chairman, shall I take it on?" And he laughed so much the telephone nearly fell off the hook and said "Nobody's ever asked me to be a Party Vice-chairman; if I were you, I'd accept." I said, "What about my work?" He told me to have a go and see what happened." So I did. I didn't regret a moment of it, although it doubled my workload. I had many meetings with the Prime Minister, put papers to her. I've met with her regularly and talked about politics.

'My great concern is that women have so limited their political involvement. The House of Commons would be much better if there were far more women in it. But it was very lucky I wasn't married else I don't know what I would have done. I wouldn't have been able to do it. A woman in politics may have to make a choice. Politics is pricey, the same as any aim you want to pursue in life. I can only imagine, that having children must be the most expensive thing of all. Anything you want in life over and above what somebody is going to pay you to do is expensive. It's just a question of where you want to put your money. I chose not to get married, I chose not to have children — that was my conscious choice.

'1987 was a very remarkable year because I was selected to fight for a winnable Tory seat in West Devon, which was the most exciting thing that had ever happened to me up till then. And I got married just before the General Election was announced. It was marvellous, the juxtaposition of being elected and getting married. It was the happiest three weeks possible. All I can remember about that period is happiness. The joy of getting selected for West Devon, the extraordinary excitement and happiness of being elected and therefore being able to actually start work on the work I'd wanted to do all of my life, plus the extraordinary glory of getting married at the same time.

'As far as combining marriage now with my work in Parliament and having a constituency far away from the House of Commons goes, well, I was brought up in a political household so this is standard life to me. I feel that if you are a political son or daughter, you have the great advantage of knowing the downside. You know the awfulness of political life as well as the nicenesses of it, and the job satisfaction. Most people who come here to the Commons have no idea of what the day-to-day humdrum is, or of the difficulties for family life. But if you're born into it, you know the difficulties, so you know how to get round them.'


## SHIRLEY WILLIAMS

'Shirley Williams is extraordinarily competent,' remarked Prime Minister Harold Wilson, thinking of her as a possible Chancellor of the Exchequer.

Marcia Falkender, in *Downing Street in Perspective* writes: 'People become devoted to her — rather in the way boys or girls at school become devoted to the Captain of the First XI. Add to this her charisma, the mesmeric aura that surrounds her, and you have this quality that compels belief - the "myth" factor. She is a private person, with an instinctive aversion to being taken over either by a cause or a machine.' While Frances Morrell, former chair of ILEA said, 'Shirley Williams is a tough in-fighter.'

Shirley Vivien Teresa Brittain Williams was born Shirley Catlin in London in 1930. She was educated at St Paul's School for Girls and Somerville College, the same college as Margaret Roberts (later Margaret Thatcher), and at Columbia University in the United States.

She worked as a journalist with the *Daily Mirror* and the *Financial Times* and then became General Secretary of the Fabian Society. For ten years she was the Labour Member of Parliament for Hitchin in Hertfordshire. For four of those years she was a Cabinet Minister. Her marriage to Professor Bernard Williams was dissolved in 1974. She brought up her daughter, Rebecca, on her own while she was a Cabinet Minister. She resigned from the Labour Party in February 1981 and was one of the founder-leaders with Roy Jenkins, David Owen and William Rodgers of the Social Democrat Party. In November 1981 she became the first elected Social Democrat MP. After curious boundary changes in her Crosby constituency, she lost the seat in the 1983 Election. She became President of the SDP, and on the subsequent merger with the Liberal Party, of the Alliance. She is now Acting Director at the John F. Kennedy School of Government at Harvard University and is married to an American professor.

How many times has she stood for Parliament? 'A hell of a lot of times! First in 1954, that was a by-election, '55 was the general, '59 I stood in Southampton Test, '64, '66, '70, '74 again, '79, then the by-elections of 1981, '83 and '87 — twelve altogether, and I think it's six win, six lose!'

Shirley Catlin had two politically active mothers — her real mother and her foster mother — and a political father. Her mother Vera Brittain, peace campaigner and author of *Testament of Youth*. Her father was George Catlin, a professor of political science, who twice stood for parliament for the Labour Party. They were both active in the Fabian Society. Her foster mother in Minnesota, where she was evacuated for three years during the Second World War, was active in the Farmers' Labour Party. Shirley Williams recalls the amazing coincidence of landing in a family with a female political activist. 'As sheer chance would have it, this woman, whom my mother had only ever met for one evening, turned out to be very interested in politics herself. So I was raised in America between 9 and 12 years old in the Farmers' Labour Party.'

Then she came back to Britain. 'Immediately I was picked up and taken by my father into the period running up to the Labour victory of 1945. There was all the excitement around at that time, the sense of a new dawn breaking, the sense that everything was going to change, which in many ways it did. I was absolutely captured by it. I lived for nothing else. I lived, drank, ate, breathed politics from morn till night from about 1944 on, I guess.'

Both parents had strong but different influences on her. 'There were so many forces that drove me into politics, it's very hard to pick on any one of them. The most single important influence was my father, not my mother. He'd stood twice as a Labour candidate. He couldn't have chosen worst elections ('31 and '35) and was soundly beaten both times, and then was looking for a seat in '45. But he was stuck with two invitations, one to stand for parliament again, the other to go as a journalist covering the United Nations. He chose the second which was probably a mistake because he would have got elected. That's the way life crumbles.' While her father was overseas reporting on the United Nations, Shirley was helping in the famous 1945 elections which astonished the world by sweeping Churchill out of office. She was in World's End, Chelsea, 'running all the polling slips back and forth between the polling stations and the committee room. Father's influence,' she remembers, 'was very strong. He was passionately interested in politics and he took me along with him from a very early age.'

Her mother was an influence of a different kind. She saw that 'politics has very deep involvements, that it's not just about pushing your own ambitions forward or it's not just a career. It's something which engages the very deepest values people have.'

Her mother's books were burnt at Nuremberg. She was on the Jewish refugees committee in '38, helping to get a lot of Jewish refugees away from Nazi Germany. 'I was very young but I was dimly aware of what was happening. The story is that when I was 3 I said to my mother, "It's no good trying to talk in this house, nobody wants to talk about me. They only want to talk about Hitler." Which shows, I suppose, at 3 I'd already become aware that my parents talked a great deal about Hitler.' Her mother was heavily condemned for coming out against saturation bombing in 1943. Standing up against saturation bombing of Germany was an almost foolhardy thing to do. She was denounced from pulpits and in the House of Commons and everywhere else. She wasn't allowed to broadcast on the BBC for about three years. Apart from the moral issue, investigation after the war showed saturation bombing had been an almost totally useless strategy. The German war production machine began to mobilise the women as well as men. Saturation bombing may even have prolonged the war.

Shirley was only 13 at the time. 'I remember my mother being very depressed, and I spent a lot of time trying to cheer her up. On one occasion, a famous woman author, who I will not name, met my mother at a literary party and deliberately just turned on her heel and walked away. This woman was somebody whose war record in no way resembled my mother's in either world war, but she just publicly cut her. A lot of people did, so I remember that, feeling terribly angry. My father was clearly depressed on behalf of my mother. Through my mother I saw some of the price you can pay for a political view and that it wasn't just enjoyable and fun, but had these very, very dark sides to it.'

Her first conscious political act was around 1946. 'I started doing weekly public meetings using an orange box, alternately in Sloane Square and World's End, with the then Labour candidate, a charming man called Fred Tongue. He and I used to get up there from 11 to 12.30 every Sunday, turn and turn about, standing on our orange box just like Hyde Park Corner. I learnt to speak through that because I had to take turns with him. Sometimes there was nobody there except a couple of men and a dog, and sometimes there were hecklers. I looked very young for my age even at that young age, so I must have looked a pathetic figure. It was a damned good way to learn how to speak in public and at the same time I took a public speaking course at the National Council Labour College. I got a report which said, "Some eloquence, but too chaotic to ever be a good public speaker."'

Her outlook on international affairs was shaped by a visit to Germany in 1948 as a member of the Labour League of Youth's National Executive at the first post-war conference of the Young Socialists of Germany in Hof, Bavaria.

'You can imagine, this was May 1948. Schumacher had just got out of hospital, after concentration camp. He was a very sick man and he didn't live long. He was the SPD leader and this was the first Young Socialist conference. It was immensely emotional. Nobody had had anything to eat except potatoes and cabbage water. Of course, our first gesture was to eat potatoes and cabbage water because we had to show we were comrades.'

It was a short time after the Communist putsch in Czechoslovakia. Refugees fleeing from the Communist take-over straggled into the town of Hof. 'We were invited by our young German colleagues to go down to the station. We went down and saw the refugees being clubbed back into railway wagons and sent across the border to an almost certain death because of Yalta. It told me something about politics which was — the opposite to Mrs Thatcher — you should not reach simple conclusions about our side being right and their side being wrong, or that our side is not capable of evil and their side is only capable of evil. It taught me that lesson.'

'Mrs Thatcher has always had a very black and white view about patriotism in international affairs and my patriotism has been for certain political ideals which some countries uphold better than others. After that experience, it's not been specifically to a country. I remember these men and women pleading not to be sent back. They said, "We'll be sent to the salt mines, for God's sake don't send us back." Our German colleagues turned on us and said, "Can't you do anything? Can't you go and talk to the American commander?" We talked to the officers and they said, "We're under orders. This is nothing to do with you. No, we've got to send them back." And they did.'

Under the present British electoral laws you are considered old enough at 18 to take full legal responsibility for a candidate's election campaign — making sure all the complicated electoral laws are not broken and keeping a detailed account of election expenses — but you are not considered responsible enough to be elected for local council or Parliament until you are 21. Shirley Williams was not old enough to stand in the General Elections of 1950 and 1951.

'So I was a speaker in 1950, in Devon and Cornwall, for the Labour Party. In 1951 I was still too young to stand myself so I was agent for Chelsea.'

In 1954 she stood for Parliament for the first time in Harwich. She was 24 years old. She was invited to stand that first time as a result of a summer vacation job working on a farm in the area.

'I worked for about seven or eight months on a farm after I left school. I didn't want to go to college right away, I was very bored with education and I never took A levels at all. I left school when I was about 17, after what was then the General Certificate of Education. I sat the scholarship to Oxford and got it so I didn't stay, I went and worked on this farm in Essex. I was very much involved in the local Labour Party. It was a co-operative farm, it wasn't an ordinary ownership farm — the farmer became the chairman of the local Labour Party. When I left college and went to America he wrote to me and said a candidate had stood down and asked if I would be interested in standing, so I stood. Harwich was a hopeless seat then, in fact it's a hopeless seat now.'

Ten years later she was elected Labour Member of Parliament for Hitchin, Hertfordshire. She spent the next ten years at the Commons as the Parliamentary Private Secretary and Parliamentary Secretary at the Ministry of Health and the Ministry of Labour from 1964-67, as Minister of State at Education and Science and at the Home Office from 1967-70 and as a Cabinet Minister at Prices and Consumer Protection from 1974-76, at Education and Science and as Paymaster General from 1976-79, when she lost her seat partly as a result of her controversial education policy.

Shirley Williams takes a philosophical approach about the ups and downs of her career. 'I've got the good fortune to almost invariably find myself thinking about the future and not about the past. After I got defeated in 1979, a woman friend who'd come to stay with me said, "I was worrying how I was going to comfort you because after all, you'd been a Cabinet Minister and here you are, not even an MP. And I woke up and heard you singing and I thought it's going to be all right."

'I still remember waking up that morning after the election defeat thinking, Gosh! there are about ten things I can now go and do I couldn't have done before! I got up and did them.' Was the sense of freedom partly the freedom of having ceased to be a Minister or Member of Parliament? 'Yes, that's a very intense part of it. I think it's particularly true if you're a single or divorced woman, that there'll be an intense interest in things like who you're going out with and so on. I've been followed by reporters in and out of the shop fronts.'

Two weeks after the launch of the Council for Social Democracy in early 1981 she resigned from the Labour Party's National Executive after months of bitter internal fighting. 'It was just grim. For example, we put down amendments saying, "that if the trade union block vote is going to elect the leader, then they must all ballot their members beforehand". And we put down an amendment saying we wouldn't get out of the European Community unless there was clear evidence they were trying to stop all public ownership, that kind of thing. We never got anywhere, it was just constantly a battle like that. The whole atmosphere was very sour. It tended to be mostly along the lines of saying, "You're selling out, you're not supporting us." It wasn't personal in the sense of people saying, "You bitch." It was much more that the far Left had the wind in its sails and therefore everything was judged by its standards and its values. In my constituency the same thing happened, every GMC meeting was like that.'

From one of the most miserable chunks of her career, she got back on her surf-board to woosh to the top of a perfect political wave at the Crosby by-election in March 1981.

Her win as the first Member of Parliament to be elected for the new Social Democrat Party in November 1981 ranks as her sweetest memory of all. Her majority of 5,289 overturned a Conservative majority of 19,272. Crosby had always been a Tory seat. It was ranked the sixteenth safest Conservative seat in Britain. 'It was by far my most exciting campaign and my most satisfying win. Of course, when I won a parliamentary seat for the first time it was very exciting because I'd already stood three times. So to actually win was a tremendously exciting moment, but it wasn't as exciting as Crosby. Crosby was the high point because in Crosby we went berserk. It was the new party, we'd overturned this vast Conservative majority, we'd won against things which were deeply held views in a deeply Conservative constituency, with a deeply right-wing Conservative Party which had been in charge for ever. We'd fought very directly on certain gut Conservative issues. Public schools, capital punishment, those were the two central issues at Crosby. They never lay down for a single day and I was not prepared to compromise on either.'

She campaigned with the three other members of the famous 'Gang of Four', ex-cabinet ministers Roy Jenkins, David Owen and Bill Rodgers.

'We campaigned for a month in an open truck with the rain just pouring down our faces, all four of us, Bill, David, Roy and me. It rained almost all the time. Our campaign consisted of driving through this big constituency — slums, fields, resort towns, suburbs — hair just streaking across our faces, absolutely soaking wet almost all the time, with "Chariots of Fire" playing. It was a by-election where we used to regularly get as many as 3,000 people to a public meeting, standing sometimes for an hour in the playground of schools, being rained upon and snowed upon. They just stayed there. It was simply staggering. I've never seen anything like it and although some of the others were a bit like it — Croydon and Hillhead — it was a unique kind of politics, it wasn't like any other politics I've ever had to deal with. I suppose what happened was we simply touched a nerve at a moment when that nerve was raw and touched it with something that people wanted.

'Whenever we got the chance we campaigned, just stopping for a few minutes whenever we saw a group of people and making a short speech or just talking to people off the truck. We did a lot of talking to people off the truck and it worked probably better because Crosby's a suburb of Merseyside than it would have done in most parts of the country. Merseyside's a very quick, very responsive, very human part of the country, people are very quick and very warm. The response was tremendous, there was a wave of desire for change at that time which somehow just warmed you up. We'd stop at a pub and just have a drink and immediately the whole of the pub would be a political meeting and there was no reserve in any quarter and nobody ever didn't respond — they either liked us or they didn't like us — but everywhere we went was just a mobile argument. It was a sort of perpetual hands-on experience and when it all ended and we got the announcement people couldn't believe it, they were falling about, rushing to their microphones and so forth. My party carried me out on their shoulders into the street and there must have been 3,000 or 4,000 people outside, it was a huge body of people waiting.'

Shirley Williams' perfect wave crashed on the rocks with a curious boundary change which in effect 'confiscated' her majority over the Conservatives. After the national census every ten years, the Boundary Commissioners rearrange constituencies to take into account shifts of population, these days mainly from city to suburb. The aim is to make each constituency as near as possible the same size, with about 65,000 voters each. For an MP it is devastating to see 10,000 or so voters from your staunchest area of support transferred to a neighbouring constituency. After her victory at the Crosby by-election in

1981, Shirley Williams watched a crucial chunk of her support moved out of the constituency in time for the 1983 General Election.

'It didn't change the size of the constituency, the number of voters remained virtually the same. All that happened was I saw an SDP ward exchanged for a Conservative one. People have said to me subsequently that it was quite intentional — the two major political parties got together to make sure that happened. It's very rare for the Boundary Commissioners to override an agreed submission by the two major parties. I knew after the boundaries changed it was almost unwinnable because the boundary change took with it a place called Church ward which had about 19,000 voters who had voted about 90 per cent for me. It was taken out and added to Bootle which was a safe Labour seat — it wouldn't make any difference to Bootle. In its place Aintree ward was added to my constituency. It had 12,000 voters and had always been Conservative — that made it really impossible. Quite a lot of people I know don't find it very easy to explain that boundary change. There's never any point in crying over spilt milk in politics, it's the most dangerous thing you can do, so I don't dwell on it. But it was very frustrating, as you can imagine after that win, to suddenly have that happen.'

In 1987 Shirley Williams stood for the Alliance in Cambridge against Robert Rhodes James. He retained his seat. She went back to the United States to a new job at Harvard with her new American husband. Her daughter Rebecca is grown up, but Shirley has now taken on the responsibility of bringing up her late brother's sons. Is her political career over?

'I don't know if I'm going to try again for the Commons. It's an impossible question to answer at the moment. So much depends on things that aren't in my power, like whether there's any kind of understanding among the different parties of the centre who after all are being greatly damaged at the present time. I'm bound to say I do blame David Owen, but there's no point in going over all that again. It was an absolute tragedy and I think if we don't get together, then it's difficult to see how we can have any real impact at all quickly. It'll be a very long haul before one or the other survives. It all depends a bit on when Mrs Thatcher stands again and what happens at the next election. I would like to think it might be possible for the remaining SDP and the Social and Liberal Democrats to reach some kind of understanding before the next election. I've told them I'm around to help them when I can.

'I haven't given up politics but frankly, domestically, I'm starting all over again. I've got three young people, 17, 20 and 23, all of whom are at various stages of education.' Unlike the United States, Britain offers virtually no well-paid political posts outside Parliament. Former Members of Parliament find the problem of how to earn a living a complete conundrum. Shirley Williams was forced to cross the Atlantic. 'You can't hope to get a job in this country when you are a political figure, it's just absolutely hopeless, there's no way you can do it. You have to do what Bill (Rodgers) has done in order to head the Royal Institute of British Architects; he's had to make an absolute promise that he won't get engaged in public politics. Polly Toynbee has also been effectively silenced politically now she works at the BBC. So has Ann Sofer, the Chief Education Officer of Tower Hamlets. I can earn a living in America while still doing a certain amount of politics over here. But in the five years when effectively I earned my living by doing a bit of freelance lecturing and things of that kind, I only had Becky to support and not the other two as well, and I could do that along with being the President of the SDP on a part-time basis but you can't do that for ever. It's as if you can manage two of the three, but all three — a political career, a family life and earning your living — is impossible.'

## VIRGINIA BOTTOMLEY

'I'm at home in the House of Commons, when I'm prowling around the corridors late at night or sitting in the Library or in the tea room. I feel this is were I belong.'

If Virginia Bottomley were a racehorse, her political pedigree would mark her up as a potential Cheltenham Gold Cup winner. Within five years of entering the House of Commons she was being tipped as being an odds-on favourite to become a Cabinet Minister, having risen swiftly to ministerial rank at the Department of the Environment. 'I come from a political family in which there are a great number of extremely impressive and formidable women, all active in one form or another, many of them in public life. So for me there wasn't really a decision about whether or not to do something in the public arena. It was almost taken for granted I would, so I'm in no way a fish out of water. For many women in politics, it's clear their initial steps are quite lonely, because they have no role models. They've felt they were turning their backs on what was expected of women in their family — that's quite a hard thing to do. There's an awful lot of good and bad luck in politics, of being in the right place at the right time or the wrong place at the wrong time. There have always been a great number of cousins and sisters, aunts, mothers who've stood by me and given me very solid encouragement, support and strength. It would have been very difficult indeed for me to follow the course I've followed without that strong sense of solidarity.'

Both Virginia and her husband Peter Bottomley, Minister for Transport, are Members of Parliament, the first ministerial husband and wife team since Labour's Gwyneth and John Dunwoody in the 1960s. Virginia Bottomley met her husband, Peter, when she was 12 and they married while at Essex University reading sociology.

Intrigued, a *Sunday Times* journalist wrote in 1988: 'The Bottomleys are the Odd Couple of the Tory Benches. Much is made of their apparent deviance from the tenets of enterprise culture: their liberalism, their good works. He wears a Transport and General Workers' Union tie and varsity spectacles, and crusades messianically against drinking and driving. She is a former social worker who had campaigned on behalf of poor families and the aged. . . . Verily she is fragrant, intelligent, capable; "a good sort", "a real English rose", soft, serene, not a bit shrill.'

Virginia had been a magistrate at 27 and Chair of the Juvenile Court at 32. She worked at the Child Poverty Action Group with Frank Field, now a Labour MP. 'The reason I'm a Tory is I'm deeply opposed to the class war — I was exasperated with the miners' strike. I don't believe in stirring up hatred and stirring up antagonism. I don't believe in racism and sexism, ageism, classism, I believe in fair play, so I believe in supporting the underdog. The reason I so passionately support Mrs Thatcher is she's the first Conservative leader to identify this point, that our common humanity unites us, not divides us. We all care about what happens to our children at school, we all want to have a stake in our own homes.'

By the summer of 1988 she was promoted to under Secretary of State at the Department of the Environment. Within five weeks her first very popular ministerial acts defended Britain from the poison-waste ship *Karin B* and took up the cause of protecting seals.

'When Peter first went into politics, it was quite important for me to work hard to earn some money. I used to work quite hard doing various things. There came a moment when I suddenly felt terribly bored. I was in my early thirties. I was Chairman of the Juvenile Court. I was a social worker. I'd written various articles. I'd done lots of things. I used to do a lot of political speaking. I suddenly felt I've got the rest of my life, I've done everything I want to do, what am I going to do now? We had a family joke that many women had got into politics on the death of their husband, taking over their seats. Peter and myself always had this view that, if in the unfortunate circumstance the Clapham omnibus ran him over, the obvious step would be for me to try and take over his constituency. But I don't think I ever thought it was possible for me to go in for Parliament off my own bat, myself.

'By the early 1980s, people like the 300 Group were beginning to talk about and encourage women in politics and I was very aware of how few women there were. When you went to parliament there were a tremendous number of identikit men and there just seemed to be terribly few women. By contrast it seemed there were a great many women I knew and admired in the Lords, people like Janet Young, Lucy Faithfull who's a good friend, Nancy Seear who's always been somebody I've admired greatly, Jane Ewart-Biggs. I wish they were in the Commons — they really would make a contribution, they really know what they're talking about. Everybody has a different contribution to make, but it seemed women were an element well represented in the Lords, but very rare in the Commons.

'Then something very funny happened. Peter had to go to help at one of those parliamentary selection weekends — in the Conservative Party you go away to a motel at Maidenhead for a weekend, where each of the group of eight candidates is scrutinised by an MP and by the Party organisation. Sir Anthony Royle was the Vice Chairman of the Conservative Party who organised the weekends and he summoned Peter to have a word with him. Peter straightened his tie and brushed his hair and went along. Sir Anthony said to him, "I'd like your permission to approach Virginia!" Peter's attitude was, "Well, she's a free woman, I've always said she should go into politics." Sir Anthony rang me up and put it to me I might like to put my name forward as a candidate. My initial reaction inevitably was to say, "Oh, I'm not sure I could. It wouldn't be right. How could I manage? Could I cope?" I said I would ring back. I spoke to my nearest and dearest about it. Without exception, all the people I worked with, all the people I knew, all said, "Of course, you should do it — why didn't you think of it sooner?" If the Party could see no objections to having a husband and wife together, who was I to have any objection? It was the right thing at the right moment for me. I was ready, I'd done a lot of things that were relevant. It's actually quite useful to have worked for ten years in Brixton and Peckham if you're a Tory MP.'

She went ahead, approaching the necessary three sponsors and filling out the six-page form. She was now becoming extremely keen to get into Parliament. 'I'd felt until then rather like that caricature of a person who's tied to a stake being drawn in four directions by four different horses. I had my magisterial life, I had my political life, I had my social work life, then all these voluntary organisations, and there was no integration and they didn't feed off each other. I was getting more and more involved in all these various areas. I suddenly saw that being an MP catered for all those various enthusiasms and interests.'

Eventually she was given a date for the selection weekend at the Maidenhead motel. 'You're given a number. I was number 28, I shall always remember. You weren't called by your names. I was more nervous probably than I can ever think possible before I went to this weekend at Maidenhead. It was all a form of vanity really, if I made a mess of it it would have been so embarrassing and humiliating.' She passed the test.

Virginia Bottomley's worst political memory is her failure to win the Isle of Wight in the 1983 General Election. She had really expected to win. 'I fought the Isle of Wight like I've never fought anything before. I used to work all day in London, going down to the Isle of Wight for evening meetings, getting back home at three in the morning. Plus I went down every single weekend. It was extremely expensive. I was enormously out of pocket at the end of the year, which is a real problem as a candidate for a distant constituency. I had to work part-time to do all that and therefore pennies were very stretched and I worked like anything. When the election came, I got nearly 35,000 votes, only six people in the country got more votes than me. I'd invested everything. But I hadn't won. The Liberal MP, Stephen Ross, had held the seat. It was a tremendous sense of anti-climax. All my family had planned for me to go to West-minster and Peter even had postcards printed saying Virginia Bottomley MP and the Isle of Wight address. It was really devastating. It was like a death. It was a complete bereavement and quite extraordinary.

'But I was determined not to give up.'

Early in 1984, Maurice Macmillan, the Conservative Member of Parliament for Surrey South West and son of Prime Minister Harold Macmillan, died. He had had a 16,000 majority at the 1979 General election. 313 candidates applied for the seat. Virginia was selected to fight the by-election. She was elected Conservative MP for South West Surrey in May 1984.


## RAY MICHIE

Ray Michie was elected Liberal Democrat MP for Argyll and Bute in June 1987. She is daughter of the late Liberal Peer, Lord Bannerman of Culloden, was only the second Liberal woman MP for forty years, and is the only Liberal Democrat woman MP. To become the Member of Parliament she defeated the Conservative Minister John Mackay, himself a former Liberal who had switched parties. She learned politics at her father's knee. John Bannerman was Chairman of the Scottish Liberal Party for over ten years. 'He kept the Liberal flag flying in Scotland during the dark days of the fifties while Jo Grimond kept it going UK-wise.' Ray accompanied him on his campaigns from the age of 15 — he was a well-known name in Scotland in politics and sport (he was also a rugby player).

Ray Michie's first experience of speaking on platforms came when she was 17, acting as a 'warm-up and holding speaker' for her father's large audiences. 'He would be doing three meetings in a night. He was always late for every meeting because he was a very popular person and he used to have very big, large meetings. I would have to go on to the next one to start it off. Looking back on it I'm appalled at the fact I stood up and talked, very often about things I didn't know much about.'

Her mother was also an excellent role model. 'My mother was a very good organiser. She was also a farmer and she was really the one who looked after the sheep farm while Father went off on his political rounds. I look on her as a great example of what a woman can do on her own. I was born and brought up on the

Loch Lomond side, but Mother actually came from Sutherland. She was an only child and her father gave her a farm to look after at the age of 18, so she was very much her own person. She influenced me very much. During the war she was Scottish Commandant of what was called the Girls' Training Corps. She accomplished all this while Father was away during the war.'

When Ray Michie left school she trained and worked as a speech therapist. When she married a consultant physician Iain, her husband's work with the Royal Army Medical Corps took them overseas and out of politics. 'We had three children and went abroad. I stopped working for a short time only which was rather surprising again in those days because one was expected really to be at home. I managed to work part-time while we were in the Army in Germany and Malaysia. I had a chance to see what went on in other parts of the world.'

After sixteen years of Army life, she and her husband decided to return home in 1972 to give the children a Scottish education (though she now believes Mrs Thatcher's government is wrecking Scottish education).

In 1973 her husband took a consultant's job in Oban, in Argyll. Argyll and Bute is a very large rural constituency, stretching for over 100 miles and consisting of 13 islands, with a coastline as long as France's. The typical campaign transport and clothing are ferry-boats and sou'westers. 'I have to visit all the islands by ferry. You can only fly to them if you're coming from Glasgow which is not in the constituency. So I go by ferry, taking the car over. It's a *beautiful* place, though difficult to get round. We nearly got ourselves killed in the 1983 election when bang!, we hit one of the big haulage contractors who came round the corner with a load of sheep on one of the narrow roads'.

In 1973, when Ray Michie had first arrived in the district, sheep were easier to find than Liberals. Fifteen years of hard work later, she had built the constituency into a Liberal stronghold.

'In '79 I saved my deposit, I got 5,000 votes and came third, so I was quite happy about that. In 1983, I moved into second place and then in '87 I made it.'

To Ray Michie's great regret, John Bannerman had died before she even started to stand as a candidate herself. He never saw his daughter elected Member of Parliament for Argyll and Bute, nor her daughter, Fiona, start out on her own political career as a parliamentary researcher to MP Archy Kirkwood at the House of Commons — Ray Michie and her daughter could well become the first mother and daughter to be Members of Parliament at the same time.

In the 1987 election, Ray Michie had a nail-biting wait for the result. 'Because of all the outlying little polling stations, the result in our constituency is never declared until midday on the Friday. We're about the last to be declared in the whole of the UK. At first I thought we'd just made it, until I saw the Alliance wasn't doing as well as we'd expected. I remember a few doubts beginning to creep in. I told the family to be prepared for defeat and to hold their heads up high.'

She did have two speeches in her pocket. 'I think actually I was going to make a better speech had I been beaten than what I eventually said when I won! I didn't go in at the beginning of the count. I went in half-way through. It was actually a policeman with a walkie-talkie who told me I was marginally ahead.'

She spent her entire first term as an MP at work in the Commons by day and hotel-hopping at night. 'It was awful, it was summer and running into the height of the tourist season and Wimbledon. There was literally no time to look for a place. I was shattered by the price of houses or flats, either to buy or to rent, and I couldn't really put my mind to it all. I was living in hotels and often only managed to get a couple of nights at a time in each hotel and before I was moved on to make way for other bookings. I didn't find somewhere to live until the recess came. In August Iain actually came down and we just spent three days looking around trying to find somewhere I could afford to rent.

'It was impossible because there was so much to do here. On top of work I had to organise getting a secretary, and a research assistant, and buying a typewriter. Meantime, Jim Wallace, the Deputy Chief Whip, took me round the Commons my first day and found me a desk and that was more or less it. I was astonished to find there was already a great huge pile of letters waiting for me at the House of Commons' Post Office. I couldn't believe it! Constituents must have immediately sat down and started writing to me with their problems.'

'There's no doubt, it's been worth winning the election. It's very worth it when I'm able to do things for the constituents, very worth it. Sometimes you think it's not worth it, when you've driven, sliding about through snow and ice, early in the morning to try and catch a plane or train, or there's a delay for two and a half hours because the cables were down and you arrive tired.' Without a doubt one of the worst things about representing a far-flung constituency is the travelling. 'It's very tiring. I might set off about 9.00 in the morning, drive to Glasgow, catch a plane, circle over Heathrow, take an hour to get in by tube and land on the bench by 2.30, absolutely panting and puffing. I generally go back on a Thursday night by train, take a taxi out to the airport, fly up, pick up the car, drive north, or do something like have lunch with the Editor of the *Scotsman*. On Saturday I often drive away to a surgery with constituents, which could be 100 miles down the road. Sometimes you ask yourself what you have done because you don't see the family very often, and when I do get home at the weekends, it's lovely to be home but there's not much peace.'

Even when Ray Michie goes home to her constituency the stress is still there; with an MP and a doctor in the house, the Michie telephone never stops ringing. She finds no time to relax. 'Since I got in I've not been able to do anything. I used to play a lot of golf, but I don't now except when we go on holiday in the summer. Last year we got right away. We went out to Malta in October for a couple of weeks.'

Like Maggie Ewing, the Scottish Nationalist MP, Ray Michie is committed to a Scottish Parliament: 'I'd really like to help to get power transferred from the House of Commons and Lords back to my own country. I think it's appalling to call this a democratic country when to me it's not democratic. The SNP wants to break up the United Kingdom, go its separate way. I believe the people of Scotland don't want to do that. The most important thing for me is to have a Scottish Parliament, not break up the United Kingdom. Scots have an absolute right to look after our own affairs'.

Ray Michie relates how she once stayed behind for a debate on women's health. 'I wasn't health spokesman but most of the people who spoke in the debate were women. I was extremely impressed with the knowledge in their speeches and I was also impressed with the sincerity on both sides of the House. I remember Edwina Currie and Teresa Gorman on the opposite benches saying much the same thing. It's a great sadness that there aren't more women in Parliament, because I do feel they have a greater response, a greater understanding of the issues which I think would be debated in a far better tempered manner.

'I think this is quite a lonely place, particularly for a woman.

I'm not trying to get sympathy or anything like that, but it's a very male-dominated place. The hours we keep, this business of legislating late at night, voting late at night or early in the morning or sitting all night, it's ludicrous. It's not just here in the Opposition — you can see the Ministers are tired and white-faced and everybody is yawning and longing to get to bed. I would certainly change that.'

# 6.
# HOT METAL —
# THE POWER OF
# THE PRESS

Shirley Williams is perhaps in a better position than many to point out the fickle nature of the press — and the pain newspapers can cause. 'The most painful coverage was seeing a picture of my husband with his girlfriend all over the front of the tabloid press. That picture wouldn't have happened if I hadn't been a minister or at least an MP. He just fell in love with somebody else and for a few weeks it was awful. The press were always hanging around the house, trying to take pictures. It's intensely awful for a short time and then it just stops. My advice to another woman in politics would be to say that you cannot believe that in three months' time they will be interested in you at all, and they won't be. It will all go away. Just hang on to that, just cling on to that fact. You do have to put up with it, that's the tough side of it, there's no doubt about that.'

Shirley Williams has had years of press criticism about her 'unruly hair' and casual appearance. 'They've gone on and on about it. At first it made me furious because they don't do it to men. One or two of my colleagues in the Cabinet looked very crummy and unpressed and nobody ever talked about that fact at all. It was an obsessional thing about women, about what they were meant to be like. Looking at the pictures of myself over the years, I've varied a great deal. There have been times when I've looked rather smart and other times I've looked simply awful. It tends to go up and down with mood, I suppose, but also it tends to go up and down with whether I could be bothered. I found in myself a certain kind of perverse feeling that I damn well won't and I'm not going to react to the trivia in the male-dominated press. Why should I? So quite often I didn't. I just didn't find myself having the time to *and* work 19 hours a day. Barbara

Castle always managed it, but I had a youngster as well, which really made the business of trying to find time almost impossible. In the Crosby period, I became famous for wearing an old army battle mac, which is what I campaigned in throughout, partly because the weather was so awful. People would stop me in the street, they still do, and say things like: "It's all right, dear, we know what our lives are like, so we know what yours must be like and don't you worry about it, don't you let them get you down."'

Teresa Gorman has been dogged by a features written about her in the *Independent* during and after the election. 'I think they were ageist and sexist; on and on about my age, my permed hair and my make-up. They'd never make such comments about the beer bellies of male MPs. It's the same in the House — women are judged on their appearance; even their voices are criticised by chauvinists in the Press Gallery, who also can't find a good word to say for the Prime Minister. My advice to newcomers to this game is to always be on your guard with the press and never never be your natural self. Most of all, never agree to be interviewed with a tape recorder running unless its your own. The system is merciless so you have to be calculating in order that the public doesn't get the impression that women are superficial and lightweight. But the media also works for you. Appearing on *Any Questions* and *Question Time* helped me to overcome the problem of being taken seriously. There's always someone on a selection committee who has seen you on the box and thinks of you as a personality and not just as a woman.'

News coverage of women politicians has improved in the last few years, in serious newspapers like in the *Times*, the *Independent*, the *Guardian*, the *Daily Telegraph*, the *Sunday Times* and the *Observer*, the *Financial Times* and the *Sunday Telegraph*. With occasional aberrations these papers now write about women politicians as politicians who happen to be women. But the tabloid press is another story. When I was selected to stand for Parliament in Hertfordshire East, the local paper's headline read 'LIBERALS CHOOSE DIVORCEE' Some months later, on polling day in the 1979 General Election, the *Daily Mail* ran a double-page spread on six women candidates, including the one from Hertfordshire East, headed 'WOMEN WITH X APPEAL'

Second only in disappointment at being hurt by the press is the let-down of hitting the cutting-room floor. Soon after I launched the 300 Group, I received a call from a very senior woman journalist on the *Sunday Times*. Could she have an interview on the new organisation and why I thought it was needed in Britain? 'The *Sunday Times*?' I enquired. 'Yes indeed!' She spent more than two hours interviewing me. Extremely excited, I rushed out on the Sunday. Although it was only early November, the *Sunday Times*' editors had replaced the topic of getting more women elected to parliament with a recipe for Christmas pudding!

Rosie Barnes remembers well the ironic twist to her first proper contact with the national press. 'The first big interview I did was for the *Observer*, with a fellow called Paul Routledge. It was all a big day's expedition to tape-record this interview and be photographed all over Greenwich. I was very excited and rang all my relations. I told them all to get the *Observer* that weekend because there was going to be a feature about me in it. Then he rang me on the Friday night or the Saturday night to tell me he was very sorry but the first opinion poll had just come out and it was 65 per cent Labour, 27 per cent Tories, 15 per cent SDP. He said that meant they weren't interested in me and they weren't going to run the article. Instead the *Observer* published an article about how Greenwich was safe in Labour's hands!' A few weeks later Rosie Barnes won the Greenwich by-election for the Alliance with a 6,611 majority, ousting Labour who had held the seat for fifty years.

Ann Clwyd was herself a journalist before she entered politics. Her first parliamentary campaign in Gloucester brought her against the Conservative MP, Sally Oppenheim, now Baroness Oppenheim-Barnes. 'It was interesting fighting another woman because you then saw the sexist way newspapers dealt with women politicians. It was described variously as "the battle of the blondes", and "the petticoat battle". One Press Association report actually started off the copy with, "Labour's secret weapon in the battle of the blondes is Ann Clwyd's heated hair rollers." I'd had quite a serious conversation with that Press Association reporter and I was absolutely astounded that they could have trivialised it in such a way, but it's fairly typical.'

Ann Clwyd gave up her seat as Euro-MP for Mid and West Wales to become MP for Cynon Valley in the 1987 General Election. Almost immediately an acquaintance told her something unpleasant was in the magazine *Private Eye*. To her horror, she read, 'Ann Clwyd used her promiscuity as a means of obtaining her political ambitions.' 'When I saw it, I thought it was one of the most vicious personal attacks I've ever seen and I think that was the reaction of other people who'd seen it. Your reaction at first is sheer anger — it's something which is unfair. Having been a reporter myself, a stickler for accuracy, I see no excuse at all for people not getting their facts right. It's almost a professional anger that people will call themselves reporters and think they can get away with facts that are not facts.'

Ann Clwyd took *Private Eye* to court and won substantial damages. 'There was only one way to handle it and that was to keep smiling. You realise these things do happen to people in politics and I immediately got hold of a solicitor because so much of it was untrue I had to do something about it. Many people can't afford the amount of money that is needed. It's why I got so interested in the issue of Right to Reply.'

Joan Ruddock was sitting in the editor's office of the local newspaper when she was told about dirty tricks that had been happening in her constituency during the 1979 General Election. 'I clearly looked shocked,' she recalls, 'and the newspaper, which was supporting the Liberals, headlined it something along the lines of "LABOUR CANDIDATE DRIVEN TO TEARS!", which was an absolute lie. There was no way, apart from a human tragedy, that I would ever cry in public. The headline gave the impression I really was so distraught I wasn't in control of myself, when actually nothing could have been further from the truth. Naturally I was extremely upset but I was very much in control of myself and I really resented that. It was an attempt to further weaken my position as a political candidate but I also felt it was done because I was a woman.

'Obviously I have had a lot of trouble with the press as all people in public life, and particularly women, do. Yes, I think particularly women because a lot of very seedy types of male reporters have sexual hang-ups. Rumours were being persistently circulated about a relationship between Bruce Kent and myself. Nothing could have been a million miles further from the truth, but this had been said and then it had been taken up by several people and squashed, and then I started to get a series of calls saying this particular journalist from the tabloid press needed to talk to me about something because it was going to be tremendously damaging. I should get in touch with her — she was so worried about me.'

In the end Joan decided to take the risk and meet her. 'I

think if it had been a man, I wouldn't have gone — I'm sure I wouldn't have actually — but because it was a woman, I decided to go. She had had a tip-off on a file circulating in Fleet Street about this supposed affair of mine with Bruce. She was pretty certain it had been compiled by MI5 as part of the disinformation campaign, and MI5 had apparently made it available. It was just a question, she told me, of when it broke and in which newspaper, and that it would break and my only hope was to tell her because she would put a sympathetic slant on it. I looked her straight in the eye and said, "There's nothing to tell, there's nothing in this." I added, "It doesn't matter how many hundreds of thousands of pounds it costs, this will mean a court action against any newspaper. Frankly I'm confident we won't be constrained by not having the money because I believe the Peace Movement will raise it, to clear our names, so you won't get away with it."

'I must say it really shook me. I realised how vulnerable I was — it would be perfectly possible to take photographs of Bruce and myself eating together. You can cut other people out of a photograph. At big functions when Bruce and I met we would embrace each other. I thought if these people — possibly MI5 — are so determined they've put this together then actually — for the first time, I think — I thought I could be defeated, which I had never considered before because I never felt defeated in arguments on nuclear weapons' questions, ever. It was the fact that possibly I couldn't control it, that they could do it to me. I then realised that there must be people in history to whom this sort of thing has happened and they will never ever surface again. It seems that by and large male politicians can ride over that sort of publicity but imagine the situation where it's a middle-aged Catholic priest. There couldn't have been a case which would have been more damaging to the woman involved because it would not just have been a sexual relationship, it would have the whole *religious* dimension as well. It would have been portrayed as the desecration of the man.'

Nothing was published except one snippet. Bruce Kent was under a lot of pressure from the Church over his peace campaigning. The snippet said: 'Kent needn't take it too hard because he's always got the comforting company of Joan Ruddock with whom he has candlelight dinners!' They decided to ignore it.

Edwina Currie handled the peak of the Great Egg Affair by

hiding out with her family for a quiet Christmas with the TV unplugged and the radio turned off. 'We didn't have any newspapers in the house, absolute peace. Everybody read a book. I read Leslie Thomas's biography. When the kids got bored we went off for a walk, came back with rosy cheeks and had a really nice Christmas.'

# 7.
# WOMEN IN THE HOUSE

After all the struggles of selection and campaigning and election, new Members of Parliament set off for Westminster bright-eyed and ready to change the world only to run smack into the archaic and disorganised character of the House of Commons.

When an MP wins an election, nobody officially tells them anything at all. In the weird and often unfriendly way that male-oriented British institutions act towards 'new boys', the first-time Members are left to flounder. Nobody from the Palace of Westminster sends them a congratulations note, let alone a kiss-o-gram. After all the struggle, the tears and dog-bites, not even a printed start-of-term list of what to do next comes through the post. This is quite surprising because in all too many respects the Mother of Parliaments is very much like an English boys' boarding school, with its hallowed rules, long summer vacs, prefects, headteacher, smoking rooms, widespread drinking and flamboyant courtesies.

When Maggie Ewing (then Maggie Bain) won a sensational by-election for the Scottish Nationalist Party in 1974 she had never been to Westminster before. 'I'd only really passed through London on my way to the Continent, so I was coming into a very strange world. I remember being sent to the Pass Office to get my MP's pass and there was this huge, huge queue of people. Being polite I joined the end of the queue and eventually discovered it was for the kitchen staff, the maintenance men and the lift men. I could have stood there for hours because nobody had told me that MPs go to a different place.'

No-one tells a new MP that if they themselves pay for the travel expenses for their first trip from the constituency to Westminster in advance out of their own pocket they won't be refunded. They are supposed to know that they have to request travel vouchers in advance from the Fees Office. This is an irritating matter because standing for Parliament may — and often does — use up the last of their personal financial resources.

Margaret Ewing had to rely on the advice of the man she had just defeated when she first went to Parliament. 'After you are elected, nothing happens, nobody sends you a letter to tell you what to do or where to come, you just arrive. Our previous Member obviously knew when there was going to be the opening of Parliament and that helped, but God knows what it's like to come in if you're on your own. The previous Member said: "Phone the Fees office and say who you are. They will send vouchers for your first journey down and then you get everything sorted out when you're there." It's so crazy, there's no help and no advice.'

Once they find their way to London and turn up at the House of Commons, the next real shock is the extraordinary physical circumstances in which these rulers of men and women must fulfil their parliamentary and constituency obligations. There is an acute lack of office space in the House of Commons. MPs may find they're so far down the pecking order in Parliament, that they don't even have an office, cramped or even shared. They have to put their desk in a corridor (if they have one). The new MP may not have given a thought to the not-so-simple matter of where to live in London during the parliamentary week. Maggie Ewing: 'You arrive down in London, you don't know London, or even where to stay. I booked into the Rubens Hotel. Donald and I just had to keep booking in for bed-and-breakfast there and then there was the hell of trying to find a flat while I was already working as an MP.'

Accommodation is only the start of the challenges lying in wait for the excited new MP. The Palace of Westminster itself is like the Hampton Court maze. As Maggie Ewing discovered: 'It's absolute hell getting to know the place and getting to know the system. There are about two miles of corridors. There are all sorts of ludicrous things, like trying to find where the Ladies toilets are, to discover doors marked "Members Only" are the Gents.'

Finding a Ladies in the House of Commons is an acquired art. Those Members who have seen male Members standing shiftily outside the Gents know they are probably standing guard for a woman Member who has had to hijack the Gents through urgent need.

Ann Clwyd has experience of both Strasbourg and Westminster. She describes 'the Palace of Westminster as a very beautiful building which should be used as a museum. It is not a working building. It's totally inappropriate for work in the latter half of the twentieth century. I would prefer to see a new working building with decent offices where you can take people. It is very difficult to have a private conversation with anybody in this place. Constituents come in to see you, and there's no way you can take them into your office because they're much too small and in any case you're sharing with somebody else. I was elected in the middle of the Miners' Strike and I was very heavily involved in organising various activities. Sometimes I had to phone in a mixed-party corridor; my office was actually in the cloisters which is an open corridor with no room for your secretary to sit, even by the side of your desk. I had to have conversations with my hand over the telephone or go out of the room and use one of the booths. Obviously that isn't the way elected representatives should have to work.

'The European Parliament had basic things, like a hairdresser for women and men, which we haven't got here. It annoys me. It's been one of the campaigns I've been waging because I think it's possible to win. I always say I'm after the achievable at this place. I know Barbara Castle fought for a long time here to get another room designated as a women's room, which is now christened Barbara's Castle after her sterling ten-year effort to get it. It's ridiculous. Once you get here, you've fought hard enough, so the conditions should be identical for men and women and they clearly are not. There are those rooms that say "Members Only" which are men's toilets and bathrooms. Even in the voting lobbies there are men's toilets but no women's toilets.'

Joyce Quin also arrived at Westminster after a stint at the European Parliament. 'When I first came down here, I walked around the building with a colleague just to try and get the feel of the place for when I take groups of constituents around. The attendants were saying, "Good morning, sir", "Good morning, sir", all the time. Obviously it was assumed that I was just an adjunct. Another time I was taking a taxi back to the House of Commons and the taxi driver said to me, "It'll be the visitors' entrance, I presume?" and I said, "No, it's the Members' entrance." Then as we actually drove into the Members' entrance, a policeman opened the door of the taxi, looked at me and said, "Where might you be going?"

'Strangely enough, it's fifty-fifty on whether I prefer Europe or Westminster. There are very good things about the European Parliament, but there are also some good things about Westminster. Because of the way debates are organised at Westminster, you've got to be much more on your toes. People can intervene and ask you questions — it makes you sharper. I also feel there are much more obvious ways of getting your arguments across here, because people understand the Westminster system better than the European system, so they tend to make use of their MPs in a more direct way.'

Edwina Currie thinks the public school culture of the House has its advantages. 'One of the things women discover when they get into the House (and even to a certain extent when they get into politics beforehand) is that rules and behaviour and manners exist which have been there a very long time. They are the product of a male, public-school kind of environment. It's not a criticism, it's simply a fact. It's in many ways very nice indeed. One of the reasons why they have these sweet, old-fashioned courtesies is that it's an extremely tough place, and if you are up until two or three o'clock in the morning with people, it helps to ease the pain if people are pleasant to each other. For example, if you write to a colleague, you write by hand — you don't use pre-printed notes to colleagues. Also, if it's to a member of your own Party, you end with "Yours ever" — which I think is sweet. No-one had ever ended a letter "Yours ever" to me before. If it's to the *opposite* Party, it's "Yours sincerely". Between Members of Parliament you always use first names. If David Owen writes to me, he's supposed to write, "Dear Edwina . . . Yours sincerely, David". I'm supposed to write back, "Dear David . . . Yours sincerely, Edwina". In fact he doesn't because he's frightfully pompous and always writes "Mrs Currie" — not that he writes to me very often! There are other sweet little rules which are a bit masonic in their style, such as MPs don't shake hands — we're all brothers. There are lots of little secret things Members share like that. A lot of them have rather sweet, old-school feelings about them. We call the bits of time in the year "terms" so we talk about "the end of term". The year is a session; the period between elections is a Parliament — which can be very confusing. What happens is that women come in and they don't know what the rules are. They come in and they do what they think is right. Some of the new people who've come in aren't into all of that and a difference is beginning to emerge.'

'There certainly *are* changes I'd like to see', says Maggie Ewing. 'I'd like them to sell tights, that's a definite one. There's no chemist shop in the House. I have drawers of headache pills and the normal monthly supplies. There should also be some more nice relaxing rooms where you could go and have a cup of coffee or an afternoon tea or something like that — it all seems to be bars and a bit men's clubby. There is the Pugin Room where you can take people, but it's very small and jam-packed in the afternoon.

'It would be very helpful if there was a nursery. Many of the male MPs have children too. Even a nursery where children could be booked in for a couple of hours to give the male or female MPs and their spouses a chance to go out and have lunch or dinner would be OK. The hours are crazy and the facilities are terrible. I suppose if the hours were normal, it wouldn't really resolve the problem of getting home to Scotland in the evening, but I would at least be able to go back to my flat and watch television and have a more normal life instead of constantly being here until ten or eleven at night. I find that extremely tiring.

'I certainly don't want to transfer this system to Scotland. I'd like to see a much more sensible legislature. We would go much more for the committees like you have in America — key legislative committees where people with expertise — not necessarily elected, but people with trade union or business background — could come together and look at the issues and then try to produce solutions which are acceptable. That maybe sounds a bit more like consensus, but having watched this confrontation going on here, there's a strong argument in favour of it.'

Edwina Currie feels shorter debates and a shorter year would help. 'The divorce rate amongst the men is very high. We all do too much. We don't need to. The country would be run just as well if we broke up in the middle of July instead of the beginning of August. But as far as parliamentary hours go, egomaniacs like politicians will go on talking till the cows come home anyhow.'

Marjorie Mowlam says, 'I'd like the day to start earlier to stop people doing two jobs, because that's unfair and silly. But I personally don't want to stop being here in the evening because otherwise you're sitting in London with nothing to do. I'd like to go on to a sensible hour of nine or ten in the evening because you need that for all the meetings.

'But I would favour fixed dates for sessions. Right now, MPs can't plan because they never know until the last minute when Parliament will break up for the vacation. So you can't organise your summer. People have this image that all you do is have three months off in the summer, but by the time you've done the conference and by the time you've done a bit of work in the constituency, it's all gone. I do nothing to relax, which is my biggest handicap in life. I've no outlet. Before I got in here I lived a reasonably normal life and went to the pub and played darts and walked and had a reasonably balanced existence. But since election it's unbalanced and addictive and counter-productive in the end. I went to a thing at the Cuban Embassy with Joan Walley and we got back in the taxi straight afterwards and rushed back to the Commons and ate here, which is crass. We could have sat over a pleasant Italian meal in Soho. There's almost an addiction to coming back here. The men in here have the same problem — it's not a gender-related thing, it's organising your life to give yourself an outlet. Women MPs who have children are lucky to have another life "outside". I think in the end somebody like Joan Walley, or Maureen Hicks from the Tories, who go back to kids are lucky. You can't say to a 5-year-old, "I'm going to do my constituency work", you actually have to say "Hello, I'll take you to the park."'

Jo Richardson says, 'I hate the Chamber. I'm not the best Chamber attender. It's partly because I've got other things to do, but partly because I find it so *macho*. I don't think I would put anything necessarily in its place. I would just change the way it's done. There are a lot of relatively quite small things which would help. If we had a desk in front of us in the Chamber it would help. I think it's quite stupid people have to wrestle with all these papers at our sides and lose everything.

'I was on the Committee of Procedures for a while. The trouble is I'm not sure you can change the things sufficiently. Some of my male colleagues have said that when we televise the House of Commons, we should give up this silly business of talking about ourselves as Honourable Members and call ourselves by our names. That would be a start. It's all so formalised and you get sucked into it. I just find it irritating and the trouble is I'm irritated with myself for doing it. I can get up like anybody else and say "Will the Honourable Gentleman give way?" or "I do thank the Honourable Gentleman." I don't thank him at all!'

'You can't produce a list of things to be done specifically to get more women into Parliament. If you've have more support for women outside then they'll be able to become involved in political parties. Many men here are just scandalised by the idea of children coming in, even though most of them have got little children themselves. They're getting a bit better about it now, but I remember when I first started campaigning for a crèche here in conjunction with some members of staff. We were knocked back at every conceivable stage by the Leader of the House who's responsible, along with the Civil Services Committee. It's rebuffed in the most contentious terms of "Don't be stupid, this is unheard of!" The first person to raise it was Helene Hayman. She didn't raise it on her own behalf although she was directly affected. At any one time we have about 1,800 women working here in the Palace of Westminster. They all work unsocial hours, split shifts and some of them are in career jobs. It's absolutely ridiculous we don't have any child care. That's one thing. Decent office space and space for our secretaries/researchers is another. OK, they're constructing a building across the road which will be ready God knows when.'

Joan Ruddock is equally critical. 'I don't think the job can be done in any way properly with less than three full-time assistants. People get hold of me, night and day, round the clock. Constituents will ring up here at ten at night because they know I'll be here. I have one full-time secretarial assistant/PA, and she really is a full-time caseworker dealing with all the personal difficulties of constituents. She keeps my diary, which is a bit of a nightmare. I have another person who works half a week. She works Monday, Tuesday and Thursday, and her job is to be a political assistant — all the things to do with political issues, preparation for debates, bills, speeches, questions. I don't think people here have the time or the opportunity to do real research. We get about 50 letters every day and that includes letters which are just one page of somebody's problems but it will include also somebody raising a major problem, about a traffic accident or congestion where they may include a petition from local people, where they may include letters, copies of letters, they've already sent to the Council.'

MPs do certainly get strange requests from constituents. Joan Ruddock got a call at the House of Commons late one night and a voice said, 'We're having a charity fund-raising party tomorrow and we have forgotten to apply for the drink licence. Can you get a magistrate and get a licence, because it's going to be a real disaster without it?' She told him she didn't think she could find a magistrate at that time of night. 'I actually went off to find out on what basis it might be possible for this man to make drink available on a free basis rather than completely destroy his party and suggest to him he sell raffle tickets or do something to actually make some money back. That's a bizarre example of what an MP shouldn't be doing, but you do it because at the end of the day what you are faced with is a constituent who's saying "I'm in a terrible mess. I'm in a real panic, I don't know who to turn to and it suddenly struck me my MP is a powerful person who could probably put it all right."'

Labour MP Clare Short reflects the views of most of the Opposition when she says, 'I think it needs reform desperately to make it a proper democratic parliament. There's a lot of flummery that's silly and out of date, from the Speaker's outfit to some of the silly ritual. And a lot of the system works on vanity, ego, pecking order, climbing the greasy pole. Part of that problem in the House of Commons is because the executive arises from the legislature and because the chances of promotion are so high. One in three people becomes a minister, everyone wants to get on. It turns people into toadies.'

After losing her seat in 1979, Scots Nats MP, Maggie Ewing, was away from Parliament for eight years. When she returned at the 1987 Election, she noticed changes. 'I don't mean the barracking I get in the Chamber — that's because I'm a Scottish Nationalist and we tend to be left of centre, so we get barracked by the extreme right-wing Conservatives who just don't understand what we are on about at all. It's much more adversarial and much more authoritarian. I find it a terrible contrast to the seventies because then it was a minority government and the government actually had to listen and make concessions and move towards consensus legislation on a lot of issues. But now, with a government majority of over 100, there is an awful lot of arrogance.'

As the Speaker of the House of Commons, Bernard Weatherill, wears a uniform of wig and black knee breeches, it struck the new Deputy Speaker, Betty Boothroyd, she should have an official dress made, to help give her authority. 'I decided not to in the end. I simply wear a different dress every day. I have a rota system. I think it's good for my morale to do that and I think it's pleasant for people who have to look at me. And I always wear my famous House of Commons' portcullis brooch — it was made in Sri Lanka with the House of Commons crest in gold.'

Betty Boothroyd is only the second woman to sit as Deputy Speaker of the House of Commons. 'Can I control the House? I think I can. It's a question of being natural with them. You've got to be part and parcel of what is going on in the Chamber. We had quite a hectic House recently with one or two interventions which I thought were rather amusing. One Member wanted *protection* from Dennis Skinner. Now, Dennis Skinner, as you know, has something of an unruly reputation here. I said, certainly I shall protect the Member from the Honourable Member for Bolsover — and everyone laughed. You need humour. Humour, a smile on your face, and pure common sense. Of course, you know some of the rules, because you've been doing it for years in Standing Committees.'

She remembers clearly the Summer day in 1987 when she walked in to take the Chair in the Chamber of the House of Commons for the very first time. 'Mr Speaker, "Jack" Weatherill, was in the Chair and he moved out and said to the Chamber, "Give her a cheer!" and a little cheer went up.' The famous exchange about how Members should address her then took place. Peter Pike, the Member for Burnley, was speaking. He suddenly realised he had never spoken in the House with a woman chairing a debate. So he said, 'Oh, what do we call you?' Recalling her show-biz background and the smash-hit musical, Betty Boothroyd drew herself up and said: 'Call me Madam, please!'

It's quite possible that the record number of women MPs entering the House in the 1980s will bring about change in the 1990s, derisory as 42 women out of 650 MPs may seem. Even 42 women, meeting several male MPs every day, sitting in the debating chamber, walking in the miles of corridors, waiting for constituents in Central Lobby, or even putting their feet up in one of the tea or smoking rooms may encourage a change of attitude. With a sympathetic Speaker of the House, 'Jack' Weatherill, — a married, family man, by contrast with the previous Speaker Thomas — things may change rapidly for the better. Many male MPs too are keen to learn. As Clare Short said, 'It's rather sweet now — when our colleagues aren't certain how to react to issues concerning women, they come and ask us how to react.'

# 8
# POLITICAL
# VIRGINS

The SDP and the Greens are the political parties which have done the most by far to include women at all levels; nearly one in three Green candidates in 1987 were women. The SDP attracted a number of women into its ranks, some of whom were already experienced politicos like Shirley Williams (former Secretary of State for Education in Harold Wilson's Government) and Sue Slipman (a past President of the National Union of Students). However an even more exciting aspect of the SDP was the number of political virgins it enticed into becoming political crack troops, women like journalist Polly Toynbee, market researcher Rosie Barnes and ex-Treasury civil servant Celia Goodhart. The SDP brought thousands of women into the public arena — pounding the pavements, standing for local councils and the House of Commons — for the very first time.

At both the 1983 and 1987 General Elections the SDP fielded more women candidates than any other major political party in the country. At the 1987 General Election, the SDP and their Liberal partners in the Alliance fielded 105 women candidates between them. Labour had 92 and the Conservatives had only 46 women standing.

General Elections do not often see candidates from minority parties elected and true to form no Alliance women were elected to Parliament in 1983. Elizabeth Shields, the first Liberal woman Member of Parliament for over forty years, got into Parliament in 1985 through a spectacular by-election in Ryesdale in Yorkshire. Rosie Barnes won her seat for the SDP in the 1987 Greenwich by-election.

## POLLY TOYNBEE

Celia Goodhart and Polly Toynbee were typical of the many women in the 1980s lured by the excitement of a new political party — the SDP — into becoming parliamentary candidates.

Polly Toynbee stood for Parliament in 1983. After six years as a political activist in the SDP, Polly Toynbee's political hopes have now plummeted, but she has emerged with her marriage to political journalist Peter Jenkins unscathed, career prospects undiminished and one more child rather later than she had ideally planned. 'The time between Flora and Nat represents my SDP years. I would have had another baby much sooner. The fact they are so far apart is a monument to my SDP life.' She has now left party politics and holds a senior position at BBC Television, but as she pointed out: 'There are a lot of things I would never have done if it hadn't been for my experience in the SDP. It was nothing but plus for me. I don't think I'd be in the job I'm in now if I hadn't learnt how to handle committees, if I hadn't learnt how to speak with confidence, how to prepare myself for all kinds of things, how to run things.'

It took a great deal of courage for *Guardian* columnist Polly Toynbee to agree to stand as a parliamentary candidate; although politically aware from an early age through her parents, and a long-time champion of women's rights, she had to tackle a chilling, life-long phobia about speaking in public. She also had to juggle the maternal triangle-plus: balancing her job as a senior weekly columnist at the *Guardian*, with caring for her two small children, and duties as a parliamentary candidate, while sitting on an ever burgeoning number of committees for the SDP. On top of all this, in the run-up to the General Election, she ran an underground network for other would-be women candidates.

'As the General Election of 1983 loomed, I dithered and agonised for absolutely ages on whether I should stand for Parliament. Peter was totally opposed to the idea. I kept using the children as an excuse. It meant a whole year of campaigning, non-stop every evening, winter and summer, holding together a local party and children, building an organisation at the same time with a husband who was deeply opposed to the idea for a lot of reasons, some of which were good, some of which were not so good. He was really against it. I was very torn. I don't know that his being against it was the most significant fact. I was just deeply uncertain if I wanted to do it.'

An ex-Cabinet Minister, Bill Rodgers, one of the 'Gang of Four', the original SDP leaders, was very encouraging. 'That pushed me towards it a bit. Sue Slipman and other women were going for it. We were all talking about how we could get more women candidates for the SDP and I felt it was a bit pathetic not to have a go. It was the excitement of it all that tipped me into finally agreeing to stand for Parliament. Remember, in 1983 it was our first try, this might be the big one, this might be the one when we will actually push through and all of a sudden there might be a whole tranche of us there — there might be 60, 80 SDP MPs. We would have bust the old two-party ding-dong, we would have achieved our goal — and how wonderful for the sake of history, if for nothing else, to be one of the ones who were there. I thought to hell with everything else, this sort of opportunity doesn't come along very often, to actually be a part of something that might actually change the face of the world, yea even the Universe! Unfortunately it didn't change anything very much.'

When the General Election ended, the SDP had lost most of their Members of Parliament. 'It was very tragic, we lost nearly all of our MPs and a lot of marvellous people who had given up their whole career for the enterprise.'

Polly Toynbee comes from a thoroughbred Labour intellectual pedigree background, and was brought up on Labour ideas and ideals. 'My stepfather was a philosopher and involved on one or two Labour committees when they were in Opposition. He was a tremendous friend of Hugh Gaitskell. We spent a summer holiday with Hugh Gaitskell in Yugoslavia once. I knew he was very important, but I didn't really understand the conversations at that stage. My mother and stepfather knew Tony Crosland very well. People like that were often around when I was growing up.'

Her father, writer and literary critic Phillip Toynbee, had been the first Communist President of the Union at Oxford and later joined the Labour Party. 'He was one of the founders of CND. As he got older he came to hate speaking in public and would have nothing to do with organised politics, but the atmosphere of the family was always very political and my mother was always a Labour Party supporter. So it was quite natural for me to think in those terms.'

Her classic 'child of the sixties', left-of-centre upbringing naturally included being taken on CND marches at a very young age: 'I can remember walking into Trafalgar Square when I was about 11 and hearing my father's voice booming all the way round and being absolutely amazed.' At 16 she founded a CND branch at Badminton, her boarding school near Bristol. 'I made some public speeches to groups of other school children assembled together from Bristol, much to the fury of the school and to the pleasure of the *Western Daily Press*. Most of my friends were very political, we were rather a political generation and idealistic.'

Two years later Polly helped in a parliamentary election campaign. 'It involved delivering leaflets for Lena Jegar (now Baroness Jegar) in Paddington in 1964. I remember thinking she was great and in 1964 the whole world was going to change and thirteen years of Tory rule was going to be thrown out. That was the first election I was really excited by and really worked hard in. I felt tremendously inspired by Harold Wilson which now seems rather odd!'

Polly believes she was always a political animal. 'I've always been a joiner — I was a member of the Labour Party from when I was 16 and I joined the Young Socialists.' Had it ever been suggested to her that she herself might stand for Parliament? 'Absolutely not! Nor did I ever say it to myself. It was a million miles from my thoughts. I don't think I for one moment considered going into Parliament or standing as a councillor or anything of that sort. I don't know why not. Maybe I was thinking entirely in terms of being a writer. When I was 17 I wrote a novel. I had a scholarship to Oxford — I was not the sort of material regarded as likely to get one, it was a sort of freak and regarded as a great joke in my rather academic family. My sister did really well and got into Cambridge a year early, but everyone expected her to. I was all disjointed and rushing all over the place doing different kinds of things and not really working hard so nobody expected me to do particularly well, so getting a scholarship was a great surprise.'

The year between school and university was spent working for Amnesty International in Rhodesia. This led to an invitation to take part in a debate at the Oxford Union about Rhodesia and sanctions. Today's highpowered BBC executive, in her smart tailored businesswoman's jacket, blouse and skirt, still squirms with embarrassment as she recalls that agonising event so many years ago: 'I was so horrified and appalled at having to speak — it was a nightmare — the misery of public speaking. I got up there with my notes, shaking from head to foot, and made an abominable speech to the disappointment of my friends and sat down again. I knew this was not what I wanted to do. I can't even remember now why I hated Oxford so much, but I was deeply unhappy there. I left university half way through without taking a degree. I hated it.'

Although a member of the Labour Party while at university, she hadn't got involved. 'I've always been basically Labour, but very much on the social democratic wing. I never ever flirted with extreme socialism, or not, now I look back, with socialism at all. I never believed in there being ultimate Utopian ends to the game. I always believed in "gradualism" working towards general improvement in flexible ways. I don't think I ever really believed in equality as a useful goal to work towards, let alone a useful place to arrive at. Fairness and justice, equality of opportunity is what matters most, thinking of every way you can to give everybody a fair start in life.'

She adds: 'All we need think about now in Thatcherite Britain is how to close the gap between the poor and the rest. The gap used to be between the workers and the rich, but now it is between most people and the poor. It has actually now become a problem which could be solved if there was the political will to do it. You've got 75 per cent of people who can afford to pay, so let's find the ways in which the other 25 per cent of the people can be enabled to live tolerably.'

It was the birth of the Social Democratic Party in January 1981 which became the trigger which shot Polly Toynbee from an observer of politics to an active participant. 'There were lots of discussions about the idea of a new party going on around us all the time. A lot of toing and froing and agonising about whether it could work, whether it would work. I somehow got drawn into it because things were going on in a number of different people's houses — our house, David Owen's, the Rodgers', who were all friends of ours.' In the last century the dining tables of the great homes of the aristocracy in the country or in Mayfair and Westminster were the backdrop to political plotting and chatting. A century later, in 1980, the SDP took shape over the dining tables of the middle classes in Kentish Town, Limehouse, Notting Hill Gate and Lambeth.

'I remember it as a time of incredible political ferment and I felt passionately involved in it. I was a member of the Labour Party because I believed in quite a lot of what the Labour Party stood for. But I was increasingly appalled at so many aspects of the Labour Party that didn't seem worth giving one's life and soul for — the trade union link, the negativism, the sexism, the backward-looking sort of socialism, a kind of knee-jerk reaction towards things. But the thought of a new party, free of all this, did appeal. At the time it seemed as though it could take all that was best of the Labour Party and leave behind all that was worst. It seemed incredibly optimistic and exciting, a new party that could actually change the nature of party politics itself and give people a chance to vote for something much closer to what they wanted because there would be real pluralism and all of those things. That seemed like something worth working for as hard as one possibly could.'

Polly met another SDP convert, Sue Slipman, when they worked on a television interview programme with Helene Hayman for Southern Television. 'The three of us sat on a settee and interviewed someone on camera. One of the people we interviewed was Shirley Williams. At the time the SDP was very much in the melting pot and we prodded Shirley about all this. She gave a very good interview which inspired us. I felt she was going to get things right about social democracy and we came away rather enthusiastic about it. Sue and I were always very sad we never persuaded Helene Hayman to join us too. We kept trying very hard to persuade her, but she became more and more fierce, as many people did who stayed in the Labour Party, and vitriolic about the SDP. We didn't see any more of her, which was a shame.'

Polly got a telephone call to ask if she would be one of the hundred people putting their names to the Limehouse declaration that launched the SDP. 'I was delighted to accept. I think I was asked for the reason women are often asked, because they found they hadn't got many women and asked themselves quickly who they knew who was a woman who might be interested in supporting them? If I'd been a man they probably might not have thought of me.'

From there she was invited to be on the committee which helped to draw up the constitution. 'Again, I was only asked because I was a woman and there were very few women on it.' At that time she still hadn't overcome her fear about speaking in public. 'In the early days of the SDP, when we had women's meetings, I got dragged into doing a bit of public speaking and I was terrible. I hated it. I would be terrified for weeks ahead. It was such misery I just couldn't imagine doing this voluntarily if you had any sense at all.'

She went to elaborate lengths to avoid speaking at public

meetings of any sort. 'I'd pretend to look up in my diary and say, "Oh, terribly sorry, I've got another one that day," and I wouldn't go. I also felt that as I was fairly well known as a writer by then I was a terrible disappointment. People would say, "Oh, yes, Polly Toynbee, she's terribly articulate and lively in the *Guardian.*" Then they would go and see me speaking and it would be a total wash-out. I wasn't really doing myself any good. If you are at all well known, people expect you to be a public-speaker.'

She found that the only thing that helped was to make herself do a lot of public speaking. 'It got so it wasn't terrifying in the end, but it took a hell of a long time. I'm now perfectly happy at getting up and speaking as long as it's on a subject I know well. I can speak with fairly minimal notes, but I don't speak as somebody who is going to rabble rouse, I just give information.'

She agreed to stand as a council candidate in her local ward. 'I was totally astounded to find myself standing for anything. But once I realised local elections didn't involve much public speaking, just a lot of tramping round and knocking on doors and putting things through doors, I agreed to do it. I thought, well I'll probably lose (she did) and it will be all right.'

Polly rapidly learned how to wheel and deal in committees to get what she wanted. 'It was fine being on the Steering Committee. I didn't talk for quite a while and then I learned to talk in the committee. Like lots of women who learn to talk in a committee, I probably started to talk too much. You have to learn to shut up again! You have to learn to keep your powder dry and then, when you do speak, you speak with more authority than if you gabble away all the time. Every issue at the time seems a main issue. Afterwards you wonder why you bothered, but at the time everything is crucial! I went through all those learning curves about how committees work, how certain dirty tricks go on with people caucusing before committees, how suddenly everyone seems to be amazingly united down that end of the table!'

Polly says, 'There were quite a lot of women put on that committee in the beginning. It indicates that so-called tokenism is not all a bad thing because we proved to be more than tokens. There wasn't any opposition to the idea in the SDP at that stage. The old Labourites in the new party would make jokes about it, but they could see this was the way it was going to be. David Owen and Shirley Williams were the ones who always thought about having enough women. Roy Jenkins and Bill Rodgers would immediately say, "Yes, of course" and look terribly guilty that it hadn't occurred to them earlier. And we were helped tremendously by Bill Rodgers' wife, Silvia. She was very good. David Owen was heavily committed to the idea of an equal number of women and men on all SDP committees and at least two women and two men on each constituency shortlist of candidates. There were a lot of us in favour. I think you could fairly say it was Shirley and David together who made it happen.'

But Polly Toynbee discovered the 'nice Party', as the SDP rapidly was called, had an irritating cabal of disdainful males. 'People like Mike Thomas and James Wellbeloved would turn around and say "Polly, the last thing on Earth we can think about is women — Jesus, are you going to saddle us with all that old Labour Party leftie stuff?" I'd say "This is not Labour Party leftie stuff, this is something else." A bunch of men thought all these peculiar women had come out of the woodwork and didn't have any proper political track-record and didn't belong. Women were going to be a bore. We were going to get in the way. We were going to slow down the debate. We wouldn't be able to keep up with the boys.

'If you belong to a Party and you don't get involved in the women's bit, you're a rat! It's a double burden for women in politics. The only thing anyone asks you to write about or come and speak about is "women", which is a bore because you have other things you want to talk about as well. I never actually minded it that much. After all, I already wrote for the women's pages of the *Guardian*, which is social death. People say you can't get any more wild loony feminist than writing for the women's pages of the *Guardian*!'

The SDP ran a significant number of women candidates, some of them in the Party's best seats. One of the reasons there are so few women in the House of Commons is the old parties have traditionally chosen men as candidates for the safest and most winnable seats. To help women apply for seats where they had at least a chance of winning rather than fighting only the no-hope left-over seats, Polly Toynbee and Sue Slipman organised an SDP women's underground movement. Polly's telephone became the central information clearing house for SDP women prospective parliamentary candidates.

'I managed to get my hands on two lots of polling information about seats, assessing what was going to be worth what to us and also giving quite a lot of information about those seats. We encouraged women to ring me and I would then read out the information.'

The SDP women's mafia also set up a network of women who didn't want to stand themselves, but who would give helpful information to others interested in standing in their area. 'We clearly did manage, through a network, to bring in all sorts of women who got up and spoke for the first time at small meetings and said, "I'm totally terrified." They got used to speaking, and then dared to get up and speak at meetings of their local party, then dared to stand for secretary or treasurer or work their way through to standing for Parliament. I would get these phone calls and I'd say things like, "Of course, you can do it, just go to the Commons and look at some of those idiot back-benchers — you can't think you are worse than them." I would try where it was possible to put them in touch with someone in the region who would tell them a bit about the constituency, and what had been going on in the local party so that when it came to the selection they didn't arrive in total ignorance.'

Finally she was persuaded to stand for Parliament herself. 'I hummed and hah-ed about it. First it had to be somewhere fairly near. If it was in Scotland or Wales or somewhere, there was no way I could trek across London after work to get from Clapham to a major railway station and out of town, so it had to be London and preferably South London which meant it was unlikely to be anywhere terribly winnable for the SDP. I went for Lewisham which at the time was the sort of seat we thought would be good for us because it was split, being very marginal between Labour and Tory. Of course, it was the sort of seat which turned out to be a disaster (amongst nearly all the seats which turned out to be a disaster) because we just got squeezed and you couldn't persuade either side they weren't going to let the other side in if they voted for *us*.'

Polly was told she had been selected for Lewisham in an even more graceless way than Angela Rumbold in Mitcham and Morden. 'The Chairman of the Lewisham Party, whom I had not met and who was a very aggressive 55-year-old single school master, came up to me and said, "If you accept this selection, I will resign and the local party will disintegrate. We simply cannot have a woman candidate in this seat and I won't have it." It was a surprising experience, in fact the only time I ever came across anything quite like that in the SDP. But it all came together in the end and we worked very hard. It was only half-an-hour's drive away and it was an extremely nice local party.'

After the split in the SDP, Polly remained a David Owen supporter. 'I still think David Owen is the best leader we'll never have.' She stresses that she doesn't put him up on a pedestal as a hero. 'I don't think I have any absolute heroes any more, I think it is rather a good thing not to. Heroes and heroines are dangerous, they are fallible ordinary sorts of human beings.' She accepts that David Owen is not always an easy character. 'He listens all right but he doesn't always look as if he's listening. I think the thing that people who get on well with David realise is that if you get through your first two rows with him, then it's fine. If you stand up to him, if you actually say "David, that's rubbish", or "David, that's outrageous," or "You can't do that," or "How dare you treat somebody like that!", he takes it in. He will have the face to say you were right even if it is a couple of hours later. What is more he will reflect about it later and be generous about it. If you have got the thickness of skin to live through it a couple of times, then you will be OK. David Owen has an astonishingly good instinct for what people's real aspirations are. He has a pretty unerring gut sense for what people feel passionately about and a great trust that that is very often right. But he will resist all sorts of prejudice and bigotry. It is not a question of cheap populism. He genuinely understands people's wish to get on in life, but also that people have a corresponding decent wish to live in a society that is fair.'

As well as marking the end of the Alliance, the 1987 Election was the end of Polly Toynbee's interest in politics for the foreseeable future. 'The catastrophe at the end of the Alliance was a great and mighty tragedy. If you fail that badly after such high hopes as the Alliance had, people fall on each other's swords and kill each other — and that's what happened. I was part of that too, so I know what political assassination is like, both the doing and the done. I was great with the axe. The low point of my career came towards the end, before the SDP finally split. Roy Jenkins thumped the table and pointed his finger down the table at me — red, apoplectic, purple and blue in the face, and said "Madame Defarge!" And I thought to myself that was the kind of abuse women get. You get a bit tough and you're Madame Defarge! I had been quite tough, but by then, my God, blood was all over the floor and only some of it was his.'

Was it all worth it? 'I'm delighted I did it. I would do it again if the same prospects offered themselves as they did before 1983 — if there was some extraordinary new project which was going to significantly change British politics for the better. I'm not optimistic about that enterprise being on offer. I now understand much more of the internal workings of the Labour and Conservative Parties. I can read behind the lines infinitely better now. Even though I was nowhere near any kind of serious power, just knowing how political organisations work makes a lot of difference.'

## CELIA GOODHART

Celia Goodhart was also a founder member of the SDP in 1981. She had been the Chair of the Gas Consumers' Council. She and her husband William are a husband-and-wife team in politics, like the Bottomleys, or Clare Short and Alex Lyons. The Goodharts were part of the dinner party circuit when the new political party was planned. Like Polly Toynbee, Celia's name was one of the original 100 in the advertisement in the *Guardian* launching the SDP.

'William and I had been urging Anthony Lester and Bob Maclennan to have a new party, because we were saying it was just what this country needed. We were political animals and neither of us could find a political home. You could sum up what we felt as "if only politicians would stop bashing each other and just settle down round a table and actually seek to solve problems". We were people looking for a rational group of people to treat politics rationally. We tended to vote Liberal. William had never belonged to any political party and I'd been involved in Tory politics when I was up at Oxford, sitting around the table with Paul Channon and Kenneth Baker and Alan Haselhurst and Tony Newton, all Members of Parliament now. Eighteen months of doing that made me realise I was not a Tory, so I went into the Civil Service as a sort of political thing without being political.'

When Celia Goodhart started in 'new party' politics at the beginning of 1981, her children were 9, 11 and 13, and she was 42. 'I was taking a break because I had got fed up with teaching history. I had rather a high-powered existence at that time — I was teaching, I'd been on the Data Protection Committee and was running the North Thames Gas Consumers' Council which was a half-time job. I was all set to launch into an existence entirely in public life because — let's face it — I knew a lot of people. I was well placed to become your statutory woman on all sorts of things. I had the credentials as well. I had a Civil Service background from my days in the Ministry of Agriculture and Fisheries and the Treasury, which was useful. I'd switched to teaching history because I wanted to work part-time while the children were little.

'When the SDP launched I decided it was so important I went to work in SDP Headquarters. I worked there for 18 months, but it was a big mistake. If you go in prepared to do anything, you immediately devalue yourself. I don't regret it because I think it was actually quite useful, but it was not good in career terms. Once you become staff, politicians perceive you differently. I found I was seen as a dogsbody. Of course, if you're a woman doing those kind of things, you're much more naturally seen as a dogsbody. My original thought was that I would go in and work in the headquarters because that was much more sensible from the point of view of the family. I'd been a teacher and I had run my life on the basis of being available in the holidays and available from 4.30 pm onwards. But looking back, if a man with my qualifications had been around, they would have been regarded in a different light. I really do think that.

'Politics is a much better thing for women to be in than lots of other things, and it's far easier to be a woman politician than to be a woman civil servant because it's flexible. You can quite often fix meetings to suit you, you can quite often miss meetings. I'm not somebody to literally just miss meetings, but I mean if you have got a crisis it's not the end of the world.

'People kept saying to me, "You ought to stand." It was really just a gradual thing, I just realised that was probably a sensible way of using my time and energy. I suppose I've always had a dream of being a minister. The one I would have liked most of all would have been the what was previously Minister of Works. I would have been greatly interested in all the arts and historic buildings and how things worked — the rather practical sorts of things. Or I'd like to have been the first woman Speaker of the House of Commons.

'My mother was the major influence on me, although she died before I entered politics. She was a very clever woman, very frustrated because she just had to stay at home and not use her brain. My entire life, really, was built on making sure I don't have to lead the life my mother led. She was in the mission field with my father, though she didn't really believe in God, I don't think, and poverty was always a problem, so she had a tough time. Where she really influenced me was in urging me to go to university. She was very keen on that, she'd wanted to go herself and hadn't been able to.

'My father was completely opposed to me standing for Parliament. He thought women were there only to look after men. He liked a cooked breakfast and a cooked lunch and a cooked dinner prepared for him.

'To become an SDP parliamentary candidate I had a rather formal interview, but it wasn't a very gruelling one. I remember being asked what newspapers I read and when I said the *Daily Mail* at the time for the children, somebody laughed and said it was a good thing it wasn't the *Times*, *Financial Times* and *Guardian*!

'When it came to looking for a constituency, I made some very ruthless decisions. It's critically important to feel at home in your constituency. I knew where I would be strong would be where I would be happy, which would be in a mixture of town and country. I had no home originally because my father was a missionary in Africa and I went to a boarding school from the age of 6 and spent school holidays with aunts and uncles. Home from the age of 12 was Huntingdonshire and I love the English countryside. So I looked for constituencies which were a mixture of small towns and countryside.'

Celia tried for five constituencies. 'The first one was Exeter, but that went to a local man. A very experienced politician came up to me afterwards and said, "You did very well. You mustn't lose heart." That was lovely because I was frightened. I hadn't ever made public speeches and I'd never been in a political world so it was wonderfully helpful.'

She was finally selected for Kettering. 'Kettering is only 30 miles from Huntingdon so I was in reasonably home territory. It was the first time I'd ever lived on my own, which was quite peaceful, but what I don't like is loneliness. One of the most interesting things that happened to me through my politics was living alone. Suddenly there I was, a full-grown woman driving around Northamptonshire in the middle of the night, all alone and being actually quite frightened. You always think here I am a great strapping woman, but what would happen to me if my car broke down on a dark night? I found I could do much more work in Kettering, but nothing drove me back faster into the bosom of my family than the experience of living alone.

'It's not easy being husband-and-wife in politics together, especially as we'd not been used to working together. When Willie got selected for Kensington we had a great row. I said I ought to do Kensington because it made sense with the children and the family home being near. He said *he* would do Kensington because, firstly, he'd been working on it a long time, and secondly, he'd got to stay here to earn our living. Timing also becomes a nightmare. Both of you being candidates means you're not able to support each other and that's quite tough. It certainly strains the relationship when you're both doing something as intense as being a parliamentary candidate, even though I see us working actually very much in tandem. I found it very difficult, for instance, when we fought the Kensington by-election. You could mis-interpret this very easily, but it seemed to me one of the interesting things about William was that he not only was himself but had a wife he allowed to be active. I kept trying to persuade our literature writers to put this over a bit more, but they wouldn't. I found that deeply frustrating because we work as a team.

'I think the whole story of the Alliance would have been different if Roy Jenkins had remained the leader. I think that the electorate in the SDP knew what they were doing when they elected him. I'm a great admirer of many of the attributes of David Owen but he doesn't have wisdom. He was a lot of wonderful things and I was very prepared to work with him, and used to try and combine loyal support with criticism. He is brilliant on television, brilliant I think in the House, very good on saying things, has good judgment on purely policy matters in many instances, tough and charismatic. But I regarded it as a disaster when Roy Jenkins stepped down from the leadership. I did raise the issue of two leaders on the national committee and we weren't even allowed to discuss it. While I think strong leadership is very important and I admire it, what I couldn't take about Owen is that you have got to be a general who not only leads from in front, but is occasionally prepared to listen.

'But on the subject of women's equality and Roy Jenkins, our only legislation (the Sex Discrimination Bill) is down to him.'

She looks back over her political experiences with mixed emotions. 'It was absolutely jumping over a cliff for us. An awful lot of other people had been involved in politics before, an awful lot of other people who became involved didn't jump into it quite as much as we did — I think we've had a very rough 10 years. But I would do it again because although I've actually lost confidence, maybe I'm a richer person, in understanding how people work, and certainly in terms of friendship. I feel I've been through the mill but I feel I've also learnt an enormous amount.'

# 9.
# YES, MINISTER

LYNDA CHALKER

It's quite inexplicable why Margaret Thatcher did not appoint any other woman to her Cabinet from 1979 to 1989, apart from the all-too-brief appearance of Baroness Young from the Upper House. Margaret Thatcher has shown herself amazingly able to brush aside stale tradition and the choice of who sits in Cabinet is overwhelmingly in the remit of the Prime Minister, 'first among equals'. Yet year on year, she has sat at the head of twenty or so pin-striped males, as the only woman in the room. By July 1989 there were three women Members of Parliament with ministerial experience a rung below Cabinet rank: Angela Rumbold at Education, Virginia Bottomley at Environment and Lynda Chalker at the Foreign Office (second to Sir Geoffrey Howe when he was Foreign Secretary).

But in the July 1989 ministerial reshuffle, Margaret Thatcher still failed to promote any other women in her Cabinet. Outside Cabinet, she demoted one woman, Baroness Hooper, and promoted Gillian Shephard to Under Secretary of State for Social Services. Lynda Chalker was moved within the Foreign Office to Minister of State for Overseas Development. In seniority terms, as she has been a Minister longest, Lynda Chalker is the highest elected woman in Government after Margaret Thatcher. In 1984 I was advised by a senior NATO man over lunch at the Reform Club that: 'You'll know women are getting somewhere in this country when you have a woman Secretary of State at the Foreign and Commonwealth Office and a woman Secretary of State at the Ministry of Defence.' The Treasury would be less of a problem, he felt. He stared at me pensively, assessing my age (I was then in my thirties). 'You won't see women Secretaries at the Foreign Office or Defence in *your* life-time.' For decades, possibly centuries, it was suggested 'Women can't keep a secret, you can't have them in positions of national security.' Such balderdash is laughable now, but for many years it was taken very seriously indeed.

Lynda Chalker represents Wallasey, a suburban seat in

YES, MINISTER

North East Wirral, across the Mersey from Liverpool. She held on to her Wallasey seat in the 1987 General Election by a heart-stopping majoriy of 279 votes, after a particularly nasty election campaign. She was visibly shaken by the style of the campaign: 'Old people on doorsteps were told by Militant supporters, "We'll know if you don't vote Labour, we'll bash your windows in!"'

As Deputy Foreign Secretary, she has a small office to herself at the House of Commons — most MPs share offices in the Palace of Westminster that are so tiny and Dickensian there would be an outcry if prisoners on remand were kept in such conditions. She also has a large, more comfortable office with armchairs at the Foreign and Commonwealth Office building in King Charles Street. She gets up at around 6.00 am to arrive at her office by 8.00, often working beyond midnight.

As Minister for Transport, Lynda Chalker was often photographed for the national press riding her bicycle to the House of Commons, but nowadays she appears in the press rarely. She ascribes her current low-profile to the nature of her work: 'Frankly no Foreign Office Minister could afford to shout from the roof tops about issues. You can play much more party politics for voter consumption in home departments. It's a different job with different skills here. In the Foreign Office you very often have people's lives in your hands in a very specific way.' Yet she's aware that politicians with small majorities benefit from publicity. 'There *is* a problem and a lot of people tease me, almost cruelly, sometimes on the other [Labour] side saying: "You're being overtaken."'

Puzzling over why so talented a politician was not yet in Cabinet, the *Sunday Times* opined: 'Lynda Chalker has shown a little too much passion over foreign affairs and been too pro-European and too anti-apartheid for the tastes of Downing Street.' Often described as the 'Shirley Williams of the Tory Party', she has an engagingly impish, cheeky streak which she hides well in her public persona. She has also been described by some as inhabiting the 'wet' wing of her Party, 'something of a hate figure for the Party's pro-South African wing,' as the *Sunday Times* put it. Yet as Antony Bevins stated in the *Independent*, she is 'regarded as fast-stream Cabinet material'. She is certainly tipped for Cabinet posts every time the Prime Minister orders a reshuffle and even more recently she has also been tipped to be Britain's first woman European Commissioner.

Since teenage days, Lynda Chalker was active in the Conservative Party. She became Head Girl at Roedean and star of the Young Conservatives which she joined at 15. 'I didn't just step gingerly into politics, I walked in willingly,' she says.

Her father was an active Conservative, mainly at the local government level. 'Dad really wanted to get into Parliament. It was ironic because he was beaten in the final selection at Southend West by just four votes by Paul Channon who was then 21 and fresh down from Oxford. Here I've been, years later, working alongside Paul. It could easily have been my Dad.' She was girlishly delighted to become a Minister of State at the Foreign Office while he was still alive.

Both her parents were a great influence: 'Mother was always involved in voluntary organisations, a Justice of the Peace, chairman of the Juvenile Bench, involved in quite a lot of what were then very unpopular voluntary activities like care of the mentally ill, which I've tried my best to carry on too.' Sadly her mother died of a cerebral haemorrhage when Lynda was only 16, 'very suddenly and without any warning'.

It was an incident that occurred when she was 23 that made Lynda decide to try and become a Member of Parliament. 'I was programme organiser or vice-chairman of South Kensington Young Conservatives. I was sitting at the back of a meeting I had organised which was being addressed by a member of Her Majesty's Loyal Opposition. I won't say who it was, except he had been a Minister. He didn't answer *one* question directly, he was actually disregarding what people were saying, particularly young people who've got views and should be listened to. He was really dismissive. I suddenly thought, "My Golly, I could answer those questions better than that!" I suddenly thought I'll have a go.'

She became Chairman of the Greater London Young Conservatives and succeeded her then husband as the YC's Senior Vice-Chairman. 'People started to talk to me about going into parliament, so I suppose from about 1965 onwards it was there as a thought, but I had to do my exams. I had to continue in business and make sure I had a career.' Lynda Chalker did, in fact, work in business for thirteen years before she got into parliament: as a statistician and market researcher with Unilever, Shell Mex and BP, with Barclays Bank, and with an American company.

Lynda Chalker recalls, 'In my thirteen-odd years in business full-time, I was always one woman alongside a whole lot of men and I've always got on perfectly well. Then I suddenly began to realise that in the political sphere, it was more difficult than it had ever been in business. I kept thinking, this isn't right, women have got just as much to contribute. In the Conservative Party, it's often been women — the very bastions of the constituency parties — who stopped other women from being chosen as candidates. When I was a candidate I found the most prejudice amongst selection committees who couldn't believe they could possible do such a job themselves, so automatically thought another woman couldn't do it either. But I think we've passed through that stage with a woman Prime Minister for ten years now.'

After trying for eight other constituencies, Lynda Chalker was finally selected for the marginal seat of Wallasey when Ernest Marples retired in 1973. By that stage she was divorced. (Hard as it may be now to believe, she was the first woman divorcee to be selected as a candidate.) 'I was one of the four women out of 108 applicants for it, but there weren't as many high-flyers as there should have been,' she said — 'It was seen as a difficult seat even in those days and they knew it was getting more difficult for Conservatives to hold because of population shifts.'

Lynda Chalker's first front-bench post was at Health and Social Services. When the Conservatives won the 1979 General Election she became Under Secretary of Health and Social Services. During her time there she ordered 'sex snoopers' to ease off questioning unmarried mothers. She then became Under Secretary of State for Transport, then Minister of State for Transport where she introduced the compulsory use of seat-belts because a seat-belt had saved her own life.

Women in public life are still enough of a novelty to have to cope with some unusual happenings. 'Back in Australia in 1983 when I was meeting Ministers of Transport from other countries, the Iranian Minister, a fundamentalist Muslim, wouldn't shake hands with me. After an awkward pause, his assistant was told to explain, "My Minister mustn't touch any part of your Minister's body!" For the sake of Muslim women I have very grave doubts whether there should be a belief in any society that should so disregard women and not treat them as equals.'

In January 1986 when the call came for her to become Minister of State at the Foreign Office, Lynda Chalker was up at a school in her constituency. 'I was actually having a lovely debate with my sixth formers at what is now the Wallasey School. The sixth formers had been asking me about relations with government. We'd been having a jolly good discussion. All of a sudden the Head of Business Studies came into the room. "Very sorry to disturb you," he said, "but there's a phone call for you." As it was the third phone call I'd had at the school that morning, I was a bit unwilling to go and take it. The Head of Business Studies looked at me. He said to me: "I think you'd better take it, it's No.10." Nigel Wicks, who was then the Private Secretary to the Prime Minister, was on the phone and then the Prime Minister came on the line.' Lynda Chalker became Deputy to the Foreign Secretary and a Privy Councillor, the highest elected woman in government after the Prime Minister in June 1987.

Does she find it frustrating not yet being in Cabinet? 'Yes, but all things come in time. I go to Cabinet meetings in Geoffrey's place quite often and I attend quite a lot of the top committees which decide  government policies. I've nearly always had quite a deal of input into the decisions taken one way or another.

'I've never ever wanted to get out of politics with the exception of the time in the middle of the 1987 General Election when the man who had threatened my life many times was at large. I was under full police protection, morning till night. It was very horrid. It had gone on for four years and it was something I couldn't really talk about. Yet another letter arrived which staff had kept from me so as not to worry me, but I found out within the last week of the election campaign. Finding it out then was even worse. It was at a time when the pressure was on me in the constituency from the Militants and all the people who'd been shipped in. The people who were carrying out this bully-boy campaign weren't Wallaseyans. Then one of my policemen simply said, "Come on, girl, you've never given in before, why are you going to start now, stupid!" Anyway this man was appre- hended the day before the election.'

The 'wet' discovers she's now beginning to dry out a bit too. 'I've been influenced lately by people you won't associate naturally with me, like Norman Tebbit and Nicholas Ridley. They've influenced me to make me think things through and to actually test out if an argument stands up, sometimes to dismiss things I had comfortably taken on board before. I don't believe — and never have, which is what makes me a Conservative — that the state should do everything. On economic issues I'm fairly tough these days. Quite honestly, if you don't have an economy that produces the wealth, you can't do all the social things I'm also deeply committed to.'

# 10.
# CANDIDATES FOR PARLIAMENT

By the year 2000, the names Angela Browning, Linda Siegle, Zerbanoo Gifford and Doreen Miller could be as familiar as Shirley Williams, Diane Abbott or Edwina Currie are today. Or like many other political hopefuls they could just remain hopeful. They are all currently on the approved candidates list of their parties.

Prospective parliamentary candidates spend much of their lives pounding the pavements in pouring rain, delivering soggy leaflets, knocking on doors, driving to meetings through frost, snow or rain, juggling family, work and politics, wheeling and dealing, learning about new problems and issues, dealing with the press, putting themselves into nerve-wracking situations, including candidate selection, or getting up to speak for the first time at a party conference. They have used every spare penny. They spend agonising hours and sleepless nights over nasty internal fights and spats in their own constituency parties. Some prospective candidates go through all that without even getting selected to fight a seat. Yet, when you ask them, most of them say they wouldn't swap it for the world. Politics is an addiction. Women, like men, become political junkies.

Conservative candidate Angela Browning sums it up: 'I love being on the doorstep and I love being in communication with people — that's the nicest part, it's the fun part of it. I really enjoyed the election, it was great fun, we had a lot of laughs. I remember knocking on one chap's door and before I could even say, "Hello, I'm Angela Browning, I'm your Conservative candidate," he said to me, "Ee, I'll not be voting for you, love. You're an Edwina Currie clone!"'

Women who stand for Parliament come from all backgrounds and ages. Some are married, some single. There are no formal qualifications required to be a Member of Parliament. You simply have to be over 21, not a member of the House of Lords, nor a long-term criminal, nor certified insane. Motherhood may not be a severe impediment either. Parliamentary holidays coincide more or less with school holidays.

Former Labour Treasury front-bench spokesperson, Oonagh McDonald, once said that becoming a Member of Parliament is quite simple: First join a party; get known nationally in the Party; get selected for a winnable seat. And win it. It's quite true. But between those four stages there is an awful lot of hard work and a strong dash of good luck.

Unlike the United States where there are fixed dates for elections and everyone knows exactly when the next election will be held, in Britain the Prime Minister calls the General Election whenever she wants to within a five-year period. Party machinery, candidates and journalists are kept on tenterhooks as the likely date draws near. Margaret Thatcher likes summer elections — so should they cancel the family holiday? What plan should they make with their employer? Suppose it isn't this year at all? Angela Browning says, 'When the election finally arrived it was like having a baby. There's the nine months of pregnancy so you rather lose sight of the fact there's going to be an end to it, there's going to be a birth.'

## ANGELA BROWNING

Angela Browning has reached somewhere between stages two and three on the Oonagh McDonald menu. Taking the first step to becoming a candidate was the hardest. 'You stand there at the beginning and wonder, "How am I going to go about this?" It's difficult to know first of all *who* to ask and whether you've got the temerity to say to people, "Look, I think I can do this." Are they going to snap off your head and say "What makes you think *you* can do it?"' She adds, 'I said this as a woman who is naturally self-confident, who's used to taking decisions in business and putting my case across to professional people.'

For a long time for Angela Browning it was worry over not having a university degree which held her back from applying to become a parliamentary candidate. With hindsight, she laughs at that as an unnecessary fear. 'I decided I probably had as much to contribute as anyone else — my advice to anyone with these reservations is "Don't allow yourself to be held back by that!" Politics calls for a lot more skills than an academic background. I've had several jobs. They always involved contact with a wide range of people. If you are a people person and you enjoy meeting people, that's probably the most important thing. Politics is about PEOPLE.'

The grammar school grand-daughter of a railway guard is a remarkable contrast with the previous traditional Conservative MP for Nantwich, Sir Nicholas Bonsor, son of a Baronet, educated at Eton, Keble Oxford and the Inner Temple, a barrister, farmer and company director.

Angela Browning originally trained as a home economist. When she married accountant David, they moved to Tiverton in Devon. She stopped working as a cookery teacher when the two children were born and switched to auxilliary night-nursing. 'By working at night, I could cope with two small children and a job.'

By 1987 she was a self-employed retail training consultant. She has noticed a change in attitude in the Conservative Party in the 1980s. 'Conservative women have been a lot more involved at the sharp end of politics. Having a woman Prime Minister sharpens up the image of the Conservative woman. Twenty years ago, somebody like me would not have been selected for a Conservative seat. I'm an indicator of the changes taking place in the Conservative Party.'

She took her first step towards Parliament through a seminar organised by the 300 Group, where Joan Hall, former Conservative MP for Keighley, advised her to get on the Conservative Party Speakers' panel. 'That was the trigger point for getting more experience. I put myself through a self-imposed apprenticeship.'

She became Chairman of the Tiverton branch. 'I also joined organisations such as Peace through NATO, and Olga Maitland's Women and Families for Defence. Defence is a very important issue. Unless you defend the country, and defend the freedom we have now, all other things we think about are meaningless.'

She took every opportunity to practise speaking in public. 'When the Party was short of speakers, at 24 hours' notice they would call on me on all sorts of subjects. And I'd say, "Yes, I'll mug up on all this and I'll go."'

By March 1986, this determination helped her build a background impressive enough to persuade the Conservatives in the winnable constituency Nantwich and Crewe to select her from over 60 other hopefuls who applied for the seat. Her softer version of the Margaret Thatcher voice pattern may have influenced them too.

Angela Browning says fellow Conservative Edwina Currie gave her some sisterly advice on image. 'I was a candidate chairing a meeting and Edwina said to me: "Angela, you chaired that very well, but let me just give you a tip. When a woman is concentrating and isn't actually smiling, when her face is in repose, her face can actually look quite severe. Men don't suffer from this, of course, because when a man isn't smiling he just looks distinguished, whereas a woman can look rather hard-faced at times, particularly if you're listening to what somebody's saying. Always remember, when you're on a platform where the cameras are on you, you may come over as looking terribly hatchet-faced. Turn up the mouth and sparkle with the eyes." I thought this was terribly good advice. At the Party Conference later in the year I was on a platform, the cameras were going, I was listening to somebody give an hour-and-a-half-long lecture, so I composed my face into what I thought was the soft, interested, intelligent expression required. Immediately afterwards, my husband, who had been in the audience, rushed up to me and said, "What on earth was the matter with you?" I asked: "What do you mean?" And he said, "You had the most extraordinary expression on your face, like you'd had a huge bowl of prunes!"'

By the time she became candidate Angela Browning belonged to 23 committees. 'I gave up the 23 committees because I was concentrating on the Nantwich constituency.' When the 1987 General Election was at last announced, the Conservative candidates flocked to Central Hall, Westminster, for the launch of the Party manifesto and a final briefing from the Leader before going into battle. Entering the hall packed with Conservative politicians was a revelation for Angela Browning. 'I remember coming into this hall full of people and the thing that struck me most was the smell of after shave! It really got home to me what a minority women are in politics.'

Once the election campaign is in full swing, individual candidates get absorbed into their own little orbit and snippets of news filtering through to them from the outside world seem remote and unreal. 'You are really quite isolated within your constituency. You're fighting your own battle there. The Party research department keeps you up to date with the political events and you're supplied with absolutely reams and reams of paper with information on policy, but you never have a chance to read it all. You just flip through bits which look interesting. To actually gauge how the campaign is going nationally and what the general feel of things is from the electorate is very, very difficult. You forget there's another world outside your own constituency. You concentrate, and on you go, day after day, until you actually get to election day.'

Election day arrived. She needed only a village hall full of voters to swing from Labour to Conservative to defeat one of the best-known Labour Members of Parliament, Gwyneth Dunwoody. Candidates' quivering antennae keep them acutely aware of what is happening on their patch. 'I sensed from the high turnout in Crewe [a strong Labour area] that we weren't going to do it. I went home and had something to eat. When I went to the count, I didn't expect to win. But my husband came to the count and just before it was obvious I hadn't won, he rushed round to tell me he thought I *had*. The way the votes were piling up, we thought we'd actually won. Then they seemed to magic another 1,000-odd votes from somewhere and it was lost. People worked so hard. It was a disappointment to all of us, the whole family really.' Gwyneth Dunwoody held the seat. 'I had to go up on the platform and make a little speech. I thought there was no way I would let the Opposition see how I was feeling inside. I almost psyched myself up into a very chirpy mood to get up on that platform to make the speech. From the platform I could see the expression on the faces of the people from the Conservative Party who were at the count and that is devastating. The expression on their faces is worse than what you're feeling inside for yourself because you do feel at that point that they've all worked so hard and you've let them down. In later days I took a different view on that and I thought that I did work very hard in that campaign, given the amount of time we had, there weren't many things I could have done that would have actually got more votes. And I knew straight away I would stand again. The next morning at about nine o'clock my husband spoke to my brother on the phone. I should tell you my brother's not even a Conservative voter. They were so distressed on the phone I packed my husband off. I told myself I had things to do, I had to get rid of him so I could cope. Otherwise I would have a day of distress.'

Did Angela Browning find that standing against another woman

Gwyneth Dunwoody, affected her campaign? 'The fact that she
was a woman and I was a woman, I don't think made any difference. We both had a job of work to do and we just got on and did
it. It was my first General Election and I enjoyed every minute
of it. I nursed the seat for 18 months before the election was
called and I was there on average three days a week. I was 39. I
shall be 45 at the next election. I really do now feel terribly
frustrated I'm not in. Looking to the future, one can see how
legislation should be taking shape ready for the 1990s and well
beyond that. I really do want to be part of it. I would love to be
getting to grips with it in the House of Commons now. I've
reached the stage I'm only looking for a seat where an MP in my
Party is resigning and not standing again. That means the
competition is stepping up a pace or two. I've got a little bit of
panic in my background because of this, only going for a safe
seat. Am I even going to be seen? And if I'm seen, am I going to
be selected?

'One must wonder how many of the people on selection
committees have actually interviewed anybody for any job in
their life before? Interviewing is as much a technique as being
interviewed. I do just sometimes wonder how much professional
expertise is brought to bear. I suspect a lot of it is on first
appearances and what they've perceived to be the ideal parliamentary candidate/MP, and whether on first sight and sound
you measure up to that. On that score alone women are bound to
have a harder fight, because we're not traditionally the way they
see their Member of Parliament. Unfortunately the stereotype
of the male candidate in the pin-striped suit with two little children and a very nice wife is still uppermost in people's minds —
even though we have a woman Prime Minister.

'I know the Labour Party and the SLD now have a selection
process which requires constituencies to have at least one
woman out of the final three on a candidate short-list. We don't
have that in the Conservative Party. I've always been somebody
who's said I want to stand on my own merits — if they turn me
down, so be it. But I must tell you there are times when that
approach is really put to the test! Even now, despite equal
opportunities, there is still prejudice against women. It's the one
subject where I feel there's agreement among women of all
parties.'

## LINDA SIEGLE

Linda Siegle stood for Parliament for the first time in 1987, as Alliance candidate for Devizes in Wiltshire. The first stages of applying to be a parliamentary candidate are like applying for any other job. Before she could start applying for seats, she had to write and apply to be on the Party list of approved candidates.

The topic Linda Siegle chose for her set speech to the interviewing committee went down like Edwina Currie addressing the Poultry Farmers' Association. 'I was terribly nervous. I prepared this amazingly feminist speech. I catalogued all the dreadful things men had done to screw up the world over the ages and really how things would be much better if women had more control over their own lives. It was what you might give to a coffee morning of women. However, they were all men interviewing me!' She is unrepentant. 'It was a brilliant speech, they just didn't like what was in it. I think they gave me 10 out of 10 for presentation and 0 out of 10 for content.' But they accepted her for the Party list of approved parliamentary candidates.

She agrees very much with Joanna Foster, Chair of the Equal Opportunities Commission, who described a woman's career pattern as a 'patchwork'. 'That happens to a lot of women. We don't move to where we want to go, or start doing what we want to do because we want to do it. Circumstances in your life happen to make it a possibility. My political career never really happened as a series of steps, it sort of happened over a period of time.'

She had held a few part-time jobs and became a dental hygienist. She then married John, a dentist, and left paid employment to spend the next fifteen years bringing up their children, Charlie, Edward and Ben.

Linda did not go to university nor does she come from a political family. She believes her background puts her more in touch with grassroots feelings and reactions. 'I've met a lot of people who were very much involved in student politics during the sixties and early seventies, but somehow or another they almost all got stuck in a groove, a rut, in that time.'

Linda Siegle didn't always vote Liberal. When she first moved from London to the West Country as a young mother, she conformed to the prevailing social group. 'I lived in a very pretty Somerset village, and because I was a professional man's wife, we were naturally assumed to be Conservatives. So we were welcomed into the bosom of the local Conservative Party.'

Gradually she started to form her own political views. 'I started to examine what the real values and real policies of the Conservative Party were and discovered I had always been a Liberal. I think liberalism is about the sort of balance between personal freedom and community and the public good. The Conservatives have got that wrong. They put personal freedom to do what one likes, above one's commitment as an individual to the community, which is what liberalism is all about. I also felt they didn't actually want me in the Conservative Party because of my political views, but because I fitted in socially. That's what shire county conservatism consists of, a big social club. If your face fits and your income's right, you're in. Nobody ever discusses any policies as far as I can see. I think the Conservative Party has now become much more broadly based under Thatcher- and Tebbit-ism, but they still have this fairly shire county snobbish attitude to life, which I find rather offensive.'

She took no active part in politics until her youngest son started full-time school. By then she was 39. 'It was a new beginning for me. I had the time and decided I would join the local Liberals and become involved in local politics. Until then, apart from helping in a couple of general elections, I wasn't active.'

She immediately faced one of the most profoundly difficult barriers that women who bear children have to overcome, and not just in politics: society foolishly does not comprehend the value of the skills and experience women gain as mothers. A woman who just writes 'mother' on her CV doesn't stand a chance of getting selected. Track records built outside the family unit carry clout with interviewers. An ex-commando, a journalist, a lawyer, miner or teacher are deemed to be suitable candidates for Parliament, but when 'the importance of motherhood' is trumpeted, society talks with forked tongue.

Linda Siegle feels strongly about this. 'You can write a CV and it won't look like a man's CV. A lot of women who've spent most of their time bringing up children — with all the human and management and time skills it entails — still have a CV that looks like they can't hold a job down for 5 minutes. A woman on the selection committee in Wells spelt it out to me: "What have you ever done? What have you ever won? How do we know you'll be any good as a candidate?"'

She decided to build a track record of activities outside the home. She joined the 300 Group, then in the course of the next five years she became a county councillor, a magistrate and stood for Parliament for the Alliance in Devizes in the 1987 General Election. 'I gained an awful lot of political experience, debating skills, all the realities of politics, even the reality of government because even in opposition you're part of a council that governs and has responsibilities to spend people's money.'

Linda Siegle believes clothes are an area where women politicians have the advantage over male colleagues. 'As a woman you certainly have got one up on the armies of men in grey suits, if you can come out in something bright orange. At the Eastbourne Party conference, I decided the way to get on the box was to wear something very, very bright because television presenters must be fed up with interviewing men in grey suits. I bought a bright orange suit in a sale specifically for the purpose of attracting the television cameras. It was fantastic, I was never off the television. Then, once they get to know you can actually speak and you can be available and if they ask you to be there at 8.00 am to do an interview tomorrow morning, you'll be there. It seemed to snowball.'

In British politics the toughest and most unpleasant moments often take place within your own party, as rivalries and vanities abound. Competitors and their handmen go for the jugular vein. Gloves come off, no holds are barred. Rumour-mongering of a completely unacceptable kind is rife. *Nothing* is too horrid to say or imply about the rival. Anyone who ever sought a parliamentary seat has crashed into this unwelcome scene. Infighting in the political parties can be bloody, wearing and spiteful.

Linda Siegle has found worst moments in politics have been during internal party wrangles. She was caught up in a fight over a selection in Somerset. 'They were doing so much internal manoeuvering because they couldn't work out the effect of me being in the race at all. I wasn't obviously going to win, but they thought my presence in the race would screw it up for one or other of the candidates. They just thought they'd be better off with a straightforward fight between these two men without me being in it at all. The rules required them to have three candidates on the short-list, but they just rang me up and said, "Sorry, no, we've made a mistake. We don't really want you to be on the short-list, so don't come to the hustings. We won't circulate your details to the membership." I was upset and hurt first of all. Then I was FURIOUS!

'First of all I had an hour-long conversation with the Chairman of the constituency, which I don't think he'll ever forget. Then I rang up everybody in the Party who was on the candidates' committee or who were in the position to give dispensation for a two-candidate short-list. I said, "If you dare to do this, I'll cause you so much trouble you'll wish you hadn't. This is only the beginning and don't think you'll ever get away with it." I just rang everybody up that had any say at all and said I'm not taking this, I may not be going to win this selection, but I jolly well have the right to stand for it.

'All the in-fighting really does drain your emotions and your resources. Next time I get a constituency, I shall be very much more Stalinist, I really will! You get the flack for being a tough bitch anyway, just for being the candidate, so I shall actually play that to the hilt. I'll just say right, I'm not going to have any of this in-fighting and you can either work for the Party or you can go and have an argument somewhere else and we'll get some new people in who aren't always arguing.'

She feels strongly about certain political issues — 'particularly things like women's employment and child care. I realised how disadvantaged women are as a result of having to always be the one who is left at home with the children. If we're going to accommodate women, society must structure itself rather differently to allow more of them to take part in the democratic process.'

Linda Siegle believes that 'more women in Parliament would make an enormous difference to the country. Our priorities would all shift and we'd stop talking about economics and defence and we'd start talking about the environment and health and the things that actually matter in people's lives. When we're the norm a balance would prevail and that's what happens in committees. You get a committee with two women and ten men and the men will keep telling you, "Shut up, that's not what we're talking about, you don't understand." And you keep thinking well that's what I'm talking about. But there's only two of you. Men and women do debate differently, whatever people say. They have a different train of thought. If you get half and half women and men you get a balanced debate and a very good conclusion from it. Men have this very formal attitude to an agenda — you have to be seen to be producing pieces of paper and you have to actually go through it so everybody else can see you've done it. Not all men but many men. They do seem to have a procedural attitude to things where women actually enter into the thing to solve the problems set for the committee. They have a more informal way of going about it which may look fairly shambolic to some men but actually produces the goods and actually comes out with the result that they were intended to get.'

Linda Siegle states unequivocally: 'In his 10 years as Leader of the Party, David Steel never could understand what we women were talking about. Attitudes of the old Liberal Leadership towards women have been very detrimental to the advancement of women. Women are invisible, because they live in a different world on a different plain in another planet almost and the men don't see them. We're there but we're not there. I remember complaining to a former chair of the Liberal Party, Paul Tyler, the MP from Cornwall who lost his seat, that there were absolutely no women on the Alliance General Election campaign committee in 1987. Tyler said, "Well Linda, we really are very aware of that problem but honestly when we looked at the women in the Party, there simply were no suitable women!" I said, "Paul, you wouldn't know a suitable woman if you fell over one in the street!"

'The Party says all the right things on women but it doesn't actually deliver them when the time comes. There was an awful lot of lip service paid to equality in the old Liberal Party. Our regional Party Agent here in the West Country is a terrific agent but he feels very strongly about me being a pro-feminist and that I shouldn't display my feminist views because it's a negative thing. We always have a joke about it. He thinks I've got a chip on my shoulder about feminism and that's something some men will not understand. The new leader, Paddy Ashdown, has been very good in actually encouraging women to get ahead and get on in politics for their own sake and he's certainly encouraged me and a lot of other women. You don't get this great barrier like you did with Steel where you felt only the privileged kitchen cabinet could speak to him. It was made worse by the fact that there weren't any women on Steel's kitchen cabinet. Paddy is actively working not to have that set-up. But I still don't think Paddy basically understands where we're coming from or what we're talking about. Michael

Meadowcroft, our former MP from Leeds, put it best about men resisting women in politics — "Anyone who's dealt four aces doesn't ask for another hand!"'

## DOREEN MILLER

I was *so* determined to get into the House of Commons, I mortgaged the family home to raise the cash for my own business. I built a multimillion pound business for one reason only, to give myself a CV for politics, a track record. For fifteen years I built a huge track record for myself. Then I said to the Conservative Party, OK here I am.

'By the time I offered my services I was a 50-year-old wife, daughter, mother and businesswoman, as well as a magistrate, and I know what it's like to go out and earn a living, to meet a payroll, to understand the problems of caring for a family. I really thought I would be God's gift to the Conservative Party. I couldn't believe they would take one look at me and say, "Don't you think my dear you're too mature?" Or something of that ilk.'

She applied to over 140 seats. 'I've only been interviewed nine times, though of those I was short-listed for seven. I haven't had an interview in quite some years; the last one I had was Hendon South where they had to see me because it was my home seat. I'm now 55, but I was the right side of 50 five years ago. I haven't had an interview since.

From 1986-88, Doreen Miller spearheaded the 300 Group's campaign as Chair. 'All my life I wanted to be in politics. As a kid at school I always thought it would be wonderful. I would listen to the radio and think I could do better than that. It was a desire to actually do things and get things to happen. When people say to me these days, as they do, "Good God, I'm not interested in politics, politics is corrupt," I always say, "If you're not interested in politics, you're not interested in life," because nothing happens that wasn't a political decision somewhere along the line.'

Doreen Miller didn't always vote Conservative. Like Shirley Porter, she started off as a Liberal. 'At school I was a candidate for the Liberal Party. I was Head Girl at Kilburn High School and I was always going on crusades. After I was old enough to vote, my first two elections I voted Liberal and then I changed my views very radically.

'I'm the kind of Conservative who believes the more wealth

you create in the country, the more money you have to help those who really need it and not for giving to those who I don't consider really need it. There is far too much nannying and spoonfeeding. I just feel that at the very end of the day, private enterprise is the way for creating wealth. I don't believe in socialism, I've seen it in operation in China. I've seen it in Russia, I believe it's dull. I believe in free enterprise, I believe in freedom under the law. If you have that kind of atmosphere, creativity and the individual can bloom. I also came to the view that really if you want things to happen, you've got to be there where it's happening, where you can put your input in.'

She is not from a political family, nor did she come up through party ranks since her teens, or belong to the Oxbridge network, or have a background as a local councillor.

She left school and studied law at London University. 'I married Henry six weeks before finals. I promised my parents I would take my degree and I didn't. However, I've not regretted it, Henry is fabulous. Michael was born 11 months after we got married and I kept saying I'd go back but I didn't. I wanted to bring him up and then we had Paul, then we had David and I enjoyed the first ten years bringing them up. Then I said, "OK, that's it now, it's my time to do the things that I want to do for myself. I was 37 and my children were off my hands. I'd had my good education, I was a magistrate as well. My ambition really was to get into the House of Commons.'

'I didn't join a party until fifteen years ago. Like many people, I never even knew you had to be a member of a party — you just vote. I wasn't a born politician — I don't think a politician should be a politician, I think a politician should be a person who's done other things and can bring something to politics. That's why I didn't want to be a local councillor, I didn't know what skills I had that would make me a suitable local councillor or a Member of Parliament, but I looked at the House like a man looks at it, plotting one's path to power — how do you get there? It doesn't just happen, you have to have a programme of what you want to happen.'

She decided the House of Commons was short of two categories: 'I thought it was very, very short of women. I easily fit that bill. Second, it's extremely short of business people. There are a tremendous amount of academics, but practically nobody I would go away and take a sabbatical and leave my business with. I said to Henry, "I want to get into politics. I'd like to give myself a business profile, I'd like to start a business."

'I had sleepless nights to build that business. When people say to me, "Now *you*, of course, you had luck", I say, "I had a hell of a lot of hard work and good luck, and a tremendous amount of courage." I ran smack into a cashflow problem before I had even begun. I had to go to the bank and ask for a further £50,000, and in those days it was not usual to lend women money and £50,000 to boot!

'Then I had to go back to tell Henry at the office I'd actually mortgaged our house. I thought am I mad! Here I am, with a successful young solicitor husband, three children all down for Clifton, with sufficient money for fees and the house paid for. And I've had this barmy idea because one day I want to get into the House of Commons!' Henry asked what she had given as a collateral. She said the house. He said, 'Of course, I knew you had guts!'

When the business had been running successfully for some years she wrote to Marcus Fox in charge of candidate selection at the Conservative Party. 'I said I was very interested in becoming an MP, I thought I had a lot to offer. This is what I'd done in my life, this is where I was. I never usually blow my trumpet about my business, but within a couple of years we had become the third largest distributor of cosmetics in this country and my turnover within three years was over six million pounds a year.' She went to a meeting with Marcus Fox. 'He asked me how long I'd been a councillor. I said I had't and he hadn't read my letter. He rummaged through it and said they obviously got me muddled with someone else. "This isn't the way it's done, Doreen," he said. "Usually you join the Party, work for the Party and then they think you could stand for local council and then you could do this." I looked at him and said, "But Mr Fox, if I do all that you'll get me in my wheelchair, I'll be too old for you. You need me now." Marcus Fox said, "What you really want is twenty years experience in five minutes."'

He arranged for her to help Dr Rhodes Boyson, the MP in Brent North, as a type of apprenticeship. He gave her a thorough grounding in an MP's work. She canvassed with him, helped in his constituency and went to meetings with him. She embarked on building her political experience with the same gusto as building her business. As well as helping Rhodes Boyson, she rushed around the country and spoke in over 200 constituencies. 'I'd speak on any subject they wanted. I did luncheons, AGM meetings. I think the whole multi-lateralist stance has proved to be right. I feel that was a very, very important campaign and I feel Joan Ruddock was totally wrong and I see signs of them all changing a bit now. That was my view — I'd have gone out and spoken on that at any time of the day or night. You'd always get me on that one and on all the women's issues. But not just women's issues, I'm very interested in education too — I think education is a very important thing. I stood for the ILEA elections in Hampstead and Highgate. I also am a great one for Europe. I got into doing training, and things like door-to-door work, getting more members than anybody else and getting more subs than anybody else.' She was so successful that Central Office asked her to teach the Party her recruiting methods.

She went on the Conservative candidate selection weekend. 'Peter Morrison was in charge of my little group and he asked me for lunch at the time and said, "You're first class, but I don't think you'll make it because I have to tell you, I think you're slightly mature to be starting as far as the Conservative Party is concerned. They're not actually even enraptured with women candidates. What Central Office wants is one thing, but what the local associations actually do is something else."

'Yesterday there were articles in the *Times*, there were articles in the *Telegraph*, there were articles in the *Daily Mail* about how Mrs Thatcher says she wants more women in all of these things. The truth is that's great, but when you read the whole article in *She* magazine, it's four pages all about Mrs Thatcher and one tiny little paragraph saying how, in her view, we need many more women, so for goodness sake why didn't many more women come forward? Now it's very difficult to actually go to Mrs Thatcher and say "Let me tell you many, many more women are coming forward, but they're meeting just as much prejudice." Who is going to go and say that to her, who's going to tell her this is typical? Letters have just come from Conservative Central Office explaining how women on the list ought to be trained, so they're having these special training conferences. That's an insult. Actually what we need is training courses for selection committees to stop them being so sexist, so ageist and so on. Ageism bears down as insidiously and damagingly on women as "domesticism" or any other "-ism". There's no doubt the Conservative Party is trying very hard to attract women candidates, but the message going out to constituencies around the country is: "We are only interested in women under 45." But who's going to say it? The Party's been running something called the Younger Women's Conference and asks chairmen to recommend women who are under 45 to go on this course. The other thing they're running is what they call "The High Flyers" conference. Although they don't put an age limit on it officially, they actually wrote to chairmen of different associations and asked, "Do you know anybody under 45 who could come on the High Flyers Course?" One of the blocks to women getting selected in the Conservative Party is the deep basic feelings within the Party that a woman should be at home and bring up a family, full stop. But if women do do that and then say "OK here I am ready for public service," the chances are they can't be under 45 and so all of a sudden there's this extra barrier of ageism.

'But I'm not going to make it easy for them, so they can turn around and say well she withdrew from the list. I wanted to come off at one stage because I was becoming a joke. People saying, "There she goes again on her hobby horse" and so on. OK, if I have to be the joke in order to make it easier for someone else to stay on the list a bit longer, so be it. And another thing, I think a lot of legislation is needed, family legislation that hasn't come about yet. We're talking about new things, for example the rights of grandparents in a divorce. Very often the parent who gets the child doesn't give access to the grandparents of the other side and they don't have any standing in the courts, they can't demand it. I think the whole concept from West Indian families, the extended family, is such a great one. People haven't realised the need and the value for other people to belong to families, complete family units. If you ask me what would I try to do, that's one of the bills I would try and bring in.

'When I was being interviewed later for a seat at Welwyn, somebody said to me, "Don't you think it's rather presumptuous of you to think we should select you for the House of Commons when you haven't even stood for local council!" I just looked at this gentleman and said, "Well, I think you should put the same question to Mrs Thatcher!" I was so narked — what a nerve. He shut up but I probably lost his vote.

'I was then short-listed for the Southgate by-election, which was conveniently near my home. Young Michael Portillo got it. He's now a minister. But it's all worth it in a way. I've had terrible disappointments and I've cried a hell of a lot — behind closed doors, not in front of anybody of course. I wouldn't dream of doing that. It's all worth it for the knowledge for myself. No-one can ever say, "Doreen, you didn't even try." My mother once said to me, "Doreen, I can't understand why you work so hard day and night, 24 hours a day, either on business or on politics or in the 300 Group or on women in public life. What the hell do you think you're doing? You'll kill yourself." I said to her, "Mother, you don't kill yourself that easily." '

'I'm not looking actually for recognition funnily enough, I don't care about that. Yesterday I was speaking to Caroline Bullingham at the 300 Group office on the phone and she said to me, "Doreen, I want to just tell you something. I do far more now than I've ever done for the 300 Group because you inspired me." THAT will stay with me. And I was talking to Anne Levit today and I said, "Anne, I didn't want Caroline to know, but I wept about that afterwards" and Anne said, "Well, it's true, and you've inspired me too." So I feel that while we're inspiring the Carolines and the Annes of this world, what we're doing is changing the climate. Younger women are coming up behind who won't have this hard grind and won't have the insults, people talking about young women MPs and bikini lines and all that kind of junk. I have a philosophy in life that you don't know what tomorrow is going to bring, we don't know if tomorrow is going to be our last. Hopefully it won't be, but we know not. I wouldn't like to actually die without having tried everything I wanted to do. To be in Parliament — this was my ambition.'

## ZERBANOO GIFFORD

'I'm a long distance runner. I don't think politics is you lose one election and you give up. Heaven help it — everybody loses elections.'

Zerbanoo Gifford was born in Calcutta and came to England when she was 3 years old. She says, 'It wasn't my dream to go into politics, but I was reminded by my housemistress that when I sat the exam for Roedean, I wrote then I was going to be the first Indian woman Prime Minister.'

Her hero is Dadabhoi Naoroji. 'He was a Liberal, who elected to the British Parliament in the seat of Finsbury Central as the first Asian candidate nearly one hundred years ago, in 1892. He came to England and fought to get into Parliament because he wanted to speak on behalf of Home Rule for India. He was called the "MP for India". I admire him as he was so deeply loved across communities and was a man of honour and wisdom. But he became a very disillusioned man and he actually in many ways suffered exactly as I did. When he started his campaign Lord Salisbury called him a black man which outraged Queen Victoria. People like Florence Nightingale and Keir Hardy canvassed for him because they were so embarrassed at the sheer racial prejudice. He only got in once, in the landslide of 1892. Then he lost his seat. One hundred years later I was suffering the same racial prejudices, still being called the nigger.'

The other person she admires is Lord Avebury. 'He is an English gentleman and a saint in politics. He works for the Asian community, especially with immigration problems. Many people are arbitrarily stopped at the airport, even families coming for weddings or funerals. We used to ring him up in the middle of the night and he would help people. He would ring up a minister and always do something and never once asked for thanks. A lot of MPs do it for publicity or for some sort of recognition. Nothing, it was just the sheer goodness of the man and I thought he was a real liberal.

'My father was Founder President of the World Zoroastrian Organisation. I probably got my zoomph and fight from him. But my grandmother was an even greater influence. She's dead now. I used to go back to India and spent a lot of summer holidays with her. She was not in politics at all, she had 12 children and was adored by all her family and grandchildren and great grandchildren. I think the way she influenced me was she was so stable and loving. I had a very stable upbringing.

'I never really ever saw my life mapped out or had a career prospect or anything. I've always been a great believer that the unexpected is to be welcomed. Everything seemed to just happen to me and when it has happened, I've taken the opportunity and done it and enjoyed it.

'I was brought up in our family hotel in Central London. That was a wonderful background to politics, having to be quick in your judgement of people and also always being on duty.

'I loved school. Its great influence was that it allowed you to be a total individual, a respected individual and it gave you a lot of confidence to mix with people. The greatest benefit has been that most of my dearest and closest friends are my school friends. I have still got friends all these years later. We were like sisters because we were brought up together.'

After Roedean she returned to India. She started to travel, firstly through Russia by herself on the Trans-Siberian Express and then to Iran, then to South America and back to the Middle East. 'Travelling is very important. People talk about travelling now as if it was a sort of joke, you know you go and sunbathe and it is a bit trivial, but in fact if you go with an open mind you learn a lot about yourself and other people. You learn that within the limits of political systems every country is very much the same — most people have the same hopes and worries.'

Zerbanoo and her English husband Richard met at her 21st birthday party and married two years later. 'He came with a group of friends; since then unexpected guests have been most welcome in my life.'

Like Joan Ruddock, she worked for Shelter, the campaign for the Homeless. 'Again I got into it by accident. I went to deliver documents to an office in the Strand and I went to the wrong floor — Shelter. I was so impressed with what they were doing I became a volunteer and I helped set up the groups in London and from that I worked for them setting up Shelter shops.'

After she married, she went off travelling by herself again in the summer of 1973 to China. 'I was one of the first people to be let into China, just at the end of the Cultural Revolution. I was curious to find out how they organised modern China. It was a wonderful trip. The Chinese always asked me, "Where is your husband?" I used to joke and say he's at home paying the mortgage. When her first son, Mark, was born, she stayed at home and did a four-year Open University course in Arts and Humanities. 'I didn't get a degree, just studied.'

Zerbanoo's first election happened by chance. 'I was at home in Harrow with my young children feeling isolated when the Liberals arrived on our doorstep. They wanted to put a poster on the huge tree in our front garden. It's supposed to be the most outstanding ash tree in Middlesex and it's floodlit at night — a superb position for election posters! I said if they could get a poster up our tree, they could use it. The Liberals were so barmy they actually climbed up the ladder. I was so astounded by their courage we started talking. I was interested in community politics, especially the need for local nursery facilities, so they decided I might be a good candidate to stand in a defunct ward. I was willing to do it — and it was great fun. I used to go canvassing with the two children Wags and Mark.'

In 1982 Zerbanoo was 32 years old with an 18-month son when she stood in her first local election in Harrow. At this stage she had few problems with racism though leaflets were distributed on a council estate by the British Movement. 'To everyone's surprise I won the safe Tory seat for the Liberals. The electorate was 7,000 and I think I met everybody, I made it my business. I also have a very good memory, so I remember everything about everybody. I enjoy hearing people's views and discussing how life can be improved with a little foresight and initiative. I used to canvas, with my son Wags in his pushchair, during the daytime, when there was no competition with people watching TV in the evening. It was a new approach. People weren't used to politicians giving them time and listening to them. There were three recounts and I got in with a 25 per cent swing. I was the only young mum on the council and made history by being the first Asian. There were 13 Liberals and we were the main Opposition and I was the only woman, the thirteenth man. So I got media coverage.

'I was totally naive and knew nothing about the art of politics and of course the Liberal group were insistent that I spoke at my first council meeting, but I'm glad I didn't speak until I knew what I was talking about. At that stage I didn't understand Standing Orders or the etiquette of council meetings. I realised Harrow was about the only borough left in London that didn't have a housing aid centre. I found out everything, all there was to know, about housing aid centres, went and saw housing aid centres in other parts of London and used that as my maiden speech. Other councillors and especially the council officers saw that when I spoke I had my facts about the subject and knew what I was talking about.

'I went to my first party conference because I'd become a councillor and everybody said that is the thing you do. I always go with Richard. I hadn't thought about national politics at all until then.'

Her next move was to stand for Parliament in the 1983 General Election against Cecil Parkinson in Hertsmere. Zerbanoo was short-listed with three men. 'I went to the full membership meeting and got selected. I think it was because of proportional representation. PR is a great advantage to women because I think most women are everybody's second choice. I was positive I was everybody's second choice.

'We had a very good election except we became the targets of obviously right-wing fascists. I had death threats on the phone. We were telephoned and threatened, and told that if I stood for Parliament, I would regret it. On one occasion a man tried to smash our kitchen window, on another we came home to find a death threat left on my desk in the sitting room.

'The police were good and we had surveillance. It was very distressing. I always had to have somebody drive me to Hertsmere and be with me. Once, as we were driving back from Hertsmere the car was flashed at and followed very closely and we were nearly pushed off the road. I would have volunteers from Harrow. I knew these people were evil, and it was a hazard of politics and I knew that if I was in the public eye I had to accept a certain amount of upset.

'I thought Cecil Parkinson was a very discourteous man. I remember on the night of the count he refused to shake hands with myself or the Labour candidate and I was asked by the press what I thought. I said that he would never be Foreign Secretary until he learned some manners. I know many other Tory MPs and they are very courteous. The count was televised and I had a lot of letters from people to say how shocked they were. When I got up I wished him well and hoped that he would think of the people who were suffering in the country and wouldn't ignore them. I think it was a shame. I don't think it is ever necessary to be rude to anybody. Of course now in hindsight I realise that everything blew for him that night because certain people were made aware of his relationship with Sarah Keays.

'The Parkinson Affair raised speculation of a by-election. The local constituency insisted that I should be endorsed as their candidate in case of a by-election. There was no question of imposing a well-known political figure. I had doubled the vote and had come second in a forty-day campaign. But after the election, Zerbanoo went for a different constituency, rushing in where savvier political angels feared to tread, by deciding to try for selection in Harrow, where she lived. A well-established Liberal candidate who had fought the seat several times before was still in place. 'I was asked why I put myself up against a standing incumbent. I answered: "We're in a democracy, we're not in Soviet Russia where people have only one candidate to vote for. It was a period in my life which summed up politics for me — *certain sorrow, uncertain joy.* It was sorrow from that moment onwards. One of the reasons I wanted Harrow was I really wasn't willing to travel with young children — Waggly was about 7 and Mark was 10. I felt if the political parties had women with young children they should accommodate them if they are really serious. I have never been ashamed of saying we should have positive action. I think it's the only way to go forward. Also I was thinking a step ahead. If I did get to Parliament I wanted to be able to come home at night and be in bed with my husband. Neither did I want a constituency I had to go to at weekends away from my family.'

Zerbanoo Gifford thinks 'political women aren't keen to be associated with fashion, but the fashion industry is the third largest employer in the country. That's something a political woman can use to her advantage. She is different and she can capitalise on that.' Zerbanoo invited third-year art students at Harrow College to design and make all her wardrobe for the election for their degree course. '*Today* newspaper did a big feature on it and lots of people actually covered it; this novel idea was even covered on Scandinavian TV. The students used it to apply for jobs later on. Their image of political women was interesting — we were just honorary men. They weren't allowed to see me when they were given their brief, so they designed pin-striped suits. When they saw me everything changed, everything was done in yellow and gold because my name Zerbanoo means Golden Lady and because the Alliance colour was gold. They did one Rajah suit, dresses and a coat. I wore them all through the campaign and even on the Alliance party political broadcast, to publicise the outstanding work of our fashion students.'

In the 1987 General Election in Harrow she met racialism again. 'The local papers got letters telling me to go back to where I came from. They didn't want people like me being politicians here. The letters said people thought the whites were being swamped by Asians in Harrow. A lot of white people refused to put up posters. I had hate mail, but one anonymous hate letter I received seemed to crystallise a widespread white dilemma. "Why," asked the writer "should I vote for Mrs Gifford? She is young, pretty, popular and energetic, too, but the fact remains she is a foreigner and I want to be governed by British born-and-bred people. She should be satisfied with having been a Harrow Councillor." My parliamentary candidature had put her and 'other decent folk' in a quandary. I think that really summed it up.

'I'm interested in issues equal opportunities — I'd like to see the introduction of positive action. Ecology also interests me because unless we look after the environment everyone's going to suffer. I come from a religion that's based on ecology and the belief that none of the elements should be polluted. It's a religious crime to us. I used to be distressed when I thought how many trees had to be cut down to put across my message on leaflets. There was something obscene about it, just for promoting oneself. Foreign policy — I think this country has got to stop being so xenophobic and realise we're a trading nation and start trading. The post I'd most like to hold is Foreign Secretary. It would be an affirmation that the child of an immigrant could be trusted to be Foreign Secretary of this country. The post that would be most useful in breaking down people's misconceptions is the Home Secretary. If an Asian woman were in charge of the police, prison and immigration officers, people would have to change their views then.

'For me, a woman politician should be there to make sure she's not the first, only and last of her kind, but there to see that many more reach positions of authority and use their power to better the position of those who are voiceless.'

# 11.
# THEIR LORDSHIPS' HOUSE

Imagine you were living in a country where the system for entering one of the Houses of Parliament blatantly discriminated against women; a country where two-thirds of the seats in the Upper House were reserved for men only; a legislative chamber where until 1958 — the second half of the twentieth century — no woman was ever allowed to take part in the proceedings; and where religious leaders — bishops and archbishops — had 26 seats reserved for them although the national religion of that country did not permit women to become priests.

Which country is this? Somewhere in the Middle East? Asia? No, it's Britain.

In the Upper House, we put up with blatant medieval discrimination against women of an order which makes the blood of any champion of equal rights boil. Worse, it doesn't make sense. Right now, as we hurtle towards the twenty-first century, there are only 66 women in the House of Lords, and more than 1,000 men. More than 700 places in the Lords are reserved for men by *law* under the ancient 'Loi Salic' which stops women having the right of inheritance, a law whose old Norman name is often misspoken as the 'Loi Phallique'!

The House of Lords, variously known as the Upper House or 'the Other Place', is an important law-making body. It has crucial constitutional power and is the highest court in the land. Consequently, it has a profound impact on all our lives. The Upper Chamber plays a crucial role in initiating and investigating legislation, as well as the much mentioned role of acting as an amending body for legislation coming up from the over-burdened House of Commons. Specialist committees of the Lords such as the European Committee which acts as a link between Britain and Europe have a great deal of influence. Members of the House of Lords have individual platforms outside the Palace of Westminster for their voices to be heard — as after-dinner and conference speakers as well as on TV and radio.

Hereditary peers make up a very large group — they simply have to be born to the right *father*, be over 21 and male. There are always a handful of little boys waiting to get to 21 to take their seats. Thirty of the current peers, all males, have had hereditary peerages conferred on them this generation, including the Duke of York and Viscount Whitelaw. There are a mere 19 female hereditary peers, several of them Scottish whose titles date back to an age before the Salic Law. Interestingly Lord Mountbatten of Burma asked for a 'special remainder' for his daughter to succeed him, but Viscount Whitelaw who has four daughters has not made the same arrangement. His title will die with him. Even where no male heir existed, women hereditary peers were not allowed to take their seats in the House of Lords until as recently as 1963, in spite of persistent campaigning by Viscountess Rhondda from 1921 onwards.

It is not possible to take the House of Lords to the European Court at Luxembourg — with its excellent record on women's rights — under the EEC sex-discrimination law, even though there is a *prima facie* case of restricted entry for women, because technically peers are not employed. They receive an attendance and overnight accommodation allowance, but no salary.

The Life Peerages Act introduced by Harold Macmillan in 1958 brought in a new system of Life Peers who sit and vote in the House of Lords, but whose peerages expire on their death. These peerages can be awarded to women as well as men. There are 378 Life Peers, including 21 Lords of Appeal. However, life peerages are being created at a male/female ratio of eight to one, because women's contribution to national life is terribly under-rated. The identities of the Committee who decide on the creation of Life Peers, and more importantly the basis of their decisions, are hidden from view by the good old Official Secrets Act. To judge from the results of their activities, it's jobs for Old Boys — Captains of Industry, field marshalls, trades unions' bosses, business/City magnates, national press barons and editors, Whitehall civil servants, ex-ambassadors, plus men who have made a lot of money (and donated it to a Party). You won't find many women among those main sources of Life Peers.

The most important sub-group of Life Peers is the male or female 'working peer'. These are mainly ex-Members of Parliament or people who have served political parties, like Baroness Seear, Baroness Young and the Australian, Baroness Gardner of Parkes. Party leaders have a discreditable history of overlooking women for working peerages. David Steel in his ten years as Leader of the Liberal Party failed to get one woman put in the Lords.

Once women do get through the eye of the needle and into the House of Lords, they are treated more equally than in any other institution in Britain. On party and cross-party benches, they are readily promoted and respected. Baroness Seear has been a member of the House of Lords for over ten years. Former Leader of the Liberal Peers, she states unequivocally, 'I can honestly say I've never been in a place where you are treated better on a male–female equality basis. And that includes the London School of Economics where I lectured for years!'

The issue of the Lords would be less important if the Upper House was nothing more than its wide-spread image of an ornate, Gothic olde worlde club, filled with watering-holes and plush reading rooms, corridors rich in gold and scarlet, smelling like a fine but ageing hotel, stretching attractively along the Thames. In fact, just a pleasant place to meet on a rainy day. But this is far from the whole story. As Baroness Seear says indignantly, 'Some people think we just sit here in our ermine-trimmed red dressing-gowns, but this is an amending and revising Chamber. We look at legislation pouring up from the Commons. Often it's been hastily considered by the Commons and badly drafted too. They're so overloaded there, they often "guillotine" (cut short) their debates and pass the result on to us to patch up.' Sometimes future Acts of Parliament start out in the Upper House, as in the case of the Wildlife and Countryside Bill.

Whether there should be reform of the Upper House or whether it should simply be abolished has been hotly debated for decades. Since 1935 the Labour Party has been committed to abolishing it altogether, though now they may recommend democratisation. The Alliance manifesto in the 1987 General Election proposed extensive reforms, with half the Members elected regionally by proportional representation and half 'chosen on merit' by an all-party committee of Privy Counsellors.

One of the customary arguments for leaving the situation as it is in the Lords is that no more than 350 peers attend each day. But figures show it is not the same 350 every day — in any year more than 800 individual peers have actually attended. The Lords, in recent times, have voted against the government on some issues, but when a Conservative government is exceptionally keen to get its legislation through, it can and does, bus in hundreds of their 'backwoodsmen' (its inbuilt majority), mainly well-off males, as in the debate on free school dinners or the bill which introduced charges for eye tests. The Government rustled up enough support from the shires to win the latter vote 257 to 207.

Baroness Seear, Baroness Young and Baroness Gardner of Parkes all earned their peerages through political work. Baroness Seear stood for Parliament seven times for the Liberals and is a former President of the Liberal Party. Baroness Young was Conservative Leader of Oxford City Council. Baroness Gardner of Parkes was a member of the Greater London Council and Westminster Council and stood for Parliament twice for the Conservatives, once against the legendary Barbara Castle.

## BARONESS SEEAR

If she had been in the Conservative or Labour Parties, with winnable parliamentary seats on offer, Nancy Seear may well have been our first woman Prime Minister. She would certainly have been a Cabinet Minister. But she has devoted her life to the liberal principles she believes in. She stood seven times for parliament without winning, at a time the Liberal Party was in the wilderness. Members of the smaller parties have all the usual political grind and the ups and downs of political life, but know they are unlikely to reap any financial or visible rewards, or even thanks, for all their hard years of dedication. Instead, members of smaller parties have to cope with being mocked for looking like 'lost causes'.

Nancy Seear says her family background was 'wet Conservative'. 'I suppose I was about 13 or 14 when I went with my father to a Conservative meeting. He was a great free trader and he stood up and had a great row with the candidate about the candidate's protectionist politics. I thought this was absolutely marvellous. I don't say that's actually what got me started, but the fact I remember it as a great event shows it made a considerable impact.'

Her political awareness started at school. 'My generation was terribly lucky in the people who taught us, because we really had the first generation of university women in such large numbers. They were surplus in the marriage market because of the slaughter of men in the First World War. We were taught by people who now would be senior civil servants, barristers, journalists, the lot. Because there were no openings, they all came into teaching — and stayed. So we had the same very high quality people teaching us right throughout our secondary school period.'

By the time she was at Cambridge University reading History, Nancy Seear knew she wanted to be active in politics. 'At Cambridge, history has a lot of political theory in it. I was on both the university Liberal Club Committee and the University League of Nations.'

One of the influences on her at Cambridge was Elizabeth Wiskemann, the author of a famous book called *Undeclared War*. Elizabeth Wiskemann used to spend half her time at Cambridge and half writing for the *New Statesman* on Germany, including getting herself arrested by the German secret police. It was the sort of anti-totalitarian pro-libertarian emphasis. I read a lot of political theory. It's rather difficult not to be Liberal if you really soak yourself in political theory.'

Nancy Seear added practical politics to the armoury when she spent four months of a summer college vacation in 1932 teaching English to a family in Germany. 'It was just at the time the Nazi Party was coming up from being an illegal organisation to winning an alarming number of seats in the July 1932 election.' The visit to pre-war Nazi Germany left an indelible imprint on her political thinking, leaving a life-long loathing for concentrated power.

'In Germany, we used to play tennis and go to dances. The young men were completely taken in by the whole Nazi thing. I remember an argument with a Catholic. I said to him, "How can you be so anti-Jewish if you're a strong Catholic?" "Oh," he said, "Christ wasn't a Jew, we know that. Christ couldn't have been a Jew."'

She witnessed the early Nazi rallies. 'As soon as the Nazis were legalised, they held great rallies all over Germany. One very, very striking thing I always remember, which in some ways

I think was the bravest thing I ever did, took place at a huge rally in a marvellous natural amphitheatre in St Esea, in the mountains. Five thousand of these young Nazis marched past carrying their banners. Of course, being an evil organisation the weather was absolutely perfect, the setting was perfect. The march-past was taken by a chap subsequently murdered in the 1934 putsch. As they marched past, everybody rose. I thought I'd be damned if I was going to rise but I was pushed to my feet. They all raised their hands in a Nazi salute. I thought, "That, I will not do!" and kept my hands down. I thought afterwards if I could do that once I could do it twice and anyway I was going home, wasn't I? I wondered how long I'd go on doing it. It did seem unreal, but on the other hand if you were living there, in some ways it didn't seem all that unreal because there were too many incidents. I remember another one, when I was teaching English in about the only remaining well-off family in the area. Every day, middle-class beggars came to your door, asking you for food, and things were pretty grim. One of the women in this family was rather complacent. "Wasn't it funny," she said, "I met Herr Stein (a local councillor and a Jew) on the street and I gave him a slap in the face." She said this as if it were an achievement.

'I remember one day we went to supper in a farm house which was half farm house, half schloss. Two enormous chaps, about 26 years old, came in with a huge dog. They were educated, but unemployed; one was a mining engineer. Supper was potato salad and a bit of fruit because there wasn't anything else. Three weeks later I saw that unemployed mining engineer dressed up in Nazi uniform, haranguing people in the street. Unemployment gave the Nazis its educated middle-class support and that's what made it absolutely fatal. That was 1932 and it just went on relentlessly to 1939. One after another the centres of power were being taken by the government — the universities, the Churches, centres that could have stood up together. This is what frightened me.'

I wondered what made Nancy Seear choose to battle away her entire life as a Liberal when thousands of young people in the Britain of the 1930s were joining the Socialist or Communist Parties in revulsion at fascism.

'I think the point politically was that an awful lot of people of my generation went to Germany for a spell around the Depression to learn some German and many of them will tell you it made them Labour, the poverty and all the rest of it. I was already theoretically a Liberal, but the thing really drilled into me by all this was that the danger of the concentration of power — corporate, centralised state power — is more important than all the other things. That's always been the centre point of my Liberalism, because all the rest depends on it.'

Baroness Seear fears that the present government has dangerous centralist tendencies. 'Margaret Thatcher is trying to control the universities, she keeps interfering with the media — they can be a pain in the neck, but still — but the judiciary on the whole are standing out all right.'

The moment the war was over Nancy Seear was back in political action. 'We were starved of politics by that time. There was no interest in politics in the war years. My first active participation was a meeting addressed by Lady Violet Bonham-Carter when she fought in Wells in 1945. She was a magnificent speaker.'

Nancy Seear stood for the Liberals in Hornchurch, Essex, in 1950-51. 'It wasn't a problem being a woman and I'm bound to say I never had any difficulty in getting a constituency. I always remember that Frank Byers vetted me. He was absolutely notorious for his lack of social soft soap. I was 34. I remember asking him if he thought it was a disadvantage I was a woman. He replied, "It isn't as if you're very young, Nancy!" which was a typical Frankism.'

Her next constituency was in Cornwall. She commuted every six weeks up and down from London to Truro from 1955 to 1959, battling to build up Liberal support in the area. 'They'd be awfully nice and they'd do absolutely damn all from one visit to the other. It was quite obvious that it was going to take a Cornishman to win Truro — partly because you had to be one of them, but also because they're so damned idle.'

She was right. The seat was finally wrested back from the Conservatives by the Liberals fourteen years later by archetype Cornishman, David Penhaligon.

In the 1964 Election Nancy Seear stood in Epping, much nearer to London. In 1966 she fought Rochdale. Rochdale was considered a plum seat for the Liberal Party. The previous candidate had been TV presenter Ludovic Kennedy. 'I went up to Rochdale which was a great mistake because Rochdale was really so right-wing.' Rochdale was finally won for the Liberals by Cyril Smith.

She fought one more parliamentary seat, Wakefield, in 1970 and then entered the Lords where she can be seen in gladiator fashion fighting for her principles and beliefs.

Nancy Seears is just one example of why there is a national need for a House of Lords drawn from a much broader base of knowledge and experience. In the lists of new Life Peers from 1987 New Year to 1989 New Year, there were 43 men and just four women. The proportion of women is falling even further behind with every Honours List. With the best will in the world —- and it does exist in the Lords — a Chamber of mainly men cannot reflect a population's views and needs with feeling and accuracy.

## BARONESS YOUNG

The ex-Leader of Oxford City Council, Janet Young was the first woman to become a Minister at the Foreign and Commonwealth Office. She has a long string of 'firsts': the first and only woman to have served in Margaret Thatcher's Cabinet; she was the first woman Leader of the House of Lords, first woman Chancellor of the Duchy of Lancaster, first woman Lord Privy Seal and first woman Deputy Foreign Secretary, number two to Geoffrey Howe, a post later filled by Lynda Chalker. Baroness Young was also the first woman to break into the all-male sanctum of the Board of Marks and Spencer. As Deputy Foreign Secretary, Baroness Young had an office at the Foreign and Commonwealth Ministry and a pleasant room in the House of Lords, both buzzing with the comings and goings of a host of young women and men organising her visits and her visitors.

In a feature on her in the *Guardian*, I described Janet Young as 'a diplomat by temperament whom history has smiled on'. She has often been in the right place at the right time without conniving it. And she has made a point of helping other women to fulfil their potential too. There are many women in parliament and on local councils today who wouldn't be there if Janet Young hadn't given them their first encouragement of their first shove into public life. As a Minister, she made a point in the reorganisation of the Civil Service of looking for ways to advance women up the ranks. Indeed, rumour has it she fell foul of Margaret Thatcher over a too-zealous interest in issues connected with women.

The Rt Hon. Baroness Young is a matriarch with three

daughters, three sons-in-law and four grandchildren. Daughter of a university don, she grew up in Oxford, where she still lives with Geoffrey, her husband, a just-retired Fellow and Tutor in Organic Chemistry at Jesus College. Her degree in Modern Greats is from St Anne's. Like Emma Nicholson, if she hadn't become a politician she would like to have been a musician. Janet Young's mother was a first-class pianist and music is still a principal recreation.

It wasn't until her early forties that her own political career really took off. After ten years as an Oxford City Councillor she became an Alderman and Leader of the Council. 'It was 1967. I was 40. I can remember clearly the day I took over. I realised that for the first time I had got a really responsible job.' Her children were by then 5, 13 and 16 and all at school. Four years later, Prime Minister Edward Heath nominated her for a Life Peerage. She was the first woman Deputy Chairman (Janet Young is firm about using Conservative Party nomenclature — chairman, not the admittedly odd 'chair' or chairperson, the English language itself does no justice to the female gender!). She even acted as Chairman of the Party when Lord Thorneycroft went into hospital. Despite the vast number of excellent women in the Party, there has yet to be a woman Chairman of the Conservative Party.

She says, 'Of all the political posts I've held, I enjoyed most being Leader of the House of Lords.' In that capacity Baroness Young was in Cabinet throughout the Falklands War. 'Clearly, to sit at the top table and hear the major policy decisions being talked about was extraordinarily interesting.' Edward Heath, a considerable admirer of Janet Young from his days as Party Leader and Prime Minister, describes her as 'firm and calm in the face of a crisis. Whenever I had to deal with her, she was always extremely balanced.'

Had she been received with masculine disrespect by Cabinet colleagues? 'Quite the opposite. I had real encouragement from colleagues.' After she had been moved out of her position as Leader of the House of Lords to make way for Willie Whitelaw, she became the first woman Minister at the Foreign Office and Deputy Foreign Secretary. 'It was a whole new world, I travelled to 60 different countries. There's absolutely no substitute for visiting other countries. I had never been a widely travelled person. On the whole women are not — they haven't the opportunities.'

Her most unforgettable trip was a gruelling 11 days to the Falklands in 1984. 'I had to pop in on Grenada first, after the American intervention. Then we flew straight on to New York. From New York we flew across the Atlantic to Senegal. From West Africa down to Ascension, and from there to the Falklands — hour upon hour, 13 hours in a Hercules bomber, too dark to read, too noisy to speak. And then, when the in-flight fuelling didn't work . . .'

Why does Janet Young think she is the only woman Mrs Thatcher promoted to Cabinet in her first decade as Prime Minister? 'Perhaps because I've been in national politics longer than most of the other women.' Several men however in the present Cabinet have had less experience in politics than some of the women MPs. 'That is very much a question for Mrs Thatcher, the reasons why she chooses to do things.'

Baroness Young reflects: 'I've certainly seen advances in my political life-time. When I was in local government in the late 1950s and the 1960s only about 12 per cent of the councillors were women. Today Conservative women are well represented in top jobs in local government — it's now over 20 per cent. At the parliamentary level, there has been an increase in women on the Conservative Party candidates' list.' She adds, 'Of course, we can do better, but it's an important advance.' Whenever there is speculation on the future leader of the Conservative Party, backbencher Julian Critchley states emphatically: "One thing is sure the post won't be held by a *woman!*" Baroness Young is dismissive of that theory. 'I think it's quite wrong to say there won't be another woman. Who would even have predicted 15 years ago that Mrs Thatcher would win three remarkable election victories?'

## BARONESS GARDNER OF PARKES

Australian by birth and a dentist by profession (and married to a dentist too), Baroness Gardner of Parkes is a 'working peer'. She is the second youngest of nine children and comes from a political family in Australia.'My father was the first of three brothers, all Labour Members of the New South Wales State Parliament. My father gave up politics before I was born so I have no memory of him as a politician at all. But his brother I do remember quite clearly as Premier of New South Wales.'

As Trixie Gardner she served on Westminster City Council and the Greater London Council and stood twice for Parliament, once in Blackburn against the Labour Cabinet Minister Barbara Castle, the second time in North Cornwall against Liberal MP John Pardoe. She was Vice-Chairman of the Conservative Women's National Advisory Committee. Since 1982 she has been UK representative on the United Nations Status of Women Commission.

Like Nancy Seear and Janet Young, Trixie Gardner's peerage was a political appointment for work done for her political party, and because it was considered she would be a useful working addition to the Conservative benches. 'You never do find out how you have been chosen, but I'm told about 200 people would be seriously considered and that would be whittled down to about 20. There were eight Conservatives chosen. I was in a list with three women, I don't think there have ever been so many Conservative women put in one list.'

Her path to the House of Lords had humble beginnings. 'I was sitting at home feeling I should be doing something for society. Our local MP came to the door to introduce himself and said he'd put me in touch with someone who would advise me how I could help the Conservatives. Eventually an old lady, well into her eighties, did contact me.' The doughty octogenarian asked Trixie Gardner to help cook lunches for an old people's day-centre. At first she was delighted with the idea. 'I had diplomas in cookery from Australia and Paris; I'd done three years cooking in Australia and a year in Paris. I thought this was a great idea.'

She discovered the cookery was more cuisine automatique than haute cuisine. 'It was those plastic boil-in-a-bags. You dropped 40 of them into a vat of water and then you fished them out after four minutes and cut them open with a pair of scissors. It was a pretty awful job. It really was to me an example of how you can misuse people's abilities or talents. I was terribly unsuited. I felt I would have been far more use to the Party out canvassing. There are a lot of women who will not go on the doorstep and yet I was good on the doorstep. I had an au pair at home helping with my washing up and there I was boiling these plastic bags and washing up 40 plates. It really was a terrible waste.' She stuck at it for 18 months.

After that, Trixie was invited to give a talk to the local Conservative women about Australia. It led to an invitation from the sturdy 80-year-old boil-in-a-bag woman to take on the Chairmanship of the local women's branch. 'Chairmanship of this local women's branch, that was really the whole turning point in my political career. I remember my husband Kevin asked what I had to lose, why not give it a try? I must have been about 30. A couple of years later the local Conservatives decided they wanted to review all the people who were on the council, some of them had been there for ever. A lot of the older people did give up. We all went through this vetting procedure and not only did I get selected, but I got a very good safe seat, so I did ten years on Westminster Council and the Greater London Council. Up to then, whatever progress I had wanted to make, I was told there was no hope. My political career was really a case of being constantly refused. When I applied to get on the parliamentary candidates list in 1966, I was refused. I was told I didn't have enough political experience. I learned subsequently the Vice-Chairman, Geoffrey Johnson Smith, who refused me was really one of the most tender-hearted men that there ever was in the Conservative Party. He had the reputation of refusing absolutely no-one. I must have gone in there looking as if I expected to be refused, which gave him the opportunity to feel he could refuse me and I would take it. There's a lesson there somewhere! Anyway, I went away for four years and did all the things they suggested. They said you could go into local government or you could go on voluntary organisations or you could do things within the community, widen your experience.'

Baroness Gardner is convinced she was not giving out the right 'I'm confident' signals. 'Now, whenever I give advice to people, I say you've got to really *not* adopt the attitude you're not worthy of being chosen. Because if people think you act like that, they follow it through. You'll get turned down. Also, people always try to discourage you and make out it's too difficult. You mustn't accept that, you must really carry on. Looking back, there were seats I could have been selected for where I was *not* selected, because I doubted my own ability. The men candidates definitely had the edge over me because they had a much greater degree of self-confidence. Looking back, no-one underestimated themselves more than I underestimate myself. It's a message I'd always give to women out to get into Parliament — do not underestimate yourself — because people will always tend to put you down rather than up, and if you do underestimate yourself, no-one's going to help you change that picture.

Things do work out. But one quality you require in politics is resilience, to spring back again and be ready to have the next go. Eventually something comes in life, eventually another door opens.'

She went back to insist on being given a chance to get on the candidates list. 'The man I had to see this time was Richard Sharples. He told me I was too late, all the candidates had been chosen for the 1970 Election. This time I wouldn't accept the brush-off. I said, "Well, I'll take a risk on that, but if I'm not on the approved list, then there's no hope at all of finding a seat, is there?"'

She passed the interview. Swiftly she was selected. The Conservatives, recognising a brave soul, asked her to fight Blackburn, Barbara Castle's seat. 'Nevertheless, I did very well there because by 1970, with the swing of the pendulum, things were coming our way.'

Trixie Gardner then took on the North Cornwall seat, against Liberal Member of Parliament, John Pardoe. The extreme distance from her job in London exhausted her money and time. Two elections later, her Conservative successor ousted John Pardoe and entered the House of Commons.

'Having stepped down from Cornwall, I was back in the political circus and getting interviews for quite good seats. Just about the stage when I was getting into the finals of very good parliamentary seats, I got a letter in a nice white envelope with 10 Downing Street on the back of it one Saturday morning. This said the Prime Minister was about to recommend a number of people to Her Majesty the Queen to be elevated to the peerage and that the Prime Minister wanted people who would take an active part in the House of Lords and speak and support the government. The final paragraph said, however, that the Prime Minister would quite understand if you didn't want to do this and not to hesitate to say so — I've always wondered if anyone says no.' Trixie Gardner said yes.

In one of those unexpected twists of destiny, Conservative stalwart Trixie Gardner believes she owes her peerage to anti-House of Lords campaigner, the former Labour Leader, Michael Foot. 'At the time, there was no need for the Conservatives to create any peers at all, they had plenty of peers. Michael Foot and the Labour Party had opposed making Life Peers. But they had lost a number of their peers to the SDP and through deaths, so they were just desperately short of anyone in the Upper

House. It was Michael Foot who asked to have peers created. This was really my good fortune because the Prime Minister said, "Yes, but I'll create Conservative peers also." One reason people like me were selected was because it was at a time when the government didn't want a by-election. There was no thought of moving anyone over from the House of Commons and they had to look further afield.'

Once she was ennobled, she had to choose a name for herself. 'Choosing a name can be a complicated business. If your name has been used by anyone else, you have to add something. The last Lord Gardner with my spelling had only been dead 97 years — if he'd been dead 100 years I could have had just plain Gardner.' She chose the title Baroness Gardner of Parkes. 'I was born in Parkes, Australia, as were my father and his three brothers. So I sign myself "Gardner of Parkes".

'On my first day at the Lords it was really quite funny; you come in to meet the Clerk of the Parliament and he gives you a little book of the rules, standing orders and so on. The book he gave me was quite unique, he was as surprised as I was when I opened it — it was printed upside down. He said that was particularly appropriate as it was the only one they'd ever printed for a peer from Down Under.'

What does an Australian think of the Upper Chamber? 'The House of Lords is a marvellous institution. You must always speak from direct personal experience. If you are a poseur, if you don't know your subject, it's a place that finds you out very quickly. There's always someone else here who knows all about whatever you're talking about. The greatest thing about it is people actually listen to what is said. There are quite a lot of cross-party bridges where people judge issues on their merit rather than always on a straight party-political line, though on most occasions people roll out of the library when the bell rings and they vote whatever way their party is going. But on really important issues, the Chamber will be packed with Members who listen to the debates. It's quite remarkable how they'll then say to you I'm not voting that way or I'm voting this way, and off they go.

'Working conditions in the Lords are really primitive. It's thoroughly uncomfortable. You can usually, but not always, find a space at a table in the library and there you write. There's a very good photocopying system so that's very useful, but there's no secretarial help provided at all, you're meant to make any arrangements yourself. I've bought myself a small lap-model computer because you can't type in the library, a typewriter would disturb others, but with this computer you can type your letters silently. I take it home and plug it into the printer and it prints everything.'

The first week she brought it to the House the introduction of new technology was such an attraction she wasn't able to do any work. 'All I had to do was open it and I had a host of Their Lordships all round me, saying "DO show me how that works"!'

# 12.
# NEAREST AND DEAREST

In a 300 Group course, aspiring women politicians made a list of everything they saw as an asset and everything they thought might be a liability to a career in politics. Husbands cropped up approximately 50/50 in the two lists. Family, friends, partners and spouses can form a support system — or a block.

## HUSBANDS

For Doreen Miller, her husband is crucial. 'Henry has been the most marvellous support ever. He's given me stability to allow myself to go out in the front and be creative. When you've got all these marvellous ideas, you need somebody there who can actually make it work, who can provide you with a steady background, but at the same time take your creativity and actually say to you, "Well, that way you can do it."

'In the seventies, when the business had been going six months, we had a party to celebrate. Henry introduced me. He said, "I feel ridiculous chairing this meeting. I'm the man *behind* the woman. I would like to start a club called 'Husbands Anonymous'." The press got hold of that story, and it went into William Hickey. The television cameras came round, and World at One, all wanting to interview Henry about "Husbands Anonymous". Of course, Henry being Henry would never give an interview because he'd never take anything away from me. He issued a statement which read: "The basic rule of Husbands Anonymous is husbands stay anonymous. Thank you, Gentlemen, but I can't give an interview."'

For Polly Toynbee, the situation was quite different. 'I did it in the teeth of my husband. He had exceptional and genuine reasons for not wanting me to do it, it was appallingly embarrassing for him. If you are a political correspondent, it is not at all helpful for your wife be a political candidate. It was a real cause of upset and he was much attacked for it. He used to get a lot of abusive letters and a lot of gossip columns would say he was a totally corrupt journalist because his wife was a candidate. We had a lot of rows about it and I thought about it very hard and decided in the end I really did want to do it and he would just have to live with it. After a while he just sort of settled down with it, but he used to flare up from time to time. I think it was also because I was in his patch, this was in his zone, and that's much more difficult again, not that I was being amazingly successful. Peter had no wish to be an MP ever — it was not any part of his make-up to ever wish to be a politician — he's not the type. Peter has always encouraged me to do anything and everything else and he has always wanted me to succeed. He was delighted when I got this job at the BBC.'

Teresa Gorman's husband was a great support to her endeavours to get into political life. 'I was married when I was 20. My husband was a friend of my brother's. He was around our household from the time more or less when I was a schoolgirl, so I've known him a long time. We run our business lives together as well. We are kind of completely moulded if you like. I'm the extrovert and the pushy one in the family, he's very much a background person, but he's very supportive. My husband was the only one encouraging me along. He helps me tremendously. He would do all the printing of the literature and the canvassing, plod around the streets shoving things through letter-boxes, long after my interest in doing that had expired.'

Joan Ruddock met her husband when she was still at school twenty-five years ago. Her relationship with her husband has been a crucial part of her political career. 'Keith's a Socialist and we've always shared a very strong interest in politics, but the most significant influence was the kind of security I acquired at such an early age which allowed me to be independent, allowed me to do so many of the things I wanted to do, with that emotional security always with me. There can't be any doubt that emotional stability is a major plus if you are going to be actively involved in politics. It's a role, of course, wives perform so often for successful men.'

Linda Siegle has only stood for Parliament once so far, yet she believes the cost of her political activities caused friction in the family. 'In the run up to the Election, they made me feel very guilty about spending money on my political activities. If I had been spending it on myself, they wouldn't have minded. In their eyes, I chucked the money down the drain. With three children, whatever level of income and standard of living you have, politics is expensive. I don't spend money on anything except politics, and clothes which I spend a fair bit of money on. I don't drink or smoke or have any other particularly expensive hobbies. My husband belongs to a golf club and I used to reckon I only spent as much on politics as he does on playing golf, so he can't complain. I should think the ideal political husband is extremely wealthy so you don't have to earn your living as well as be a politician. Probably Dennis Thatcher is the ultimate.'

'We've got about 40 videos of obscure and useless films that no-one in the family is allowed to record over, but the only tape I had, just of my own political things and Russian language broadcasts and things I wanted which no-one else was allowed to touch, got recorded over by the rest of the family because it never occurred to them those were important to me. So I've actually got nothing of myself on tape at all, from all the conferences and the interviews and the things I've done over the last five years. Nothing of myself, but all these useless Clint Eastwood films which they never watch. It just shows what's important, what isn't important to them. They were always very scathing about my politics. I had nothing to show for it, nothing to come home with. The best thing that ever happened to change their views of me was when I won the public speaking competition at the Women's Liberal Federation Conference and came home with a huge solid silver Georgian cup valued at over £700. For all the games and sports they're involved in, none of them had ever won a cup as big as that. They began to look at me a little differently then. To them that was real material evidence I was actually worth something.'

But Linda Siegle does appreciate husband John's support on occasions such as the time she arrived for the final selection meeting for Devizes constituency. 'There were six men candidates and me. We arrived before the hustings. Final selection meetings are always in these great big intimidating halls — I walked in the door ahead of John. The constituency secretary came up and looked straight past me at my husband. Then she looked at me and said, "And who's wife are you?"

'Considering she was expecting at least one woman candidate, and she had had the photographs of everybody, it was a particularly unnecessary thing to do. I shall be for ever grateful to John.

He just put his hand on my shoulder, and said, "Oh well, I'm the wife in this case." That was very sweet.'

## CHILDREN

Apart from a widespread lack of confidence, the maternal triangle is the crucial feature holding women back from standing for elected office. It is very difficult, almost impossible, to take an active role in politics if women have children, unless they and the family are able to work out a reliable support system. Political parties have not yet seriously addressed these extra impediments facing their women activists.

Most politically active working mothers spend lives skidding from corner to corner of the maternal triangle: work, politics and family life. Yet there are very significant personal advantages if people in politics can combine the family experience with political stress and strain. Rosie Barnes has three children, Daniel, Daisy and Joseph. They were between 2 and 14 when she won the Greenwich by-election in 1987. Rosie lives near enough to the House of Commons to be able to pop home across the river to South East London in the evening. 'I get home and get settled with the children. I listen to what's happened in their day. Children put a great perspective on politics. Through all the miseries of the SDP-Liberal merger debate, for example, I saw MPs who hadn't got the same family ties as I had being torn to pieces by it. Having children and a family to go home to, and living close to them, puts a very good perspective on life. Children jerk you back into a sense of reality. It puts it in perspective, that life does go on, there is life outside politics. It gave me a sense of proportion, I feel, that made me able to survive. You feel the world's coming to an end because the parties are at each other's throats, throwing away something you've built up and worked for and believed in. You feel desperate. You go home and find your daughter's fallen out with her best friend and she's distraught, your son's throwing his French book around the room because he can't do his homework, and the little one's fallen over on to his Lego and hurt his legs and they're all every bit as upset about what's happened to them as you are over what's happened to you.'

Angela Browning got terrific support from her family. 'My son went with the Young Conservatives and spent all election day in committee rooms and the telling and polling stations. He worked liked a trooper. I'd even told him, "Philip, for goodness sake, do remember that when you fall out with a girlfriend in this constituency I don't just lose her vote, I lose her mum's and dad's vote as well!" The next day with all the weeping and Oh-dear-we've-lost-we've-got-to-pack-up-and-go-home, I put my arm around him and told him that at least we'd be able to be a normal family. "You won't have a mother who's charging off and leaving you to cope with the fridge." And he said, "Mum, this is our way of life, you in politics is what we're used to!" '

Shirley Williams' marriage was dissolved in 1974 and she looked after her daughter Rebecca on her own as an MP and a Cabinet Minister. 'I had a marvellous daily help, a wonderful Irish woman who used to come in. She used to come in when I left for work and if necessary she would stay. She was married, lived fairly close to me. Her husband worked on the Underground and he was often on late shifts. If I was stuck I'd ring her and say I can't get away from the House of Commons until 10 o'clock tonight and she'd say OK I'll stay around.'

Linda Siegle says: 'What annoys me most of all is that in other people's perception, the message comes across to me I'm not allowed to be a good mother and a good politician, I have to choose. But men are allowed to be, in other people's eyes, at least a good father and a good politician. Nobody says Douglas Hurd is a bad father to his children because he isn't there most of the time. Although he's a lot older than me, he's still got a small family and everybody says how delightful and wonderful. I've had people imply you have to be one thing or the other, a successful politician or a good mother, there's no question about the fact you can certainly be both.

'John really is very good when he comes with me, but he doesn't like leaving the children with baby-sitters. Quite often I have to go out to somewhere where I'd prefer him to come with me, but because he doesn't want to get a baby-sitter, he'd rather stay at home with them. That puts psychological pressure on me. There's an enormous guilt about the whole thing, every time I do it, I feel guilty, because I know I'm doing something else that's important to me. It's made worse because if I gave all my energy to bringing up my children and looking after my house and cooking and doing all the things they'd like me to do, I know without doubt that's the role they like me in best.'

However, women MPs with families often pointed out the pluses of mixing family life and politics. Like Rosie Barnes and

Edwina Currie, they find it extremely helpful to have children when political life gets tough. They can hurriedly retreat into the family nest. Edwina Currie says, 'I like being married. It's like having a house, it's a home, it's there, I exploit it dreadfully. During the whole of the last parliament, from 1983 to 1987, I was the only woman MP with young children and a seat away from London which meant I had to make arrangements during the week. There wasn't anybody in the House to go and share my troubles with or to whom I could give advice because there was no-one in the same boat. Virginia Bottomley was the only one who also had young children, but she could get home every day to Surrey. Anna McCurley has a daughter who was 12 when she came to the House. Anna didn't resolve the problems because her marriage broke up. Most of the others had older children or were older women. During the salmonella crisis,' Edwina recalls, 'any negative feelings got dissipated over a very nice Christmas holiday which was super. I love my kids. My daughters are growing up. They're at an interesting age. Debbie's doing GCSEs this summer. I like them and I'd hardly see anything of them. The last summer holidays were disrupted by the fact I had to come down here to London for the nurses' pay dispute, which did not put me in a good humour when I went back again.'

Zerbanoo Gifford said, 'On the local council, I made a big issue of my family life. It is very important to me. Richard and our boys Mark and Wags are the most important things in my life. They are my support system. I wouldn't have survived the rigours of political life without them. Richard also provides the humour and diffuses the situation. There is no set time for politics, you always have to be there to help people with their problems. I was a mother and I was always there when they came home. When I was a councillor, I had to go to evening meetings. I would help the boys with their homework and put them to bed, have supper with Richard and then go to my council meetings. I was out three or four evenings a week. There were a few occasions when we had afternoon meetings. I remember one when we discussed the closure of Harrow's only outdoor swimming pool, which was being sold for housing. I had to take the boys with me and they were fascinated. They sat quietly and listened. Even at their age they're already aware that politics is about getting things done and changing the world.

Clare Short put the other side of the argument. 'It would have made it very much more difficult for me to be an MP with children. Quite likely it wouldn't have been worth it. There are a highly disproportionate number of women in the House without children. You can do it. But for the women whose children are out of London, it's the hardest. People like Joan Walley and Ann Taylor have got small children out of London and I know they miss them and that thing when they first tie their shoelaces. I don't know if I could bear that. Is it worth it? Because it's a pretty funny old job.'

# 13.
# GOING NATIVE IN BRUSSELS

'Remember the folks who gave us CAP!' joked the *Economist* in a feature on the Single European Act of 1992. Smoked salmon and caviar everyday, washed down by a limitless flow of the best French clarets, German Hocks, and Italian Chiantis is the image most of us have of the life of a Euro-MP. And yes, they *do* have plenty of multi-cultural parties and receptions in Brussels and Strasbourg; the European Parliament can be seen as an amazing cross-cultural experiment. Once away from their own shores, working alongside Euro-colleagues, allegiances and beliefs switch from narrow nationalistic party lines to 'the European Ideal'. British Members of the European Parliament are often described — correctly — as 'going native'. If you love long hours hanging around airports interrupted by unending committee meetings, and you enjoy eating dinners late into the night discussing politics, the European Parliament is the place for you. It certainly seems much more 'woman friendly' in ambiance than the Palace of Westminster.

There is a higher proportion of women in the European Parliament than at Westminster. Some women like Winnie Ewing, Dame Shelagh Roberts and Margaret Daly and Carole Tongue have chosen to devote their energies to Europe's others like Ann Clwyd and Joyce Quin have made the Euro-route a pathway to our own House of Commons.

Euro-MP Joyce Quin says: 'I was only 34 when I got into the European Parliament and therefore probably looked much less like a Member than I do now, but no, I never really felt any discrimination of any subtle or unsubtle form. The European Parliament has got a freshness about it, it's got an international atmosphere and it's less bound by tradition. It's also rather a magnificent communication effort; all these people trying to make a system work and in many cases, surprisingly, trying to see each other's point of view, and I liked that.'

ANN CLWYD

'When they knew I was coming to the House of Commons (Ann is now MP for Cynon Valley) Euro-MPs from other countries, particularly the Germans, used to joke and say, "Why are you leaving this place and going to the parish council?" Here in Britain Members of the European Parliament are looked on as being inferior to being a Member of Parliament. But it shouldn't be looked at in that way. I see the European Community developing so that being a Euro-MP is much more important than being a Member of Westminster.'

Fighting a Euro-election is a different ball game from fighting a Westminster seat. For Europe you're fighting apathy and the logistics of Big Mac, American-size constituencies; it takes eight Westminster constituencies to make up one Euro-seat. 'I was selected for the seat and all the press said in the run up to the election, the Tories are going to win, because it was a Tory seat. Not one commentator predicted a Labour win in the seat, so it was a particular delight to prove them wrong. The morning after I was elected we just went round and thanked people. Imagine doing that in eight constituencies — my size Euro-constituency (about the second or third largest in the UK in land area) covers a huge portion of Wales.

'I can remember arriving and going into the Socialist group in Luxembourg and seeing all the names, particularly the German names which were very long. I thought I'm never going to be able to pronounce their surnames, names like Heidi Wieczorek-Zeul and Ludwig Fellermaier. I *was* anti-membership of the EEC. It took quite a bit to imbibe the atmosphere of an international grouping, but I became a complete convert to the idea of working with people of other nationalities. After two years there I wrote a piece for the *New Statesman* on how I had changed my mind on the EEC. I liked working with other nationalities because of their differing experiences. The things they could teach us about how pensioners were treated in their countries compared to ours. The trades union laws, for example, in Germany where trades unions have had certain rights and benefits from the beginning of the century, whereas we in Britain have had to fight for over fifty years to get those basic rights. It was much more relaxed and more informal there, you didn't have the protocol and the various ceremonies that go on, the traditions that are part and parcel of life in the House of Commons. It is a much better working environment. Everybody has an individual office and very generous office expenses. In fact much more generous office expenses than you have here at the Commons where the need is greater.

'In the European Parliament, you can make a lot of noise about various issues: steel was a very important part of my Euro-constituency, and farming. The whole restructuring of the steel industry took place in 1981 when I was a Euro-MP — a drastic change for which there was really no planning in Britain and no provision for the social consequences. Yet in other countries, they'd planned for change. I visited the Ruhr to see a big steel works where 5,000 men were losing their jobs. Everybody who wanted a job had another job to go to. That simply wasn't true in my Welsh constituency, where thousands were losing their jobs and there weren't alternatives. There were moments like that where it was possible to get workers together from different countries to discuss mutual interests and sometimes to co-operate. Members in a factory in my constituency were about to lose their jobs making fans for cars, the manufacture of those fans had been transferred to a town in the Netherlands. I got the two groups of workers together and the workers in the Netherlands said they would refuse to take the jobs away from the Welsh workers. That is an example of the kind of co-operation that ideally you could get at the European community level.'

## JOYCE QUIN

Joyce Quin was elected a Labour Party Member of the European Parliament, for Tyne and Wear, in 1979. In June 1987 she was elected Member of Parliament for Gateshead East. For a year she held the dual mandate, until June 1989 when she retired from the European seat. 'It's a huge task fighting a Euro-seat. Someone did a calculation, that if a Euro-MP went round walking up garden paths and knocking on front doors, it would take them all day, every day for nine years to get round the constituency.'

The UK has yet to come to grips with how elections should be fought when a candidate is trying to reach half a million voters. As Joyce Quin says, 'There was a tremendous atmosphere of intense apathy and no-one wanted to know. It's very difficult fighting a Euro-election. It's like banging your head against a brick wall all day, every day, for three weeks. It seemed to be particularly difficult among Labour supporters who certainly at that stage were not at all keen on Europe and didn't know what the European Parliament was about, as in fact I think most people didn't. We didn't really have enough money for our election leaflet. I had donations from constituency parties and trades unions to fight the election, but we were very short of funds. It was a very meagre budget. We had to be careful even about things like lapel stickers and the basic bit of razzmatazz of elections which are very useful to spread about to try and create a presence.

'The '79 campaign was much less well run than the '84 campaign. We learnt quite a bit. We organised things better so we were pretty sure most of the leaflets had gone out, which I don't think a lot of them did in 1979. In '79 my majority was only 7,000 which is very little in the Euro-seat. By '84 it went up to 49,000.'

'I was probably one of very few Euro-MPs to whom Strasbourg was not unfamiliar because I had gone there regularly when I was working at Transport House with the Labour MPs who were delegates to the Council of Europe. I knew what the building looked like and I also knew what to expect in the way a continental parliament is organised — the system of committees, the system of rapporteurs where somebody gets a report to write on behalf of the committee, and the way that's amended and then presented to the full Parliament. I didn't have the feeling of strangeness perhaps many people had. And because I had lectured in French I didn't have any language problems.

'The problem with the European Parliament has been we've had these two meeting places, Strasbourg and Brussels. Luxembourg is only the home of the officials, parliamentarians in practice hardly ever go there. I've probably been there four times in the last nine years. We alternate between Brussels and Strasbourg. It's not really very feasible to have a flat in both places and in England. You can imagine having a home and two flats, even the difficulties of trying to cope with the gas man when he came . . .! While I had my dual mandate, as a Euro-MP and a Westminster MP, I had my main office with my secretary and researcher in the constituency in Gateshead which doubled as a Westminster and a Euro-office. One full week, Monday to Friday, each month is spent in Strasbourg where the whole Parliament collects together. The other three weeks are in Brussels for committee meetings and political group meetings. The

Brussels' weeks would typically be three days in Brussels — perhaps Tuesday to Thursday or Wednesday to Friday — and a day or possibly two days at home in the Euro-constituency, meeting people who wanted to meet you to talk about different aspects of European policies or visits to schools, Women's Institutes, Rotary Clubs, anybody who wanted to hear their Euro-MP speak.

'In the European Parliament, you get a daily allowance when you're actually over there. It certainly covers your needs and you get money for travelling and so on. So you're not having to pay for travel or daily subsistence from your salary. I certainly found it very easy to cope.

'As a Euro-MP my job was to go and represent a specific area over there and try and get the best deal in all negotiations. The main issues are how European rules and regulations affected the constituency. When I went to Strasbourg in 1979, I had a third of Britain's shipyard workers living in my constituency, so shipbuilding was a huge issue and was very much affected by the amount of state aid allowed to be given by each country to their shipbuilding industry under European rules. I've learned all kinds of things which I had no idea about before. I represented a fishing port in North Shields at the time the European fishing policy was being negotiated. At first I didn't know the difference between a pelagic or a demersal fish. But I soon could say "Hold on! You haven't taken into account the type of fishing we do in the North East of England!"

'Women's rights was another issue that interested me in the European Parliament. There's a very good body of legislation relating to women: equal pay, equal treatment at work, equal treatment in areas of occupational and state social security. As a woman member I was very interested in how these regulations were working in practice. I was keen to take up cases where the rules were not being respected and where women could gain redress through the European Court.

'I don't know whether I'd call it fun, but there's a lot of enjoyable social contact with people from other political parties and other countries and that can be fascinating because it can give you a real insight into other people's political concerns, what makes them tick, and the different interests that have somehow got to be accommodated within a complicated structure like the EEC.

'I found MEPs relax mainly by eating. We usually finished at

8.30 in the evening, having started the day at 9 in the morning. It's quite a long day during the Strasbourg and Brussels sessions. After 8.30 in the evening, there's really only time to go out and relax over a meal. Politicians being as obsessive as we are, we still discussed political matters even when eating. I had friends at home who badgered me into seeing them to make sure I just didn't cut myself off and work all the time. I've also always had a lot of outside interests which frustratingly I don't have much time to pursue. I like walking a lot, cycling and I act as a Newcastle City Guide taking people around the old buildings. I like to take at least half-a-dozen tours each August. I did that before I came into politics. It's a voluntary thing. The guides are people like myself who love Newcastle and are very much bound up with the history of it. I'm learning to play the Northumbrian pipes too.

'Being an MEP was definitely worth it. What I didn't enjoy was the constant travelling. The travelling is very unglamorous, hanging around in airports, particularly if you haven't got a direct air journey. It could take sometimes as much as six or seven hours, a lot of that just waiting around between planes. That'll get better as the European Parliament concentrates more of its activities in Brussels, which it looks likely to do.

'I left the European Parliament for Westminster because I wanted a change after ten years. One of the MPs in my Euro-constituency, the MP for Gateshead East, was retiring. I thought I'd have a change and try for the Commons.'

## CAROLE TONGUE

Carole Tongue, Labour MEP for London East, says she is 'a Socialist, a European, and a feminist. All of that stems from my family. My family's European, my mother reinforced my feminism as a one-parent family. She was a part-time poorly paid woman worker, a part-time physiotherapist, who struggled and is still struggling, all her working life, to get proper wages, proper recognition, a fair deal in the labour market.'

Twenty-eight-year-old Carole Tongue was the youngest woman elected from the UK to the European Parliament when she went to Brussels in 1984. 'I'm a member of the Committee on the Environment, Public Health and Consumer Protection, a member of the Women's Rights Committee and substitute member of the Economic Monetary and Industrial Affairs

Committee. My constituency in East London has manufacturing industry. With the enormous changes happening within the European economy, it was important I was in that committee where decisions were being taken affecting the working lives of a lot of people I represent, plus the fact that there's hardly a woman in that committee. I felt it was crucial the women's perspective was brought in.

'I prefer being here in the European Parliament to the House of Commons. It's where my skills, my experience, my heart and my gut is. The EEC has been much more progressive on equal rights for women than the UK government — whichever Party is in power. Way back in 1957, Article 119 of the Treaty of Rome called on all countries to implement equal pay for equal work for all women and men in the Community. What's wonderful about being in the European Parliament is the number of women here. We have a marvellous sisterly solidarity which cuts across nationalities and cuts across parties. I've been in a situation where we've been four or five women round a table, all different nationalities, all different parties, and we've really bucked each other up by exchanging anecdotes, offering support and solidarity, and showing an understanding of the problems. Women of all parties in the European Parliament have been very involved in discussions on equal pay, maternity rights, childcare and parental leave. It's one area where the Conservative women in Euro terms have "gone native". The directive on parental leave was originally proposed by two Conservative MEPs, Gloria (now Baroness) Hooper and Dame Shelagh Roberts, but it was blocked by the UK Government.

MEPs are on the run all the time. 'Because of all the travel, I do most of my reading on the trains and planes. I rely on briefings from non-governmental organisations and from industry and the trades union movement. I had to be in Strasbourg last week. I arrived in Strasbourg at 2.30 pm having caught a plane from Heathrow on Monday mid-day. I had three-quarters of an hour to gather my thoughts and papers together and speak with my assistant. Then I went straight into a meeting of the Socialist Group where we discussed the day's agenda. From there I went into the meeting of the Economic and Monetary Committee to negotiate on how we would approach a vote within the new procedure and the single European Act, the new constitutional set-up where the Parliament has more power. This actually requires agreements between political groups, so it involves more work. The next day I spoke in a debate on economics — public works contracts. I went through more meetings I can't even remember. I met up with the management of Plessey who'd come to talk to me about the bid by GEC/Siemens.

'Then in the evening we had a night debate where I was speaking for the Socialist Group on the law on package tours. As the next debate came on I spoke to my own rapporteur on animal experimentation — it was 10.30 at night, I nearly sent all the animals off on package tours at this point.

'I then had the BBC and LBC outside the door who wanted to interview me on both subjects, plus what had happened in the whole Plessey set-up. I finally left the Chamber at about quarter past midnight and had a drink with Mary Benotti, the Irish Fiana Gael MEP. We collapsed in a bar in the Holiday Inn and had a Perrier. We thought that was all we could stomach if we were going to wake up and start the next day — the following day was going to be *particularly* heavy!'

The debates in the European Parliament take place in one great semi-circular chamber known as 'The Hemicycle'. Each speaker is limited to five minutes. 'You've got to be very, very disciplined. I've taken a number of years to get to this point. I jot down the three or four points I want to get across. I make a general political speech without attempting to go right into the detail. The detail is there in the report, I don't need to repeat it.

'Our main difficulty is how to find time to relax. I learned the hard way you've actually got to carve out that personal space. There's a danger of becoming a sheer political automaton in doing your work, Monday to Friday, often at ridiculous hours, and then accepting invitations to do major conferences on a Saturday, constituency engagements on a Sunday. This means there's absolutely no time for anything else in your life. People tell me I'm a very giving person. I invest a lot of energy — emotional, intellectual and physical — in what I do. At first I hadn't realised you have to ration the giving of those energies. I gave too much and wore myself down.

'After a couple of years, I realised I was coming very close to mental and physical exhaustion. There were days I couldn't bear to go in the office and see my diary plan up on the wall. I was booked from January to July and you could hardly see a free lunch or a free evening. I'd sit down and I'd think, I haven't got the energy to go to this meeting and get up in front of all these people. I realised as I had not come up through the more conventional routes, I was trying too hard to establish my credibility, to show I could do the job, that I was capable of winning the respect of my peers and of people throughout the Labour movement. I've realised that and I'm trying to put that right. It's a question of carving out time. In the last year I've taken on fewer weekend meetings. I joined a badminton club on a Friday. I decided I actually need Saturday to go and mend my shoes, take my glasses to the optician, say hello to my friends in the local florist and actually visit my family. On Sunday mornings I decided it was about time I went back to my love of horse riding, so I found the nearest stables and decided that was a priority. It helps to clear the cobwebs from the brain, a bit of fresh air in a nice open country environment is absolutely invaluable. I don't think you can do your work properly unless you find a way of clearing everything out of your mind — that's the theory. But next month for example, I'm working three Saturdays on the trot.'

Carole was born in Switzerland where her father still lives. 'There are a number of different nationalities in my family as a result of re-marriage, it's quite a complicated set-up. When I told Barbara Castle the story of my family she said, "Carole, now I understand why you're such a European." At a very young age my parents split up and I came back to Britain with my mother, so I spent all my childhood in Britain, though I had a family which was essentially European. I was always very interested in politics. I grew up in a family with a very long socialist tradition, I'd been involved at university in student politics with a relatively short membership of the Labour Party. The Labour Party was my natural home, but I was unsure about their anti-EEC stance. I was saying things about the Community which could have been considered to be a little heretical. My message was "We've got to be in on the inside in the Community, paddling it in our direction."'

When Carole Tongue went to college she had already worked out what direction she wanted to take in life. 'I went to Loughborough to read Politics and Languages because that was in my blood already. I wanted to improve my languages and I knew I wanted a career in politics and in the public service. I wanted to improve my experience in both areas and then bring them to bear in a way that would improve the living and working conditions, particularly of women, but of people in general. I speak French and German. I can also get by in Italian and Spanish.

I'm lucky, I have an aptitude for learning languages — I consider it's one of the most important parts of my job. If I'm to succeed on behalf of the people I represent, on behalf of my party and on behalf of my ideas and what I feel I want to change, then clearly it's an advantage to be able to speak other people's languages. If I'm to sell my ideas and to sell what I want, I've got to be able to speak at different levels in other languages.'

After a brief spell as a courier in France, she won a scholarship in 1979 through the European Parliament to do research. 'It confirmed to me I wanted to work in a multi-national arena and I looked around for a job I could marry with my politics. I wanted to work with Socialists. The only job available doing that within the European Parliament was with the Socialist Group as a secretary. I took it even though strictly speaking the job was below my qualifications.'

Carole was originally based in Luxembourg and then a year later, when the Parliament and the political groups decided to move their secretariats, she moved to Brussels. 'I built up a fantastic network of contacts and a lot of things I didn't realise were experience and knowledge and skills. That would be a message very much to women, we invariably undervalue what we know and what we can do.

'In 1983, in a discussion with a number of journalists, I was displaying some anger and frustration at the Labour Party's views and policy in general towards the European Community. I said, based on my knowledge and experience, I'd like to put some input of my own into the European Election campaign due to take off in 1984.

'There was a chorus of agreement from the journalists, all men. They said, "Don't just stand there — stand!"'

Carole Tongue won her seat with a Hollywood script swing which reversed the Conservative majority. 'I went from a secretary to an MEP in one month. It was a major inspiration to the women staff and their aspirations in Europe.' Then she was off on the flight to Europe, this time not as a secretary returning home, but as a Member of the European Parliament representing around half a million voters of East London.

After several years in the European Parliament, Carole Tongue has learned from seasoned professionals like Barbara Castle how to handle the gruelling schedule. 'I have an intense admiration for Barbara. We were on a German language course together. I started German at 12, Barbara started it when she was in her early seventies and I think that's absolutely amazing. Barbara's good at knowing how to relax. She has her dogs and she lives in the country and she does some gardening and she takes her dogs out round the country and relaxes with them. She's remarkable, an absolute dynamo. I think she's learned various tricks of the trade, the idea of sweeping the big pile of paper to one side, going straight to the political nub of a problem and simplifying what we're doing. In this job you get so many piles of paper and so many subjects.'

# 14.
# WOMEN IN LOCAL GOVERNMENT

Local government elections are traditionally held on the first Thursday in May. Springtime is the season when thousands of women and men up and down Britain spend frantic hours knocking on doors, putting leaflets in letter-boxes, getting to talk to as many voters as possible.

Being a local councillor can be a route to Parliament, as it was for over half the MPs currently in Parliament. Gillian Shephard, Janet Fookes, Teresa Gorman, Dawn Primarolo, Edwina Currie, Angela Rumbold, Jo Richardson, Ray Michie: they are all current Members of Parliament who started their political careers in local government. In fact, about 50 per cent of the male MPs and 60 per cent of the female MPs were on local councils before entering Parliament. For many thousands more, being on the council is a political job in its own right.

About one-fifth of all councillors are women, though this varies sharply according to where you live: Wales has a mere one in twenty, a dramatic contrast with the South East of England where more than one in three local councillors is a woman. Often political parties find it hard to get enough council candidates, not least because the job is always unpaid. In the new friendly climate for women at all levels of political life, women candidates are especially welcomed.

Certainly, leaders of local councils, and to some extent the chairs of council committees, have more power to generate action — and see the results of their work — than back-bench Members of Parliament. At the very top of the list of job-satisfaction, councillors put the ability and power to 'get things to happen here'. Far from worrying or being overwhelmed, they find having large budgets to handle is a great experience.

Like standing for Parliament, you need no formal qualifications to become a councillor, not even one O level or GCSE.

You must be over 21 on the day your nomination papers are sent in, and you must be on the voter list in the county, district or parish you want to stand in. To develop as a councillor you need a deep commitment to your community, plus energy and a good amount of available time. Actually, to stand for council takes very little out-of-pocket cash. And once elected, councillors find the work all-absorbing, time-consuming and very stimulating. Your work has a direct and often immediate effect on your community.

## JEAN VERNON-JACKSON: COUNTY COUNCIL POLITICS

Councillor Jean Vernon-Jackson has just passed on the Mayor's job in the *Howards Way* sailing resort of Lymington, in Hampshire, after a two-year stint. She says, 'The biggest cost for anyone active in local politics is nothing to do with money. It's time and energy and it's YOU.' She should know. She has clocked up a lot of experience since she first co-opted onto the Town Council in 1983. She is now a Town, District and County Councillor. 'I was persuaded to stand for the County Council. I said yes because I honestly didn't feel the existing councillors were doing enough. It wasn't likely to be easy because it had been a Tory seat for as far back as anyone could remember.' She won by under 100 votes.

Originally a nursing sister, Jean Vernon-Jackson had been at home bringing up three children and looking after her elderly mother until well into her fifties. Her mother died and the children had grown up. She herself was divorced. Jean Vernon-Jackson is elected as a Liberal Democrat but like many women on councils outside major cities she doesn't see her work in terms of party politics: 'I have never seen myself as a political animal. The community comes first. I like to think I'm doing it because of my Christian belief. I did quite a lot of work in the Mothers' Union, on the Committee for Social Concern, looking at laws and how they affect people. I got tired of giving evidence and not having any direct contact with people, to try to improve things for them. As a councillor you are actually up against things with people, and with luck I can change these things.

'What I enjoy most is the case work — not a *shadow* of a doubt. It's incredible what you're asked to do: marriage-guidance councillor, financial adviser, honorary granny, you name it. I suppose what people are after is a sympathetic listening ear. You remember the things you've actually succeeded in doing, probably for the rest of your life. I'm pleased I helped a local woman get a vehicle so she could be mobile. She's a paraplegic, with three children under the age of 4. A charity assessed her and said they'd offer £1,000 towards a vehicle, but that was still £800 short, and she was really desperate. I wrote a dozen or so letters to every local, and some national, charities, told the County Council, and we made it, all £800 needed. She's now living as near a normal and varied life as she possibly can, and I'm very pleased about it.'

When Jean Vernon-Jackson was persuaded to stand for the Council in 1986 she decided if she was going to fight a campaign she would do it properly. For two months she used every spare minute to knock on thousands of doors to introduce herself, visit schools and homes for the elderly. 'The main cost,' she recalls, 'was in tiredness!' She visited almost all the 7,000 households in her division. Her constituency party raised funds for leaflets and posters. Apart from some extra Damart underwear to keep her warm — required clothing for any intrepid political campaigner — she didn't buy new clothes. 'I wear jumpers and skirts and comfortable shoes. I didn't have to look like Joan Collins, and I didn't!'

Nevertheless, once elected, she did go and buy a decent typewriter and a filing cabinet to help cope with a cascade of paper. You can sink beneath an unending flow of reports and mail from Council offices and constituents. 'Being a councillor can pull you into all sorts of satellite activities,' she points out. 'I take every opportunity to go to Council training sessions on everything from information technology to planning, housing and environmental services.' More of her time is spent giving talks to schools and women's groups. 'One thing spawns another,' she says. 'I'm also a school governor for five schools and colleges. I go to school fetes, school concerts, school football matches. I'm chairman of the Lymington County Junior School and I really love it when tiny children in the street say "Hello Mrs Um Um" to me, when they recognise me.'

It is extraordinary that councillors are not paid a salary. The hours can be long, and councillors may have very wide responsibilities. At county council level, members are chairing committees with annual budgets many times larger than the entire *national* budgets of many small countries; the Education budget in Hampshire alone is around £500,000,000 a year, ten times the entire national budget of the Gambia in West Africa. Town councillors and parish councillors receive no attendance allowance at all, though district and county councillors can claim modest attendance allowances and some travel expenses. The standard attendance allowance for district and county council meetings is £19.50 (less tax) per 24 hour day plus £4 per day to cover meals if the sitting lasts more than four hours. There is a mileage allowance according to the size of your car. Councillor Vernon-Jackson's telephone rental is paid by the Council, but not the phone-bill itself. As Mayor she could claim up to £1,425 a year for official entertaining and staff tips.

Perhaps one day the country will see sense and offer a decent salary to people who are prepared to offer their earnings and abilities to help run our parishes and boroughs and towns and counties. Three years ago a report by top QC David Widdicombe recommended councillors' allowances should be abolished and replaced by a salary, with extra pay for chairs of committees. Any such development would directly help many thousands more women to put themselves forward for elected office. All too often women find it particularly hard to allocate the money, even if they can allocate the time.

## SHIRLEY PORTER AND FRANCES MORRELL: POLITICS IN THE METROPOLIS

Council work in the great metropolises is a very different game from a town council in a genteel south coast resort, or the shire councils. After the Prime Minister, two women have probably wielded more real political power than any other women in Britain. The first is Frances Morrell who, as Leader of the Inner London Authority, was responsible for a budget of a thousand million pounds. And the second is Shirley Porter, who has been Leader of Westminster City Council since 1983. Shirley Porter is a Conservative — 'an economic Thatcherite. What I think I am really, is somebody who thinks we should turn this into Great Britain plc.' Frances Morrell, on the other hand, is staunch Labour. Their political views may be in opposition, but Shirley Porter and Frances Morrell share the distinction of having been the focus of some of the roughest, toughest, 'politicking' imaginable.

Possibly these two women would get on well together if they were to have a coffee somewhere away from the public eye. Both know what it's like to be strong and controversial personalities who arouse violent pro- and anti-emotions in people. Shirley Porter avers: 'If you make waves, you make enemies, but you cannot really have an effect upon events and have everybody love you. It's not pleasant, but it's one of the decisions you have to take.'

Both women are very anti-pomposity and can be very funny. For instance, as a journalist-guest at a Labour Party conference in Bournemouth, I watched Frances Morrell star alongside Glenys Kinnock and Harriet Harman in a hilarious 'end-of-the-pier' feminist lampoon of Neil Kinnock, Ken Livingstone, Arthur Scargill and the Labour male hierarchy. Frances Morrell had, in fact, written most of the skit herself. Shirley Porter once turned up on an official visit to a school dressed as an American Indian.

Both women had parents humble origins, but their formative years couldn't have been more different. Paradoxically, although Frances Morrell's parents remained poor, she went on to have an excellent education; Shirley Porter's father made a vast fortune, but her education was distinctly lacking. She went to an expensive Sussex boarding school; she was so bitterly unhappy that she had dropped out of formal education altogether by the time she was 16.

There's usually nothing new when politicians boast they're going 'to clean up the city'. In most American movies that's what every celluloid politician sets out to do. Those tough guys didn't mean they wanted, *literally*, to leave litter bins and loos as a monument to their years of hard work. Shirley Porter did.

Shirley Porter is proud of her legacy as Westminster City's boss — hundreds of white and green designer litter-bins, each sponsored by a local business, plus the rather modern 'Porter-loo' with their menacing air, standing strategically placed on pavements from Parliament Square to Paddington. 'I believe you should highlight things, not hide them. I had to fight to get the first sponsored litter-bin. They wanted planning permission for every single litter-bin! It was a fight to the end. Now everybody talks about sponsored litter-bins as if it's all accepted wisdom.'

Lady Porter was born Shirley Cohen in the East End of London. Her father, Sir Jack Cohen, started out with a stall in Petticoat Lane and built the Tesco Supermarket chain. Her husband Leslie, now Sir Leslie Porter, in his turn became Chairman.

'I suspect that I am what I am, and do what I do, for several reasons. I was the youngest of two daughters and I've no doubt my father would have liked to have had a boy. I was a home-loving child who because of the war went to boarding school and loathed it. I used to sit there very quietly, thinking I was doing nothing, but I was always picked on for being the leader. You can't tell what you're like yourself, I thought I was quiet and mouse-like, and they thought I was a pain who was always leading people astray. Apparently there are certain children who have this unsettling effect and I was one of them. I was expelled from my House when I was 11, they went through this Dreyfus-type operation where they cut your colours off. I stood outside waiting for this to happen, saying to HELL with them all. I was shouting away outside as they were getting prepared to do it — I would never knuckle down, never.

'As school I encountered anti-semitism and a lot of teasing. It was a very nasty atmosphere. I think it was because our name was Cohen. Boys bully, girls tease and sometimes, to this day, when we're in the council chamber, it's recreated, that feeling, and I feel the unfairness of it all. So I spent the early formative years saying, "I'll get my own back, I'll show you."'

When Shirley Cohen left school, she did shorthand and typing, and then got married. 'I was married at 18, had a daughter at 20, a son at 22, lots of courses, Women's Institute, City Lits. I was always involved in charities, played golf for the county — for Hertfordshire — always running committees and then the Workers' Educational Association — wonderful courses in philosophy. I've always loved history, literature and music, poetry, that kind of stuff, what the hell I'm doing in this, I don't know.'

Shirley Porter is a top-class golfer, a single-figure player. Golf led to her first political action. 'The first thing I ever did that was public-minded was getting involved in fighting anti-semitism in golf clubs. I stood up at some public AGM and said how disgraceful it was. My daughter got married very young, so I discovered I had to do something with my life. Having been a prisoners' wives visitor, I became a magistrate. I already had a reputation as a doer.'

Shirley Porter was originally a Liberal. 'I'd been asked to stand for local council by the Liberals. Then we moved from the clean suburbs to town in 1974. I was walking in Hyde Park with my sister-in-law. I said, "It's rather dirty here, isn't it?" She said, "Why don't you do something about it?" I said, "What on earth can I do?" There were no Liberals on Westminster City Council. You were either Labour or Conservative. I had to be pragmatic. I was certainly not a Socialist, I don't believe in being a capitalist Communist. As far as I'm concerned if I'm a wealthy privileged person, it's ridiculous for me to pretend to be anything other than that. I can't quite understand the Wedgwood Benns of this life. I was really a rather wet Conservative until ten years ago. Then I went to Russia which affected me deeply — the lack of freedom, I couldn't believe it, especially for the Jewish people.

'At a dinner somebody gave me the name of the local Conservative agent. They were looking for new blood and they asked me if I would like to stand for the Party. I went along for the selection procedure in murkiest Paddington. I actually appeared at my interview clutching a copy of the *Daily Worker* which I bought outside. I knew absolutely *nothing*! I didn't even know I had to be a paid-up member of the Conservatives to stand. I joined the Party the night before they selected me as a Council candidate. Somebody sidled up to me and said, "I think you'd better join the Party."'

At 39, she won a seat on Westminster City Council. 'I wandered around in a bit of a fog, thinking what's this all about? It was a totally new world and I kept quiet because I didn't know what to say. I was put on the Housing Committee. I've always cared very much about housing and thought I'd be fine when I was talking to tenants and people in the meetings. But when I got to the committee it was all a lot of mumbo jumbo and people saying words like "hereditament", so I sat there in a stupor. One day I asked what it meant, and discovered nobody else knew either, but nobody would ever ask the idiot question. The Party hierarchy must have recognised the fact I could be a potential trouble-maker, so they made me a Whip. I learnt quite a bit as a Whip, a very good way to learn how to handle people. I became the vice-chairman of Highways and Works and then I became the Chairman. Women traditionally only had jobs in the so called "caring" committees. No woman had ever been Chairman of Highways and Works or anything, as they saw it, so sordid — licensing sex shops, public toilets, *prostitution*. In '82 I was short-listed for Europe, just before the dustmen's strike. It was freezing cold and I went out there to Ilford and I came back and I collapsed on the sofa and thought who wants to go all the way, backwards and forwards, to Europe, what a daft thing. I'm not somebody who likes talking shops.

'I was approached to stand for Parliament when I was about 45. I decided I'm not really committed enough to be a proper politician. In the final analysis, I would put the family before politics and I object very much to the ridiculous hours at night. I'm not back-bench material and I thought at that age I would be considered too old to qualify for promotion.

'At Westminster Council my hours will often start perhaps with a breakfast meeting or phone calls on council business, or something which has emanated from council. About 8.30 I'll start talking about this or that. I've had meetings up until now — late afternoon — today. I've been dealing with industrial relations, press and PR, management, various things all day. I might be visiting a sex shop one minute and the Queen the next. Clothes to my mind are the biggest nuisance. I'm very laid back. I wear trousers when I feel like it, albeit a rather smart suit. The thing which bugs me most is the woman has to do so much more to look civilised. Your hair has got to look right. Twelve of us had a party, my sister and her husband and other friends including the men, and we had a wonderful evening where this woman came and she colour-coded everybody. My husband's all colour-coded too. *Wonderful!* It makes it much easier, everything goes with everything.

'I don't think I'm a rabid right-winger. I believe in market forces, certainly. But I believe in being practical and pragmatic as well. Many politicians have never actually had to put their money where their mouth is, and I see many instances of people who have "ideas" but aren't at the sharp end, putting them into practice. I am, and I enjoy it.

'Really what I think I am is a frustrated businesswoman who's translated it into politics. In my six years as Leader I've tried to change the culture at Westminster Council, but I must have been a bit mental when I tried to do it. It's like taking the British Empire and turning it into Great Britain plc. You're changing a cosy establishment of both Members and officers. They may not be people who use a lot of energy in making things happen, but boy! they work hard to stop them happening. We've had our battles. I don't have a particularly long fuse. I can work all day and all night with people who are on the same wave-length, great! But I can't bear negativity. I've battled against negativity and finally have had to understand I cannot make negative people work. Positive people will go to the end of the world for me. Now, I'm pleased to say, I've got a very good team. I remember asking, "Why don't we run this Council like a business?" One of my own side, a certain uptight gentleman with a moustache, spluttered, "This is the Council!" That was the beginning of my wanting to change the way things were run.'

Suddenly, the famous case of 'The 5p Cemeteries' became for Shirley Porter what salmonella was to Edwina Currie — an issue which unexpectedly blew up into monumental proportions. In the *Sunday Times*, 19 February 1989, Valerie Grove wrote: 'If you opened her heart, you might expect to find the words "The 5p cemeteries" engraved on it, because that messy saga threatens her reign as Leader of Westminster Council.' Instead, Lady Porter wears a cheeky badge on her lapel that says 'YCDBSOYA'. 'I'll give you the polite version,' says Shirley Porter. 'It means "You can't do business sitting on your armchair." My father gave one to Callaghan and one to Heath but I haven't had the temerity to give one to Mrs Thatcher yet.'

Shirley Porter knows exactly how unpleasant in-fighting can be after experiencing a bitter battle with the leader of the Opposition on the same council. 'He is trying to build a national reputation on my back. He wants to destroy me like Kinnock screams and shouts at Maggie Thatcher. This is the bit about being a woman and I hate it when they shout and scream at you. You are offended by it, you feel upset, it's not nice and then something comes to you. I'll fight back the same way. He wants to get rid of me because he knows if he can get rid of me then he's got Westminster in his pocket. I won't give in to this fellow. In fact I think there's a bit of my father in me. If he wasn't trying so hard to get rid of me, I would have gone. I've said to myself: "Who needs it at 58?" I have a husband who likes the warm weather, and he's ten years older than I am. I think to myself, it's ridiculous, I don't have time for friends or family. I should be doing something else. But he's made it a point of honour now, therefore I think it's a bit like the markets. My father stood there fighting.

'I've noticed a dramatic change of atmosphere in local council in the past decade. Politics at local level has become polarised. In the mid-seventies when the Labour Party slung out the Militants, they came down to the local level. They changed and politicised local government. It's been getting worse and worse. It's now revolting, nasty, it's total vilification. You asked me if I speak to the other side. I talk to the genuine Socialists, but there are only a couple of them left. Now it's all go for the jugular stuff, it's no longer anything to do really with running a city. It's to do with power.

'Why do I do it? More to the point is, why am I *still* doing it! Why don't I give it up? My game plan is to lead my Party into the election and to win resoundingly in 1990, to put them on a firm footing, see off all these nasties, see the City run properly.

'I recognise the fact that I'm anti-Establishment. I don't like the Establishment and they probably don't like me. In some people's eye I'm part of the Establishment, but I mean those people who are time servers, who're at the top of most political parties. I'm not somebody who's going to kiss everybody's posterior just to get on. I can't do it. There's something in me that has to be true to myself. Had I been that kind of person I probably would have gone further and I think that's what keeps me away from the main stream. I don't want to be the boss of local government organisations and all this stuff, it's not me, I really want to make things happen. I don't want to get honours by buttering people up, saying the right things, I'd rather not have the honours.'

So how does she deal with the stresses and strains of the job? 'I try and clear my head by walking. I talk to people, I remind myself I've got very good friends, I remind myself this is politics and revolting. I notice how they try to destroy the Prime Minister. Well, I think she looks pretty good on it. The mind is stimulated. I try not to go into overdrive, so I meditate. TM. I use it as a technique. I don't commune with Buddha or anybody, I go to health farms for weekends and I completely switch off.

'I adore the sea, if I can I get away for a few days on the sea. I like to play sports, but I don't seem to have much time. I like it really warm and beautiful — not so much places as the total freedom of the elements. I spent some time on a boat in Majorca, swimming in the sea with not a soul there. I sat on the back of this boat, practising knots because the fellow was an absolutely brilliant rigger. I also went back to what I used to do very well, composing doggerel, a form of poetry. It pours out. I spent a couple of days doing that and then I felt marvellous.

'I need a complete switch. Father used to have a saying: "With friends like these, who needs enemies!" That's the bit I don't like about politics, I don't like this feeling you can't rely upon people. The bit that has offended me most is not the Opposition, but that I've got a couple of people on my side, who from jealousy, envy, call it what you will, work hard to undermine what we as a Party are trying to do — that upsets me most. When I was ill, they worked doubly hard to try to destroy me. I don't contact the media — but they've made me into a cult figure. I am synonymous with Westminster Council and even if I offer up — as I'm trying to — other chairmen, other people, they don't want them. I've got a very good inner team and have a terrific Party. If you believe in what you're doing, it helps very much because you know where you want to go and why you're doing it.'

'Yes, I'd like to be Prime Minister, but it is inconceivable — the obstacles are enormous.'

Born in Yorkshire, Frances Morrell became a teacher and then got a job at the Press Office of the National Union of Students. Through the Fabian Society she met Tony Benn and became his political adviser when he was Secretary of State for Industry.

For four stormy years Frances Morrell was Chair of the Inner London Education Authority with responsibility for a budget of a thousand million pounds. Reform in education has been her driving motivation in politics. She claims two victories over Margaret Thatcher. 'When I was at the NUS in the seventies, Mrs T. was Secretary of State for Education. We fought for student grants and got a big settlement. At the ILEA I defeated Mrs Thatcher with a loose popular movement. I always said governments can be defeated if you know how, even though they are the most powerful institutions in the country.' She fought hard for — and twice saved — the Inner London Education Authority. (Ironically, an internal Labour Party coup deposed her in 1987.) Her passion for quality State education has its roots in her own background. 'My family were poorly educated factory workers. My mother worked packing chocolates in Rowntree's factory in what was still called the Workhouse Laundry. They felt their lack of education deeply. Her ambition was that I should go and work in Rowntree's offices — not the factory. The school said I should become a teacher. My mother had wanted me to go to grammar school, but warned me, "That school is trying to make you ashamed of us."'

In her book *The Battle for Britain's Schools*, Frances Morrell writes: 'I'm standing beside the utility table in the small and smokey living-room of a terraced house. It is mid-evening and my father, still in his work clothes, is looking at a text book. I knew it was his ambition to get "on the staff" of the company, to become monthly paid, and to lose the permanent fear of being given a week's notice. I asked him if he was studying to gain promotion. "It's too late," he replied. I knew what he meant. He worked in the neighbouring town of Leeds and got up at five o'clock to travel there by bus, returned at seven o'clock to eat his supper, sit exhausted by the fire for half an hour, lay out his breakfast and go to bed.'

The teachers at Frances Morrell's school, Queen Anne Grammar, in York, had a profound effect on the young girl. 'They liberated my ideas and broadened my horizons. They were the types who'd been to university in the thirties, very serious intellectual women who went to Oxbridge, then went into teaching girls. I found them very inspiring — Miss Gertrude Guyon taught English and Miss Ellen taught history. They didn't teach intellectual rigour in a moralising way, they just breathed intellectual rigour and humanity and absolute fascin-ation with what the world was like — ideas for their own sake. They were wonderful for me. It was like being in the desert and thirsty for knowledge and they poured it all out. I divided my life between school and books.

'School was a very supportive community, but it was very hard to come out of my sort of family into a university back-ground — its lack of familiarity with work patterns, the whole working-class sense of inadequacy about intellectual endeavour. It's hard to convey the mixture of lack of intellectual self-confidence combined with a sort of aggression if you come from a working-class home and you're storming the middle class. As a teenager when I wasn't reading or at school I was bored. My family didn't do anything, they worked, cleaned the home and listened to the radio.'

Another scene she describes in her book traces why she believes so strongly in an education service where every child has an equal chance and is treated with equal respect, and takes place in Rowntree's factory where a group of girls from the grammar school were being shown around. 'Our guide paused by the side of a young woman packing chocolates into boxes at incredible speed. She was wearing a white turban and overalls. I was dressed in my school uniform of navy blazer with it's badge and Latin motto, ugly brown lace-up shoes and unbecoming beret. We recognised each other at once, though we hadn't met since we were 11 years old: we had shared a desk at junior school. She didn't speak to me, I didn't know how to speak to her.'

Hull University was an unhappy experience. 'It was a very miserable period. I think the people teaching us at Hull lacked confidence, as though they felt being presented with working-class students like myself was a reflection on them. They thought they should all be at Oxbridge, not at a redbrick university. Also I'd simply never had the middle-class training in structuring your life and working with it.' However, she left Hull with a degree in English and went on to qualify as a teacher.

'For me life began in London when I was 22. Being in the capital was so exciting. Most women I know who are active in politics are adventurous — you have to live in such shark-infested waters. I've certainly taken a great number of risks, not all of which have come off. I left teaching and set off for London like Dick Whittington to seek my future. I'd virtually never left Yorkshire until I was in my twenties. I came South and I thought Romford was London. I got a teaching job in Romford.'

She married when she was 25. 'Brian suggested I join the Labour Party, his father was deputy Father of the Chapel at the *Daily Mirror*. He joined us both to the local branch in Hornchurch and we went to the local branch meeting. If you come from the sort of family I come from, you don't even know there is a Labour Party with a membership structure. I didn't know what "active in the Party" meant. I wouldn't have recognised the phrase. Working-class women in the kind of environment I come from don't have any conception of the complicated network of decision-making and how it operates. Men do, through their work and their trades union. I was born a total outsider into the class of people who never go to a party conference — they didn't even know it was happening.

'When Labour lost the 1970 Election I was horrified. I thought to myself, something has to be done. I was inspired to volunteer by listening to Richard Crossman at a Fabian Society lecture. It was very hot, absolutely packed with over 300 people. He said, "We must rebuild, rethink, reorganise." Everyone cheered. Tom Ponsonby, who's now Labour Chief Whip in the Lords, organised a follow-up meeting of volunteers — three of us turned up. I was taken on as a volunteer to help the Fabian

Society. We produced a pamphlet by Tony Benn which stated, "The best leaders are the ones people don't know about." That's when I met this wonderful man, Tony Benn, who became such an influence on me. I took all the letters Tony Benn received from constituents for a year and those he had written. It was the first ever classification of an MP's correspondence. It proved to me that (a) I could do research and (b) I didn't want to.

'I don't believe in the Party as an elite cadre of leaders, but that is in reality how all parties operate — every single one. The furthest away from that was the now-defunct Liberal Party with its open conference. Liberals appeal primarily to the middle class. Labour appeals to working people, but has also become an accessible playground for a principled, educated but narrowly based, white male group.

'I don't approve of Democratic Centralism. I agree with the Liberals and Trotsky. Trotsky said, "First the party substitutes itself for the voting class. Then the Party Committee substitutes itself for the Party. Then the Leader substitutes himself/herself for the Party Committees." All parties end up that way. In fact the Tories start out that way.'

After Frances Morrell defeated the government in their attempt to abolish the ILEA, she fought hard to keep her job as its leader. However, she was ousted by members of her own Party in a coup. 'They chose to sack the victorious general on the eve of the battle,' she says wryly. 'I could have saved the ILEA from the government a third time. I really did hope we wouldn't go back to work under white-men-rule-the-world. I hoped my successor would be one of the black councillors or a woman.'

In public she bounced back. 'That's show-business!' she told the newspapers. 'It's a glorious day. We shall take the dogs for a walk, we shall do some shopping with friends and we shall drink some wine to console ourselves and to toast the downfall of our enemies in the future. I've become a human being again!'

# 15.
# WOMEN WITH X APPEAL

An entire generation has grown up only knowing a woman Prime Minister. Anecdotes abound. The Speaker of the House of Commons, Bernard Weatherill, tells how his grandchildren came to visit him at Speaker's House, attached to the Palace of Westminster. They were dressing up in his robes 'playing Parliaments' when his grandson said, 'I'll pretend to be Prime Minister.' His granddaughter retorted, 'Don't be silly *I'm* going to be the Prime Minister — only *women* can be Prime Ministers!'

No book on women in British politics can end without reference to the one woman with X appeal who so completely dominated politics in the 1980s. Unlikely admirer and old foe Frances Morrell says: 'Margaret Thatcher is an absolute phenomenon. She is an amazing woman. In 1979 along came a *woman* and challenged that chauvinist, nostalgic, conservative bureaucratic male institution — the Labour Party — and beat it. That's what it finds unforgivable. She is a woman of stature even if you don't believe in her cause! If only Labour felt able to challenge the vested interest of the class society with half the vigour and confidence she challenged the Labour world.'

Edwina Currie, who herself can readily take on the entire North of England, is in awe of her boss: 'She's a very magnetic person in political terms, very powerful, very successful. She's always believed what she believes now. She knows how to win elections and everybody else believes this as well. That gives her a tremendous power. She doesn't always realise how powerful she is. In conversation and with somebody who is making a silly or unsupportive remark she can just eat them.' After the 1983 General Election victory, Edwina Currie was invited with a batch of the other new Conservative MPs to tea at 10 Downing Street. 'Mrs Thatcher was well ahead, record majority — wonderful — the adrenalin was running, everything was buzzing.

The Prime Minister came sweeping in, started pouring out the tea, turned to Robert Jackson (at that time a Euro-MP and rapporteur between the European and British Parliaments on the budget) and said, "Now then Robert, when are we going to get back our £400 million pounds?"

'Robert replied, "It's not *our* £400 million, Prime Minister." She said, "*What!*" and I can still remember, she paused, with a pot of tea in her hand. "*What!*", she said again. Robert repeated, "It's not *our* money, it's the European Community's money and I don't think we should go around demanding our money." She put the tea-pot down and she laid into him. I had the mental image of Pac-man, you know how Pac-man goes — chomp, chomp, chomp!

'When she'd finished, the tea was cooling fast, the other six of us were sitting there, and Robert had been reduced to a little heap of cinders smoking on the chair. "Right," she said. "Now Edwina, how are you getting on?" I jumped. I was still watching in horror and fascination. I'd come ready to talk about what it was like as a new MP back in 1959 because they had a majority of 100 then. I thought she would enjoy talking about that and she did I told her we were having trouble getting desks and asked if it was the same when she first came into Parliament in 1959. She chattered on quite happily: "Oh back then, it took me 6 months to get a desk. We didn't have the Norman Shaw building and all the extra buildings you've got now."

Then something suddenly went click in her head. She turned to me and said, "Have you got a desk?" I said, "Well yes, I've got my predecessor's desk." "Good!" she said. "Have you got a secretary?" I said I'd brought somebody down from Derbyshire. "Oh jolly good," she said. "Have you got a telephone?" "Yes, Prime Minister." "Has *she* got a telephone?" "Yes, Prime Minister." "Have you got a filing cabinet?" "I've got two filing cabinets." "Well," she said, "you've only been here for 5 weeks. I wouldn't complain if I were you." So I was down to nothing and then she turned to the next one. I don't remember the rest of the conversation, I just remember shaking visibly.

'Margaret Thatcher has that effect on people. There was a long period in the mid 80's when occasionally somebody who cared for her needed to lean across the table and remind her, "It's all right, Margaret, we're the team, you don't need to argue with *us*, we're with you.'

Like Shirley Williams, Ray Michie, Emma Nicholson and

Lynda Chalker, Margaret Thatcher learned politics at her father's knee. Even when pressed by an interviewer, Margaret Thatcher never refers to her mother. Alfred Roberts was a Councillor, Mayor and Alderman who stood as an Independent and is thought to have had leanings towards Lloyd George Liberalism. Her home life is described as strict, hard-working and very thrifty. She attended Grantham Girls' High School, then her father managed to pay for her to read Chemistry at Somerville College, Oxford. At University she became the third woman President of the Oxford University Conservative Association. When she came down from Oxford she worked for three years as a chemist testing J. Lyons ice cream.

At 23, she married Dennis who was already Managing Director of a family firm. From then on she didn't need to earn her living. When Margaret Thatcher gave birth to twins Carol and Mark, her husband could afford a live-in nanny. His money and this support system allowed her to read at the bar. By the time Dennis Thatcher retired from the board of Burmah in 1975, his salary and life-style were in the Rolls Royce bracket. Money is indisputably useful in a political career. Even his retirement came at just the right moment to help her in her campaigns as Party Leader — 'always half a step behind'.

In his biography of Margaret Thatcher *One of Us* Hugo Young writes: 'Once she became famous she readily admitted "It was Dennis's money that helped me on my way."' Hugo Young points out: "She may not have inherited a private income, but she married an alternative to it. Financially she belonged to the leisured classes. This fortunate condition enabled her to pursue a political career with undistracted singlemindedness."

Dennis Thatcher is a perfect candidate for Doreen Miller's husband Henry's 'Husbands Anonymous' Club. Dennis Thatcher's role has been remarkable for a man with his very conservative views and from his generation of pre-equality male. He appears to have had no political ambition for himself but to have thrown himself wholeheartedly into supporting his wife as the out-front partner. Edwina Currie observes: "Dennis Thatcher is a much shrewder person than most people realise and he agrees with his wife's politics. He worked out a very long time ago the way to ensure the politics they both believe in got promoted was to give her as much support as possible and the support she needed was to have him there being supportive." Shortly after Margaret Thatcher became Prime Minister, she told a reporter: 'I have no-one to turn to except Dennis. He puts his arm round me and says, "Darling, you sound just like Harold Wilson," and then I always laugh.'

In her mid-twenties Margaret Thatcher served her apprenticeship as a parliamentary candidate in the Conservative nohope constituency of Dartford. At the age of 32 she was chosen from 100 candidates to stand in the safe Conservative seat of Finchley and was elected to Parliament the following year. She held posts in Parliament throughout the sixties, speaking on Pensions, Housing and Land, Treasury, Fuel, and Transport. In 1969 Prime Minister Edward Heath promoted her to Cabinet as Secretary of State for Education. Five years later she ousted him as Party leader.

It is a serious and quite inexplicable omission that for years and years Britain's first woman Prime Minister has failed to put another woman in her Cabinet, with the short-lived exception of Baroness Young. Margaret Thatcher has been the single woman in a Cabinet of 20 males. It's possible her policies as well as her style might have been quite different if she hadn't been a lone woman trying to prove she is, as Harold Wilson once said, "the best man among them".

In 1961, as an up and coming politician, she attacked the Treasury's treatment of working wives. In 1966 she urged income relief payments for women. In the early 1970s, as Secretary of State for Education, she launched 'Framework for Expansion', the policy document with a commitment to nursery school education. In those days her plans for nursery education were ambitious — nursery provision for 50 per cent of three-year-olds and 90 per cent of four-year-olds. She is quoted as saying: 'I sent my two children to nursery school, just a couple of hours each morning, and this is something that should be available to all who want it.' MP Ray Michie comments: 'I admire Margaret Thatcher's ability and her determination. I don't admire her policies or very few of them anyway. There are one or two things she's done that are worthwhile but I don't think she understands the needs of working mothers, quite frankly because she's been in a privileged position. She's been married to somebody who's very wealthy and she was able to afford to have a nanny for her children from an early age. I didn't have that and most women don't have that sort of support.'

Clare Short thinks the answer lies in the generation gap:

'Margaret Thatcher is very much from a previous generation of women politicians. The lack of a women's movement to back them up meant that generation of women have to make it like men. They had to almost make sure they spoke about Transport and Industry and so on, to prove they weren't soft and frail and not up to it. I think they almost felt the need to prove they weren't too much like women, which was hard. It was their inheritance.'

Margaret Thatcher's disinclination to consider the fundamental needs of millions of women may be the cause behind some significant shifts in female voting patterns. When interviewed by Jonathan Dimbleby on the BBC Television programme *On the Record* in April 1989, Edwina Currie espoused the cause of women, admitting that young women especially were turning from Conservatives to Labour. She called for the Prime Minister to turn her attention to such women's issues as child care.

Because of Margaret Thatcher's dominance as Prime Minister, her tendency to intrude in every Department and take the reins hither and thither, that most experienced Commons watcher, Chris Moncrief, Chief Lobby Correspondent of the Press Association, says firmly: 'After Margaret Thatcher, it's unlikely there'll be another woman Prime Minister in our lifetime.' His view is echoed by male media colleagues and politicians (not surprisingly including her arch-rival, former Prime Minister Edward Heath). Shirley Porter, Leader of Westminster Council, agrees. 'The Conservative Party won't have another woman Leader in the immediate future. The men can't be enjoying it. I think they'll freeze out women for years after she's gone.' So where next for women in politics?

Gender has become confused with personality and policy. Women politicians are still such a rare species, generic labelling of this type is not only illogical but dangerous to the advancement of women in politics. It's too easy to confuse gender with other primal forces. Jean Lambert of the Greens, is no admirer. 'I can understand why Margaret Thatcher inspires, but she certainly doesn't inspire me. Except she inspires in me a sense of opposition — there is no way you can let this carry on, you can't sit back and be relaxed while things are going on as they are, so I suppose in a sense it's a perverse inspiration.'

Margaret Thatcher's personality overwhelmed the politics of the '80s. After the Euro-elections of June 1989, the Invincible

Woman no longer seems so invincible. Other women in this book may dominate the '90s. Politics itself is changing fast. No longer can voters be relied on to vote for the great coalitions which made up the historic Labour Party and the traditional Tory Party. 'Single issue' parties like the Greens have burst on the scene. To the dismay of egocentric Westminster, Europe itself is more and more where the action is. Brussels is replacing Westminster and rivalling Washington.

Suddenly the political cards reshuffle. The blossoming of the Green Party in the 1989 European Elections could push forward the next important wave of women politicians. More than all the other political parties in Britain, the Greens have always aimed at equality between women and men. In 1989 the three elected co-chairs of the Greens were women: Penny Kemp, Janet Alty and Liz Crosbie. Three of their six national speakers were women: Lindsay Cooke, Sara Parkin and Jean Lambert. More than a third of their Euro-candidates were women, as were their parliamentary candidates at the 1987 General Election. The iconoclastic nature of the aims of the Greens — including an end to 'growth' — sets them quite apart from any of the traditional parties, though nearest to the Liberals in the 1950s. The success of the Greens in 1989 may set the trend for the politics of the West for decades to come.

Jean Lambert says: 'I like to feel part of the movement that actually made people look at the world differently, to look at our environment as the basic, the most important thing that has to be cared for. That's what motivates me very strongly, this feeling that you want to be able to say: "When the world was in danger of dying, what did you actually do to prevent that?" I have a very deep distrust of the political Establishment to actually do what it says it's going to do. It's very rare for traditional political parties to really deliver what they talk about delivering. I certainly don't trust the present government any further than I can see it. It has taken so long to get any sign of awareness from people within this government even to admit there actually are problems.'

But regardless of whether the New Wave comes from the Greens or any other political colour, the way the parliamentary system is structured acts as an automatic population control on the number of new women in the House of Commons. There is no mandatory retirement age for Members of Parliament. Despite all the hard work and very long hours, MPs really do seem to die with their boots on. Only a handful of winnable seats come vacant at each election. There is never a vacuum into which large numbers of women — or any other under-represented group — can move. The Continental system of voting — proportional representation — would help to increase the representation of women. The United Kingdom and the United States have the lowest percentage of women in their legislatures in the developed world, and both use a first-past-the-post voting system. By contrast, approximately a third of the Scandinavian Members of Parliament are women and they use proportional representation. The intrepid campaigner for electoral reform, Enid Lakeman, points out that in first-past-the-post systems selection committees 'are often predisposed to choose a man because they have just one choice of candidate. In a proportional system there is a positive advantage to be gained from presenting a balanced choice which would need to include a quota of women, if only to appeal to as many different kind of electors as possible." In the Australian Parliament their Senate is elected by proportional representation, and the House of Representatives by first-past-the-post. Elections for both Houses took place on the same day in 1987. 22 per cent of the Members elected to the Senate were women in contrast to just 6 per cent in the House of Representatives.

Does it matter if women are in our House of Commons in large numbers? I see Political Woman as the spearhead of great social and economic change. In countries like Britain, tightly controlled by laws passed by Parliament, a critical mass — even a majority — of women in the House of Commons, could precipitate social and economic changes which otherwise might take place only slowly over 40 or 50 years. Even within the same land, women inhabit a different culture. We have different experiences to contribute to society. As more than half the population, women offer a vast extra pool of talent that has hardly been tapped.

Cosmic changes have taken place since the early 1980s. Politics is no longer seen as 'a man's game'. The old belief 'voters won't vote for a woman' really has died away, killed off by the public in a remarkable string of by-election successes by women politicians throughout the eighties, culminating with Kate Hoey's victory in Vauxhall for Labour in June 1989. 'Labour's task was to select the best candidate in the Labour Party to represent Vauxhall,' Roy Hattersley remarked. 'That was why we selected Kate Hoey.'

For thousands of women, politics has now become a way of life a real addiction. As Jean Lambert sums up: 'It becomes very difficult to separate out who we are, from what we have become in our political life. It impinges so completely on your own private life, that when you get a spare week-end you're almost stunned because you don't quite know what to do with it and you think: "Is this what most people do? They are allowed to watch television?" And then the phone goes again. I still have a very great feeling of insecurity about it, a sense of wonderment and amazement about why am I doing this. If you'd asked me 10, 15, 20 years ago what I would be doing in my late thirties, would I be doing up-front television stuff for a political party, I don't think it would have been on my list. I find it quite amazing how one gets drawn into all this.'

# FURTHER INFORMATION

## Women Members of Parliament

### CONSERVATIVE

*Batley and Spen*, Elizabeth Peacock
*Billericay*, Teresa Gorman
*Birmingham Edgbaston*, Jill Knight
*Broxbourne*, Marion Roe
*Congleton*, Ann Winterton
*Derbyshire South*, Edwina Currie
*Devon West and Torridge*, Emma Nicholson
*Finchley*, Margaret Thatcher
*Lancaster*, Elaine Kellet-Bowman
*Maidstone*, Ann Widdecombe
*Medway*, Peggy Fenner
*Mitcham and Morden*, Angela Rumbold
*Norfolk South West*, Gillian Shephard
*Plymouth Drake*, Janet Fookes
*Surrey South West*, Virginia Bottomley
*Wallasey*, Lynda Chalker
*Wolverhampton North East*, Maureen Hicks

### LABOUR

*Barking*, Jo Richardson
*Birmingham Ladywood*, Clare Short
*Bow and Poplar*, Mildred Gordon
*Bristol South*, Dawn Primarolo
*Crewe and Nantwich*, Gwyneth Dunwoody
*Cynon Valley*, Ann Clwyd
*Derby South*, Margaret Beckett
*Dewsbury*, Ann Taylor
*Durham North West*, Hilary Armstrong
*Eccles*, Joan lestor

*Gateshead East*, Joyce Quin
*Glasgow Maryhill*, Maria Fyfe
*Hackney North and Stoke Newington*, Diane Abbott
*Halifax*, Alice Mahon
*Lewisham Deptford*, Joan Ruddock
*Newcastle-under-Lyme*, Llin Golding
*Peckham*, Harriet Harman
*Preston*, Audrey Wise
*Redcar*, Marjorie Mowlam
*Stoke-on-Trent North*, Joan Walley
*Vauxhall*, Kate Hoey
*West Bromwich West*, Betty Boothroyd

LIBERAL DEMOCRAT

*Argyll and Bute*, Ray Michie

SOCIAL DEMOCRAT

*Greenwich*, Rosie Barnes

SCOTTISH NATIONALIST

*Moray*, Margaret Ewing

# Women Members of The European Parliament

LABOUR

*Birmingham East*, Christine Crawley
*Glasgow*, Janey Buchan
*Leicester*, Mel Read
*London East*, Carole Tongue
*London North*, Pauline Green
*London South West*, Anita Pollack
*Midlands Central*, Christine Oddy

CONSERVATIVE

*Essex North East*, Anne McIntosh
*Essex South West*, Patricia Rawlings
*Somerset and Dorset West*, Margaret Daly
*Wiltshire, Newbury and Wantage*, Caroline Jackson

SCOTTISH NATIONALIST

*Highlands and Islands*, Winnie Ewing

# Further Reading

Shirley Ardener (ed.), *Women and Space*, Croom Helm, 1981

Pamela Brookes, *Women at Westminster*, Peter Davies, 1967

Beatrix Campbell, *Iron Ladies — Why Women Vote Tory*, Virago, 1987

Julian Critchley, *Westminster Blues*, Futura, 1986

Marcia Falkender, *Downing Street in Perspective*, Weidenfeld and Nicholson, 1983

Ann Kramer, *Women and Politics*, Wayland Press, 1988

Ruth Mandel, *In the Running — The New Woman Candidate*, Ticknor and Fields, 1981

Frances Morrell, *The Battle for Britain's Schools*, Hogarth Press, 1989

Melanie Phillips, *The Divided House — Women at Westminster*, Sidgwick & Jackson, 1980

Vicky Randall, *Women and Politics*, Macmillan, 1987

Andrew Roth, *Parliamentary Profiles*, Parliamentary Profiles, 1988

Dr Elizabeth Vallance, *Women in the House*, Athlone, 1979

Hugo Young, *One of Us*, Macmillan, 1989

# INDEX

All Optima books are available at your bookshop or newsagent, or can be ordered from the following address:

Optima, Cash Sales Department,
PO Box 11, Falmouth, Cornwall TR10 9EN

Please send cheque or postal order (no currency), and allow 60p for postage and packing for the first book, plus 25p for the second book and 15p for each additional book ordered up to a maximum charge of £1.90 in the UK.

Customers in Eire and BFPO please allow 60p for the first book, 25p for the second book plus 15p per copy for the next 7 books, thereafter 9p per book.

Overseas customers please allow £1.25 for postage and packing for the first book and 28p per copy for each additional book.